Invasion of the Body Snatchers

Rutgers Films in Print

Charles Affron, Mirella Jona Affron, and Robert Lyons, editors

My Darling Clementine, John Ford, director
edited by Robert Lyons

The Last Metro, François Truffaut, director
edited by Mirella Jona Affron and E. Rubinstein

Touch of Evil, Orson Welles, director
edited by Terry Comito

The Marriage of Maria Braun, Rainer Werner Fassbinder, director
edited by Joyce Rheuban

Letter from an Unknown Woman, Max Ophuls, director
edited by Virginia Wright Wexman with Karen Hollinger

Rashomon, Akira Kurosawa, director
edited by Donald Richie

8½, Federico Fellini, director
edited by Charles Affron

La Strada, Federico Fellini, director
edited by Peter Bondanella and Manuela Gieri

Breathless, Jean-Luc Godard, director
edited by Dudley Andrew

Bringing Up Baby, Howard Hawks, director
edited by Gerald Mast

Chimes at Midnight, Orson Welles, director
edited by Bridget Gellert Lyons

L'avventura, Michelangelo Antonioni, director
edited by Seymour Chatman and Guido Fink

Meet John Doe, Frank Capra, director
edited by Charles Wolfe

Invasion of the Body Snatchers, Don Siegel, director
edited by Al LaValley

Invasion of the Body Snatchers

Don Siegel, director

Al LaValley, editor

Rutgers University Press

New Brunswick and London

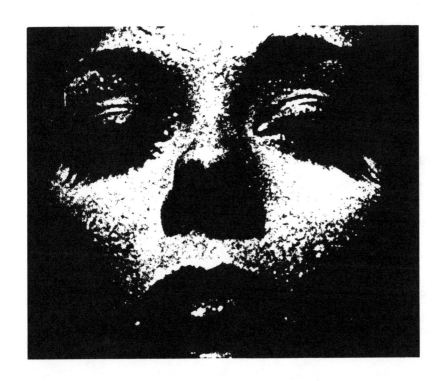

Invasion of the Body Snatchers is volume 14 in the Rutgers Films in Print series
Copyright © 1989 by Rutgers, The State University
All Rights Reserved
Manufactured in the United States of America

Library of Congress Cataloging-in-Publication Data

Invasion of the body snatchers / Don Siegel, director ; Al LaValley, editor.
    p. cm. — (Rutgers films in print)
    "Siegel filmography": p.
    Bibliography: p.
    ISBN 0-8135-1460-6 (cloth)
    ISBN 0-8135-1461-4 (pbk.)
    1. Invasion of the body snatchers (Motion picture : 1956) I. Siegel, Don, 1912–
    . II. LaValley, Albert J. III. Invasion of the body snatchers (Motion picture : 1956) IV. Series.
PN1997.I519 1989
791.43′72—dc19   89-30374
                            CIP

British Cataloging-in-Publication information available

The illustrations on pages 21 and 104 are reproduced courtesy of the Museum of Modern Art/Film Stills Archive.

This continuity script is based, in part, on the screenplay "Invasion of the Body Snatchers," by arrangement with Republic Pictures Corporation of Delaware.

Material from the Walter Wanger Collection is reprinted courtesy of The State Historical Society of Wisconsin, The Wisconsin Center for Film and Theater Research, and Stephanie Wanger Guest, daughter of Walter Wanger.

"Don Siegel on the Pod Society" by Stuart M. Kaminsky from *Science Fiction Films,* ed. Thomas R. Atkins, Monarch Film Studies (New York: Simon and Schuster, 1976); "Interview with Don Siegel" by Guy Braucourt reprinted by permission of Ligue Française d'Enseignement Permanente and the author. Letter to Bosley Crowther, film critic of the *New York Times,* by Walter Wanger, is reprinted courtesy of Stephanie Wanger Guest. Review, "Snatchers' Eeerie, Scary Science Film," by Sara Hamilton (1 March 1956) is reprinted courtesy of the *Los Angeles Times Examiner.* Review, signed "Whit." (29 February 1956) is reprinted courtesy of *Variety.* Review, "Body Snatchers' Exciting Science-Fiction Melodrama," by Jack Moffitt (16 February 1956), copyright © 1956 by *The Hollywood Reporter,* reprinted by permission. Review of 23 August 1956 is reprinted courtesy of *Daily Film Register.*

"B-Movies" by Peter Bogdanovich from his *Pieces of Time* (New York: Arbor House, 1973), pp. 148–153 is reprinted courtesy of Arbor House Publishing. "The Genre Director: The Films of Donald Siegel" by Stuart M. Kaminsky in his *American Film Genres: Approaches to a Critical Theory of Popular Film,* published by Dell Publishing in 1974 by special arrangement with CEBCO/Standard Publishing; reprinted by permission of Stuart M. Kaminsky. "Invasion of the Body Snatchers" by Ernesto G. Laura, *Bianco e Nero* 18, no. 12 (1957):69–71, reprinted by permission. "Watch the Skies" by Nora Sayre from her *Running Time: Films of the Cold War* (New York: Dial Press, 1982); copyright © 1982 by Nora Sayre, reprinted by permission of Doubleday, a division of Bantam, Doubleday, Dell Publishing Group, Inc. "Pods, Blobs, and Ideology in American Films of the Fifties" by Peter Biskind from his *Seeing Is Believing: How Hollywood Taught Us to Stop Worrying and Love the Fifties* (New York: Random House, Pantheon Books, 1983); copyright © 1983 by Peter Biskind, used by permission of Random House, Pantheon Books. Selections from *Stephen King's Danse Macabre* (New York: Berkley Books, 1983) reprinted courtesy of Stephen King. "Kiss Me Deadly: Communism, Motherhood, and Cold War Movies" by Michael Paul Rogin from his *Ronald Reagan, the Movie and Other Episodes in Political Demonology* (Berkeley and Los Angeles: University of California Press, 1987), pp. 236–271; copyright © 1987 by The Regents of the University of California. "Women and the Inner Game of Don Siegel's *Invasion of the Body Snatchers,*" by Nancy Steffan-Fluhr, *Science-Fiction Studies* 11 (July 1984): 139–151; copyright © 1984 by *Science-Fiction Studies.*

Acknowledgments

I would like to thank a number of people who helped make this volume possible: Matthew Bernstein for alerting me to the file on *Invasion of the Body Snatchers* in the Walter Wanger Collection at the Wisconsin Center for Film and Theater Research at the State Historical Society of Wisconsin; the director of the Collection, Donald Crafton, and the faculty of the Communication Arts Department at the University of Wisconsin, who made my stay there so fruitful and enjoyable; Maurice Rapf, who read several versions of the introduction and generously shared his vivid memories of Daniel Mainwaring, Walter Wanger, and Don Siegel with me; my editors at Rutgers University Press, Leslie Mitchner and Robert Lyons, who read the manuscript with care and offered excellent suggestions for its improvement, and Marilyn Campbell who copyedited the manuscript and prepared it for publication with patience and sensitivity; Al Samuels, Dartmouth '87, who worked on the project with me from its inception; Mark Decker, who unravelled bits of unfathomable dialogue and other tangles; the various Film Studies technical assistants at Dartmouth who demystified the computer and offered regular help; Bob Drake, Will Rexer, Jeff Good, Amit Malhotra, and Tom Summerall; Cheryl Coutermarsh, Crista Renza, and Margo Rahmann who offered regular administrative assistance; Bill Pence for constant good advice and information; Dartmouth College for two Faculty Research Grants which enabled me to travel to the University of Wisconsin; Ted Abenheim and Tim Wohlgemuth who helped me with early research in Los Angeles; James Goldstone, who filled me in on Allied Artists in the 1950s; Peter Saccio, Sam Gill of Special Collections at the Motion Picture Academy, and Eve Sullivan at the American Film Institute library for identifying quotations, credits, and allusions; Garrett Stewart for last-minute help; Charles Wolfe for his good advice about methodology and for helping me with the stills, along with Roland de la Rosa, Jeannine Hunt, and Willis Flachsenhar; Marti Mangan and Amy Lawrence for proofreading and making good suggestions; Tina Blake for her persistence in getting permission for reprints; and three people I met during the course of this project who pointed to readings incorporated here that open up new approaches to the film, Harold Schechter, Michel Ciment, and Virginia Wright Wexman. Lastly, I'd like to thank Don Siegel for encouraging me with this project and warning me "Don't let the pods get you." I hope I have heeded his warning.

Contents

Introduction

Invasion of the Body Snatchers: Politics, Psychology, Sociology

Al LaValley

ndependent producer Walter Wanger, responsible for such important Hollywood films as *Queen Christina* (1933), *Gabriel over the White House* (1933), *Private Worlds* (1935), *Blockade* (1938), *Stagecoach* (1939), *Foreign Correspondent* (1940), and *Scarlet Street* (1945), read the first installment of Jack Finney's serial *The Body Snatchers* in *Collier's* magazine of 26 November 1954. He was so excited by what he read that although there were two more installments to follow, he immediately began negotiations to purchase the rights for a film. He showed the project to Don Siegel, who had recently directed Wanger's critically acclaimed Allied Artists prison reform movie, *Riot in Cell Block 11*. Siegel in turn sought out an old friend, Daniel Mainwaring, who had scripted a low-budget RKO caper movie, *The Big Steal,* which Siegel had directed in 1949. All three met with Jack Finney in Mill Valley in Northern California in the first week of January 1955 to discuss the film. Mainwaring finished his first screenplay by 10 February, several weeks before Finney's expanded Dell paperback version of the serial was in the stores. The film itself was quickly shot in twenty-three days in the studio and in locations around it in late March and early April for around $382,000.

Both the speed with which the project was completed and the shared excitement of the major figures behind it suggest a remarkable harmony of outlook. What happened after the film was shot, however, suggests that underneath the surface harmony were distinctly different voices. Siegel and Mainwaring were content with the film they had shot; Wanger, for a variety of reasons, was not. Allied Artists, a low-budget studio, seemed befuddled by a film that did not clearly fit into science fiction or horror genre formats. The differences among the film's creators—and between them and the studio—plagued the film in postproduction, causing extensive cuts and eventually the addition of a framing story and voice-over narration by the principal character. The film was not released until late February 1956, ten months after shooting was completed.

Though the differences among screenwriter, director, and producer were never fully voiced nor so acute as those between the filmmakers and the studio, they nevertheless played an important role. From the start, *Invasion of the Body Snatchers*—or *The Body Snatchers* as it was first called—was a highly unstable text.

How to read this film continues to be a major problem. Throughout its history, but especially in postproduction, the film became a locus of conflicts of authorship, genre, aesthetics, political ideology, and B-movie studio practice. It has been read at one end of the ideological spectrum as a paranoid parable of invasion by Soviet totalitarianism, fueled by the Red Scare and McCarthyism; and at the other end of the spectrum as an indictment of American conformity and the loss of individualism that the Cold War fostered.

Even though we have learned that good works have multiple meanings and even though deconstructive criticism has fostered an appreciation of contradictory meanings in a text, *Invasion* clearly cannot have totally contradictory central meanings. *Invasion* may have clashing ideologies within it, varying emphases that its different creators intended, but it does have a central theme that is foregrounded: the fear of social conformity and the loss of the self that results from it.

To uncover the roots of the varying ideologies that nonetheless persist within the film, it is useful to look at the politics, aesthetics, and roles of the major creators—author, scriptwriter, director, producer, and studio—and see what each intended. The differences that emerge here will illuminate the tensions that still exist within the film as well as the problems the film encountered in postproduction.

Even Jack Finney's ideology, as evidenced by both the serial and the later book version of *The Body Snatchers,* is somewhat confused. As Glen M. Johnson has pointed out in an interesting article, Finney's endings to the serial and novel differ.[1] In both versions, Miles pauses in his flight to take a defiant stand against the pods in the field, even though he knows the delay will mean capture by the mob of pods waiting between him and the highway. He sets fire to the pods and though he does not destroy all of them, the survivors take flight from an inhospitable planet—testimony to the efficacy of the fighting individual. The remaining pod people quietly surrender. In the serial, however, Miles is rescued by Jack and the FBI, who have seen the flames and quickly arrive on the scene. In the novel, Finney removed the FBI and celebrated Miles's individual defiance more fully.

Most science fiction tales of the period reveal their ideology by the way they depict institutions and authorities—medical professionals, scientists, the army, the FBI. Stories frequently centered on an invasion, often triggered by tampering with atomic power or the atom bomb. The invasion theme suggests not only the fears unleashed by atomic power itself, but also the fear of possible Russian

---

1. "'We'd Fight . . . We Had To' ": The Body Snatchers as Novel and Film," *Journal of Popular Culture* 13 (Summer 1979):5–16.

attack with the A-bomb. The so-called pluralist center, a combination of conservatives and liberals, that emerged in postwar America as a bulwark against communism, believed in established institutions, though they often differed about means and priorities. The basic Americanism of this belief was portrayed as non-ideological, almost natural and normal. Both the radical right and the radical left tended to distrust institutional bureaucracies and for this reason were themselves seen as threats to normal American behavior and belief.

Finney's elimination of the FBI rescue and his stress on individualism mark a more rightward direction in his book, but he nonetheless remains well within the pluralist center. Of the major collaborators on the film his version of the tale is the most conservative. Finney celebrates the triumph of individualism and of typically American small town ways. Unlike the Miles of the film, Finney's Miles never distrusts all institutions. He is always looking for ways to combine individual and collective action appropriately. At one point he sets out for San Francisco with Jack, Teddy, and Becky to get FBI help, but turns back from a strong sense of duty to battle the pods on their own turf. He regularly recalls the example of the army in World War II and the bravery of individual soldiers. What worked then will work in this more obscure battle of the fifties.

Finney's Miles is not hostile to authority or science; indeed, science and rationality are privileged. Miles is always stressing his need to act logically, to avoid hasty or false steps, and to contact the appropriate authorities. He returns to town to pursue a lead that will give him more knowledge about the origin and purpose of the pods: a newspaper clipping Jack had saved about a local college biology teacher, Professor Budlong, who had commented on the strange pods in a local field as possibly having come from outer space. The central part of Finney's serial consists of a long visit by Miles and Becky to Professor Budlong's where they find out more than they want to know about the pods. Though Budlong turns out to be a pod himself, he nevertheless gives accurate information about their nature and mission on earth. Only the psychiatrist, Manny (Danny in the film) Kaufman is debunked—another position that marks Finney's book as having a conservative slant.

Finally, it is the upbeat ending, with Teddy and Jack saved, Miles defiantly victorious and married to Becky, and small town values restored that shows Finney's book as firmly in the centrist tradition. All of this, of course, is what is missing from the movie as it was originally conceived. The politics and aesthetics of Dan Mainwaring were almost the opposite of those of Jack Finney.

For Mainwaring, the fable was a cry of despair; he saw no remedy for creeping conformity. This is clear from the major alterations he made to Finney's serial, changes probably made with Siegel's cooperation since they were close friends and Siegel always liked to work on scripts for his films.

The elimination of Miles's and Becky's visit to Professor Budlong and Budlong's long scientific discourse was probably dictated by the demands of an action film. Though Mainwaring assigned some explanations to Danny Kaufman, most disappeared, leaving the origin of the pods and their mission vague and throwing the intellectual and emotional weight of the film on to Miles alone. This diminution lessened the science fiction aspect of the film as well.

Most significantly, Mainwaring followed out the pessimistic strain underlying Finney's paranoid fantasy. In all three drafts of the script, Jack and Teddy do not get through to the police or FBI and Jack cooperates with Danny in trying to turn Miles and Becky into pods. Then, in the most disturbing scene in the script, which has no antecedent in the book, Becky is turned into a pod when Miles leaves her; she then traitorously urges their pursuers to chase and capture Miles. Before Miles encounters the transformed Becky, he goes to investigate the music and sees the pods growing. Unlike the Miles of the book, he makes no attempt to ignite them or take a stand against them, but, after returning to Becky to find she cannot be saved, runs to the freeway bridge away from his pursuers and—in all three drafts of the script and in the original filming—collapses, to be picked up by a crowd of passing motorists, whom we suspect may also be pods. This is indeed a despairing end and a major transformation of Finney's happy ending.

Mainwaring's despair is the despair of a onetime strong leftist over the America of the fifties. This was a period when McCarthyism—despite the senator's recent censure by the Senate—was still powerful. The House Un-American Activities Committee had decimated Hollywood; the Hollywood Ten went to jail; a blacklist was in force; and everyone was being asked to sign a podlike loyalty oath to prove they were good Americans and not subversives. Hundreds lost their jobs, many of them friends of Mainwaring's. A chilling, podlike uniformity reigned in Hollywood. Risk was no longer acceptable; perhaps serious social subjects could be approached only in disguised form through the crime and science fiction genres.

Mainwaring's despair and defiance is found in the increasingly lonely individualism of the Miles character. This is not a right-wing despair, but a left-wing one. Mainwaring's feisty individualism was based on his experience as a crime reporter. Journalistic traditions of independence from a corrupt society that needed remedying formed these writers' social ideals as well as giving a dark and cynical note to their writings, a note often at war with their very utopian hopes. Many on the Left never had a strong commitment to communism as a system of beliefs or political doctrines, but were drawn to it, especially in the thirties, by the need to take a strong stand on the issues it championed: antifascism, social equality, justice, and civil rights. The dominant image of communism for them was hardly the popular one of the fifties—a vast impersonal bureaucracy and totalitarian dictatorship—but, on the contrary, one of outspoken fighting for radical social change. Among the radical journalists in this tradition were the pioneers of the gangster genre, Francis Faragoh and John Bright, and Gordon Kahn, one of the original group of nineteen accused by HUAC. Dashiell Hammett provides another example. Though not a journalist, he was, like Mainwaring, a crime writer, a strong radical, and a sardonic commentator on corruption.

Mainwaring had originally hoped to combine his social criticism and his writing in the way many writers of the thirties did. His first novel, *One Against the Earth* (1933), was a strong, socially critical work in a realistic vein. It was only when his novel was not well received that he decided to turn to crime writing and detective novels. His strongest statement about the social role of journalism can be found in his script for Joseph Losey's low-budget Pine-Thomas production, *The Lawless* (1950), a film in which he was deeply involved as a virtual assistant director to Losey. Here a reporter, played by Macdonald Carey, comes to the rescue of a Mexican-American youth accused of attacking a white woman and a cop. The town forms a lynch mob, attacks Mexican-Americans on the street, and turns increasingly against the reporter, eventually destroying the newspaper offices. A perfunctory happy ending returns the town to normal.

Mainwaring saw the battle for social justice as an important one for journalists. He clearly viewed some of his screen work as an outgrowth of the social role of journalism, as both the later *Phenix City Story* (1955) and *Invasion* evidence. As the fifties progressed, the totalitarian mob became a strong feature of his plots. The crusading journalist was the last just man, increasingly out of step with a nation given to the mob violence of racism (*The Lawless*), organized crime (*The Phenix City Story*), and vegetative totalitarianism (*Invasion*). The dark, despairing voiceover narrative of the hero of his famous film noir, *Out of the Past* (1947, based on his own novel, *Build My Gallows High*), prepares for the embattled hero of *The Phenix City Story,* almost defeated and driven to near madness by the criminal mob. Miles, in *Invasion,* with his descent into hysteria and desperation after his pursuit by the pods, is an extension of these heroes. Mainwaring's crime fiction was wedded to his journalistic crusading mission in these two later films.[2]

Mainwaring's official political affiliations are a bit obscure. He may have been a Communist in the thirties. Certainly he was very close to major leftists, who remember him as an ally. Don Siegel referred to Mainwaring's associations with the radicals in a letter to Wanger on 17 January 1955, just as the scriptwriting was getting underway. With a joking tone, he calls him "Mr. Mainwaring—né Geoffrey Homes—Member (non-paying) of the Older Communist League." Siegel may be just playing with Mainwaring's many names, but he may also have been warning Wanger about Mainwaring's leftist past and assuring him of his clear status from the blacklist. Siegel may in fact be associating Mainwaring's return to his first and last names with a move away from his Communist ties. I don't want to make too much of a light reference, but the letter clearly states Mainwar-

2. Significantly, Mainwaring began signing himself by his first and last name in these two films; he became Daniel Mainwaring. Hitherto he had used Geoffrey Homes, his two middle names. The scripts of *Invasion* bear the author's name as Daniel Geoffrey Homes Mainwaring. When queried by Wanger if he wanted all these names on the film, or just Geoffrey Homes or Daniel Mainwaring, he replied he would sign the script as Daniel Mainwaring.

ing's close association with the Left, as well as his "non-paying status," which probably meant he was not a Communist, in Siegel's view.

In their alienation from the system and their resistance to its monolithic qualities, Mainwaring was obviously close to Siegel, although Siegel was even more of an outsider and politically unaligned. Mainwaring scripted two more Siegel movies, *Baby Face Nelson* (1957, another movie dramatizing the conflict between control and instinct in a lonely outsider and a key film in the Siegel fifties canon) and *The Gunrunners* (1958). What we can learn from Mainwaring's case is not to label all strong, even paranoid defenses of individualism as conservative or right-wing. The combination of paranoia, despair, and individualistic defiance frequently came from the Left as well. Mainwaring was especially strong in this expression because so many of his friends had been blacklisted for refusing to conform. The threat to freedom in the fifties was not only from the radical right—as it had always been—but also from the centrists, both liberal and conservative, who refused to protect the rights of individuals under attack. America was being swallowed by a podlike uniformity of political belief, by a vast conspiracy of silence masquerading as non-ideology. The totalitarianism in Mainwaring's belief was homegrown, not imported.

It was Mainwaring who added Miles's important speech, central to the film, and without an antecedent in the book. To Becky he says: "In my practice I see how people have allowed their humanity to drain away . . . only it happens slowly instead of all at once. They didn't seem to mind. . . . All of us, a little bit. We harden out hearts . . . grow callous . . . only when we have to fight to stay human do we realize how precious it is." Here Mainwaring says that we are the villains. Social behavior and institutions that had been only partly responsive in the past were now silent. There was no anticommunist message in the film. For Mainwaring, communism was a scapegoat, an imaginary villain reflecting the fears and tensions of the Right writ large. If the pods in *Invasion* seem to incarnate the popular image of a communist totalitarian state, it is only because the government-dominated, bureaucratic, and conformist fifties was itself creating an America like this picture of Soviet Russia. Then, as now with so-called "terrorist" nations, Americans knew little of the complex political, historical, and social reality of Russia or other nations. The images constructed were largely ways of escaping criticism of existing American institutions, a convenient gathering of villainy for the tensions besetting Americans and their own institutions—and ironically, an enlargement of the frightening trends within contemporary society. For Mainwaring, the pods were indeed us, everything we feared and everything we were becoming.

The only resistance was an embattled individualism. That was where one had to begin. That is why in *Invasion* there really is nothing left of Finney's small-town nostalgia, much less of a restoration of Santa Mira and its values. Miles must eventually run for the freeway and the larger society beyond. The familiar props of the centrist vision, of the dominant America, are gone. Becky, Teddy, and Jack are all pods. There is no going back to the suburban house and the backyard barbecue.

If Don Siegel was less political than Mainwaring, he nevertheless shared much of Mainwaring's bleak vision of society and his admiration for combative individualism. More narrowly focused than Mainwaring, Siegel saw a world of pods around him, chiefly embodied in film producers against whom he had to struggle to articulate his artistic and social vision. After *Invasion,* the word "pods" was readily on his lips to define all the forces in American life that kill individual ideas and demand soul-deadening conformity. Like Mainwaring, Siegel saw hope in the defiant individual, but, unlike Mainwaring, he saw the conflict between society and the individual as perpetual, more a metaphysical battle than a political one. In all his films, his heroes contend with the warring demands of reason and instinct, fearing the deadening power of the one and the anarchic force of the other.

Though locked in the B-movie format of taut action tales, Siegel showed an individuality that he was proud to celebrate. His heroes are sketched with more depth than those in the usual action film. Dunn, the leader of the prison riot in *Riot in Cell Block 11,* is a typical case. Angry yet rational, furious but fair, he is a man of complex tensions. At one point we learn, correctly, that he is a psychopath. Yet he also puts forward the central liberal message of the film: the prison system must be changed. The bureaucracy and the state are the real villains, cajoling and placating him with lies, and finally yielding to his show of superior force. Dunn and his cause are victorious, yet he is sentenced to thirty more years for his part in the riot. Victory and despair. Heroism and psychosis. We already see connections to *Invasion*'s Miles.

If Siegel identifies closely with his emotional and often violent antiheroes, he also distances himself from them, another quality that marks his films as different from typical B-movies. The films have memorable characters, a furious pace, and startling situations, B-movie qualities that always involve us, but they also have a measure of detachment. Their director's own craft and steady point of view attest to the strength of his own social commitment and differentiate him from his heroes even as he sympathizes with them. There is no obvious social message, as in the typical liberal and left-leaning movies of the late forties or fifties—*Crossfire, Gentleman's Agreement, Pinky, The Snake Pit, The Lost Weekend,* or even *The Lawless* and *The Phenix City Story* with Mainwaring scripts. Instead, there is a firm defiance of conformity and the system along with a strong sense of the cost to the individual hero of that defiance. It is these notes of detachment and steadiness that gave Siegel a reputation with film critics of the fifties as a liberal social conscience of a unique sort.

But Siegel, like Mainwaring, was not interested in the anticommunist battles of the fifties. For Siegel, the villains were not so much on the other side of the world as all around us. The real enemy was totalitarian conformity. Resistance, with all its pain and suffering, was preferable to the surcease from tensions that Danny Kaufman proffered, as a kind of lotus land, in *Invasion*. The enemy lulls us into giving up our individuality, not into taking up an alien cause.

Conformity is so powerful that Siegel and Mainwaring both change the atmosphere of Finney's fable, which portrayed the pod people capturing Miles in a lackadaisical fashion, without energy or force. After all, they *are* vegetables and what makes them detectable is a quality of reduced life. Siegel also made them zombies of a sort, but galvanized them into furious energy when balked by a recalcitrant individual like Miles, who refuses to join them. The chase in the film is sustained and exhausting. Siegel even amplified the energy of the pod people further than Mainwaring, rewriting the battle in the office between Miles and the pods Jack and Danny. Siegel makes Miles plunge out one door, push Danny and Jack through the double doors and then wrestle wildly on the floor. Becky, for a moment, looks helpless, then turns on an energetic Officer Grivett, who is strangling Miles, and jams him fiercely with a hypodermic needle in the neck. For a moment he refuses to go down. The aim of the pod people may indeed be to make us all vegetables, but when they encounter resistance they turn from vegetables into beasts, where Miles is an animal savagely hunted by them and equally savage in his attack against them. For Siegel, the world is not a garden, but more a Hobbesian jungle, the individual at war with society and with his own divided self.

Self-definition, resistance to a system that insists on defining us, is the center of Siegel's system of belief—not just political and social causes, but all of life. It includes resistance to all kinds of conformity. For Siegel, embroiled in the often demeaning world of B-pictures, it means holding on to virtues like courage, stoicism, pride, intelligence, and virility, all celebrated in his main characters, all of whom are, significantly, men. Is there a politics beyond resistance? The early films of Siegel do not sketch this in detail. They are action pictures, spare and taut in their narrative lines. They do not create a new social world, yet they embody wishes for one. Dunn imagines a more humane system in *Riot* and Miles hopes for a harmonious world, too. But these heroes are busy fighting against the system that seeks to enslave them or coopt them; they have no time to build a new society.

Translated into the task of making B-pictures, his heroes' virtues become the virtues of Siegel's craft. They bring quality to the B-movie. First, a worthwhile message, some significance, as in those pictures of Wanger's, *Riot* and *Invasion*. Then, dedication to craft: work with the screenwriter, careful selection of locations (Siegel found Sierra Madre, a lookalike for Mill Valley, and the stairs at the head of Beachwood Canyon for the chase), close work with actors, thoughtful camera setups, imaginative lighting (he forced the night-by-night shots into the schedule, thereby adding three extra days), gruelling work (the final scene on the Mulholland Bridge over Route 101 was filmed all night until 4:30 A.M.), careful supervision of editing and the postproduction process (Siegel and the head of

Allied Artists editing Dick Heermance worked closely on fine-tuning the film for months after shooting), and persistence in the vision (even after the film was cut by Allied Artists, Siegel was still asking to have lines and scenes restored). Much of this dedication to craft—hardly something the B-film usually demanded—is documented in Siegel's postproduction notes to the film published here for the first time.

The world is flawed and the B-movie exists as a flawed product of that world. Despite that, Siegel gives it all he can and hopes to make something better, something with an individual stamp on it. That is why his films stand out. Siegel learned much from his years as head of the montage department at Warners, another studio where speed and high-quality craftsmanship were inimical forces. From work as an assistant director to Michael Curtiz and Raoul Walsh, he learned how to shoot action excitingly, to make the narrative taut, to keep a steady focus on the story, and to place his camera and lights expressively, deepening the themes without retarding the narrative. Siegel's camerawork is sharp, incisive, even graceful at times, and never participates in the frenzy of his action and characters. His dedication to realism led him to mix studio and "documentary-style" location shooting artfully, while adhering to low-budget demands. From the beginning, Siegel shunned the use of major special effects for the film. He did not want the film to look like science fiction fantasy, but like a serious and significant drama.

Siegel's craftsmanship brings distinction to the fast-paced action of his films, but ultimately it can go only so far within the B-movie format. Some have argued that the B action film, with its stress on violence and individualism, has an ideology of its own that no amount of detachment and control can counter. The genre itself may be retrograde, and carry right-wing elements. Siegel has certainly only occasionally shown an urge to move beyond its confines; when given bigger budgets in the sixties, he stayed within the cop-and-crime movie format, complicating it by a more surreal mise-en-scène and additional characters and conflicts. Yet the format remained. *Dirty Harry* (1971) signalled to some, particularly through the charismatic performance of Clint Eastwood, that Siegel had succumbed to the lone wolf vigilantism implicit in the genre. Siegel has been at pains to separate himself from his heroes throughout his career, and Dirty Harry is no exception. The later Siegel of the sixties and seventies may be a different figure from the Siegel of *Invasion*, but *Invasion* has always been a touchstone for Siegel, a harsh "no" to any demand for conformity.

Did the producer, Walter Wanger, who first discovered Finney's serial, find in it the same things that Mainwaring and Siegel did? The answer to this, I think, is partly yes and partly no. Wanger certainly responded to the metaphor of the pods for the growing complacency and conformity of America. A moralist, he was always eager to combine a significant message with lively entertainment. Neither Mainwaring nor Siegel would have much quarrel with this mix of entertainment and serious purpose, although Wanger, a shrewd producer, seems from the first to have been more wedded to larger doses of these ingredients than either of them. He wanted both *big* box office and *more didactic* messages. Feisty and daring, he was nonetheless a man of the system, in short, a conformist. He both fought against the system and represented it. No wonder that his films so frequently go soft or become muddled on the issues.

Wanger saw himself as a pacesetter in the world of entertainment, and especially in the social agenda of Hollywood films. He saw himself as Hollywood's conscience and seer. Because he had been born to wealth, educated in England and at Dartmouth, and was more widely read than the other moguls, most of whom had sprung from lowly origins, he became Hollywood's spokesman to the world and long served as president of the Motion Picture Academy. Constantly on junkets to business groups, conventions, and schools, he carried the message of a progressive Hollywood that interpreted the nation to itself. Even his brief prison term for shooting his wife's agent in the early fifties earned him widespread public sympathy and immersed him in a new cause, prison reform, about which he would make some of his best movies, *Riot in Cell Block 11* and later *I Want to Live* (1958).

Wanger had pioneered issue-oriented films. *Gabriel over the White House* and *The President Vanishes* tackled issues of public policy, both domestic and foreign, virtually making recommendations to Roosevelt at the beginning of his administration; they did not shy away from extreme solutions either—for example, executing gangsters publicly before the Statue of Liberty. *Private Worlds* was one of the first films to explore the world of mental illness. *Blockade,* diluted as it was by various pressures, was nevertheless the only Hollywood movie to deal with the Spanish Civil War. Friendly to the Left, he employed two radical writers to script *Blockade,* first Clifford Odets, then John Howard Lawson, the dean of Hollywood leftists. For Lawson, it was his best memory of Hollywood. In Hitchcock's *Foreign Correspondent,* Wanger openly supported American intervention in the war, a daring idea for 1940; to back the message up, he inserted a speech at the end, warning America that the lights were going out all over Europe and that we were next on the Nazi hit list. One of the first things he did in rewriting *Invasion* after it was shot was to add a similar speech for Miles. No longer did he collapse at the side of the road in despair and exhaustion; beleaguered, he looks at the motorists, the camera, and us and screams, "You're in danger; you're next." A long array of screamed warnings was sent to Kevin McCarthy in New York to record as wild sound in May 1955 to be added to the picture to point up its significant message.

The Cold War brought more ideological changes to Wanger than it did to Siegel and Mainwaring. Wanger had long counted himself a friend to the Left and was a strong antagonist of attempts by the Right, particularly Sam Wood's right-wing Motion Picture Alliance, to bring HUAC to Hollywood. Before the investigation took place, he wrote articles attacking the Right and the MPA and defending Hollywood. After HUAC, however, he changed his tune, conceding that the Right was partly correct about subversion in the industry. He was one of the four moguls who drafted the Waldorf statement in November 1947 that initiated the blacklist in Hollywood (the others were Dore Schary, Louis B. Mayer, and Joseph Schenck). Like Schary and other Hollywood liberals, he was later appalled at the impact of the blacklist on those who refused to sign the loyalty oath.

Yet, while he was anticommunist, he was no conservative. Although he supported the industry's unacknowledged blacklist, he continued to speak out for individualism and free speech and against censorship. He did not feel it was un-American to be critical of American institutions; it was right to expose their weaknesses in order to correct them. See, for instance, his speech to the American Bookseller's Convention reprinted here for a strong statement of his liberal beliefs in this period in relation to the theme of conformity in *Invasion*. Wanger was not obsessed any more than Siegel was with anticommunism. Totalitarianism was an enemy wherever it came from. If one looks through all his speeches of this period, it is difficult to find a specific reference to Soviet Russia and its threat, real or imagined. When he spoke of totalitarianism, he usually meant by it Hitler's Germany. The Churchill quotation with which he wanted to preface the film suggests defiance of the Russian threat, but it is equally reminiscent of the Churchill quotation from World War II in Finney's last scene and its defiance. Most importantly, Wanger did not dwell on any external threat. His focus was always on the internal threat and the answer to it: the renewal of old American ideals and a progressive streamlining of them for a new atomic era. For Wanger it is never the Communists who are the major threat; it is an America that has become complacent, dull, and podlike, out of touch with the needs of a new scientific world.

As someone who got sympathy but not concrete backing after his prison term, he knew what it was like to be persona non grata in an industry to which he had devoted most of his life. Driven to a low-budget studio, Allied Artists, because no other group would finance him, he continued to fight for basic social causes and reforms, often in a radical way. Always a feisty individual, he was attracted to other feisty figures like Siegel and Mainwaring.

Wanger's personality and politics as well as the changes that prison and the Cold War brought made him quite different from Siegel and Mainwaring, even though sympathetic to them and often in agreement with their nonconformity. Given that he was excited by the upbeat ending of Finney's serial, it is curious that he did not offer any criticism of Mainwaring's changes to the story to make it more bleak. True, he did hire a favorite writer, Richard Collins, also a friend of Siegel's and the writer of *Riot,* to rework Mainwaring's script. Since Collins had been a recent HUAC informant, he was certainly less politically suspect than Mainwaring. Collins, however, seems merely to have tightened up the action and the dialogue. It was only when the film was finished that one began to detect in

Wanger a faint note of dissatisfaction with it. But none of this was ever voiced strongly because Wanger's need to ballyhoo his latest production as his best overrode any doubts.

Perhaps the picture was not what he had expected; it was too much an action movie with too little development of the message. Beyond that, Wanger felt the narrative line was occasionally confusing and the chase at the end slack. He soon started to tamper with the film, strengthening the ending—and the message— with wild lines for Kevin McCarthy. Then followed other speeches by Sally and Danny, often embarrassing in their explicitness. A short voice-over introduction for Miles was also written to heighten the theme. Then came various prefaces, a Churchill quotation, and a framing device with Orson Welles, with whom Wanger carried on extensive and complex negotiations in England. Several previews in late June and early July confused Wanger further, with a disastrous one in mid-August climaxing his worries. When Wanger tried to remove the film from circulation to work on it some more, Allied Artists panicked and presumably then insisted on the new frame story and voice-over narration. Somehow, Siegel and Mainwaring agreed to do this, lest the film be butchered in even more drastic fashion.

For all of Wanger's insistence on significance, it is not the meaning of the film that seems the focus in all these additions, but the box office appeal. At a certain point popular success overcame the issue of social significance. Nowhere is the message spelled out more clearly, except in general words like love and defiance; instead, the additions, with their emphasis on strange occurrences triggered by atomic energy, push the film closer to conventional science fiction. They prepare the way for Allied Artists to treat it as a grade-B science fiction film, not the major and unusual film Wanger originally wanted. Wanger's grandiose ambitions for it persisted in his attempts to get Orson Welles for a preface, but the various prefaces, two of which are reprinted here, ally the film with Welles's *War of the Worlds* broadcast in a highly conventional way. One senses that Welles provides publicity for the film, not anything meaningfully new in ideas or themes. Ironically, Wanger's attempts to strengthen the film only weakened it and set the pattern for Allied Artists' meddling with it.

What about Allied Artists and its role? The studio has usually been cast as the villain of the drama by Siegel and Mainwaring. Obviously in many ways it was. However, as Peter Bogdanovich has pointed out in an article on B-movies reprinted here, Poverty Row studios offered a kind of freedom in which radical and individualistic films could be made. He points to the examples of Sam Fuller, Don Siegel, Budd Boetticher, Edgar G. Ulmer, Joseph H. Lewis, André de Toth, Phil Karlson, and Allan Dwan.

Clearly, Allied Artists was happiest with a movie they could put into a traditional slot. When it became apparent that *Invasion* was confusing audiences and its producer, they started cutting it. As Siegel has pointed out, their generic demands led to the cutting of the funny scenes, because as a matter of policy they refused to mix horror and comedy. But the deeper cuts and additions occurred only after the worries were generated elsewhere. Allied Artists was clearly the source of the idea for the frame story and the voice-over narration that has brought on such a hue and cry of critical denunciation. But Wanger's tampering with the film prepared for this. Curiously, once the film was taken back by the studio in mid-August, there were no memos from Wanger either discussing or protesting what was planned for the film. One wonders why, since everything else that happened to the film is so fully documented in his files.

If we look at the film as having the most radical voices of Mainwaring and Siegel at its center—though working with Finney's often conservative material—we can move outward to the less radical, liberal voice of Wanger, trying to give the film an upbeat optimistic message popular with the moderates of the fifties. Finally we arrive at the most conservative voice of the studio. Here it is not the politics per se that is so much in question, but the film's generic status and its bleakness. And that bleakness, of course, implies an ideological position. One cannot be that negative about America; one must show that Miles got through. Consequently the studio insisted on a framing story in which Miles gets his message out—just the action Wanger also wanted to stress and could not, even with the altered ending on the bridge with Miles talking to the camera. A framing story and a fantasylike coda were added to soften the impact, to bring the movie back into more conventional mainstream social and political terms. In the framing story, Miles is finally believed and the doctor calls the FBI to the rescue, bringing us full circle to Finney's original serial, where the FBI validated Miles's heroism and rescued him.

Even in this ending Siegel and Mainwaring managed to keep some of their radicalism alive. The stress is hardly on the rescue; it comes at the last moment, in an off-screen voice of the doctor on the phone, with the camera on Miles in a state of nervous collapse and relief. Throughout the frame story, Miles acts in a paranoid manner close to insanity. Siegel and Mainwaring underscore the cost of defiance and truth telling. Miles has been reduced to an exhausted maniac. And even at the end, it is not clear that rescue will come . . . or that the doctor and everyone else are not also pods. The radical despair of the film is only barely relieved. Even here, while fulfilling conservative studio demands, Siegel and Mainwaring triumphed over the studio and over Wanger as well. The ideology of *Invasion of the Body Snatchers* stays well to the left of center.

This introduction has stayed close to the intentions of the creators of *Invasion* in order to illuminate how both its ambiguous politics and its instability as a text orginated, as well as to correct an exclusively paranoid, right-wing reading of it. While the political parable of the film has occupied critics, it has hardly been the reason for the film's continuing power with audiences, not to mention its inspiration of the first of many recent remakes and rewritings of fifties science fiction and horror films, Phil Kaufman's 1978 version. This film featured both Don Siegel and Kevin McCarthy in cameo roles; Siegel as a cab driver in San Francisco, encountering, running over, and killing a still-screaming Kevin McCarthy, who in the twenty-two years between the films had apparently not found anyone who would listen to his cries.

Horror is the key continuing ingredient that links the two films. Horror can easily go beyond political parable—or beneath it—to deeper fears: the fear of sleep and of death, of the loss of identity, for the stability of the world as we familiarly know it, that our friends may not really be our friends. It is these fears that the older film still taps. At the same time, for some people the older film seems hokey or campy, too much a product of fifties styles and fashions, too much a cheap B-picture. Some people cannot connect with it, its style undermining any realism, social or psychological. Carmen Dragon's pounding score with its foreboding piano chords hardly helps the sense of realism; Siegel himself found it inappropriate.

The new wave of remakes and revisions—*Invasion* has been followed by John Carpenter's *The Thing* (1982), David Cronenberg's *The Fly* (1986), and Tobe Hooper's *Invaders from Mars* (1986) among others—seeks to establish this missing realism by bigger budgets, more advanced and detailed special effects, more complex and psychologically sophisticated characters and scripts, and location filming. At the same time, the new productions update the social nature of the fear, the monster now even more ambiguously related to our own moral malaise. In the case of *Invasion*, the special horror of the original endures. Kaufman's film provides an interesting contemporary reworking and reading of it—one that critiques our present narcissism—but one that does not necessarily supplant the original.

A number of recent commentators have tried to account for *Invasion's* continuing power, its appeal to basic human fears. Siegel's own oft-repeated comment that he is an insomniac and fears sleep because he might not wake up points to the fear of death that lies behind the horror genre; it offers a convenient rationale for the strong defense against sleep, the terrible fight for individuality, that animates Miles in *Invasion*. It is this which gives the film the feeling of nightmare, of running from an engulfing threat with identity itself at stake.

Still other more recent commentators have pointed to *Invasion's* deep fear of sex, which seems to be linked to the fear of death. Memorable among the film's most powerful images are the extreme close-ups of Becky and Miles when he discovers after kissing her that she is a pod and draws away in horror from her witchlike, mocking, and seductive look. His later remark in the voice-over narration, that he only really knew fear when he kissed Becky, only overstates what is obvious in the images. If the pods can be linked to a state of blissful passivity, as Danny Kaufman invites us and Miles to see them, then they can also be linked to the seductive charms of love, represented by Becky, as Nancy Steffen-Fluhr has pointed out in a challenging reinterpretation of the film ("Women and the Inner

Game of Don Siegel's Invasion of the Body Snatchers," reprinted in this volume). The flight from the pods, then, is a flight from sexuality, a basic fear of loss of self. The setting of the kiss with Becky, where Miles is exhausted and falls into mud and a puddle before a primitive cave in which they were both recently practically buried alive, underscores the primal nature of this fear. Michael Paul Rogin in an article reprinted here suggests that this fear is not only more basic than the political fears, but determines their shape as well.

Ironically, the most formally innovative and radical element of Mainwaring's screenplay and Siegel's film is the turning of Becky into a pod and Miles's despairing and desperate flight alone into the night. I have tried to suggest earlier that this is an index of the most radical despair about American values in the 1950s. But, ironically, it is also an intensification of a lone machismo that animates B-movies of whatever political stripe. In *Invasion*, it aligns woman with instinct, letting go, passivity, sleep, loss of self, and death—and once again propels Siegel's dialectic of control and instinct in the direction of a more firmly entrenched sense of control.

Don Siegel: A Biographical Sketch

Don Siegel was born into show business. Both his parents were former vaudevillians, top-notch mandolin players, who had settled down to teach music in Chicago, where their son was born on 26 October 1912. Moving back and forth between New York and Chicago, Siegel attended schools in both places and also briefly in New Jersey. He graduated from DeWitt Clinton High School in New York in 1929. Shortly thereafter, the family moved to England, where the elder Siegel was employed by an American company to train English businesses in American efficiency methods. Siegel was able to get a college education at Cambridge, where he showed a maverick trait by specializing in New Testament studies, even though he was Jewish by birth and a self-proclaimed atheist. After Cambridge, he moved with his family to Paris, where he became fluent in French.

In 1932 at age of nineteen he returned on his own to America, making his way across the Atlantic by playing drums in the ship's band. After a brief period, he sought out an uncle, Jack Saper, who had been a film editor at Warners. Saper introduced him to the producer Hal Wallis, who reluctantly hired Siegel as a Warners film librarian in 1934. Siegel was to remain at Warners in various capacities for fourteen years.

He found the job of film librarian—mainly marking and storing stock shots for use in later films—boring. He asked to be moved and became an assistant editor, with the almost equally boring job of rolling up reels of film. Next he moved into the insert department, which proved more exciting and hooked him on the craft of filmmaking. He had a camera crew at his disposal and was able in a creative way to modify Warners' handling of inserts. When Siegel came to the department, it mainly supplied still photographs, stock footage, and routine shots for the sequences in feature films that were at that time regularly used to divide major sequences and to show time passing. Siegel expanded the scope of the work and made it more inventive, eventually setting up and heading a montage department. Siegel began making montage sequences that involved sound and dialogue and even the stars of the film. He learned how to work fast, because major actors were available for only short periods, but he was never afraid to experiment.

Since the montage department was part of the special effects department headed by Byron Haskin, Siegel's montages often went uncredited or were credited to his supervisor, Haskin. Among the many films for which he made montages were *The Roaring Twenties* (1939), *Confessions of a Nazi Spy* (1939), *Knute Rockne— All American* (1940), *Yankee Doodle Dandy* (1942), *Casablanca* (1942), *Across the Pacific* (1942), and *Action in the North Atlantic* (1943). Siegel is credited on some of these, notably *Casablanca,* where he was responsible for the memorable opening montage sequence of the turning globe, animated maps, and the shots of people waiting, waiting, waiting.

His work with the montage production crew shaded into second unit director's work, which usually involved shooting action sequences that stood apart from the film's main narrative or were considered too dangerous for the director to film. Siegel worked on a number of Warners films in this capacity with Michael Curtiz (*Passage to Marseilles,* 1944), Howard Hawks (*Sergeant York,* 1941) and Raoul Walsh (*Northern Pursuit,* 1943). However, he refused to do *Objective Burma!* (1945) and Jack Warner laid him off for three months. Warner became for Siegel the prototype of the studio boss as pod.

Eventually rehired, he was allowed to direct two shorts, one a modern version of the nativity story, *Star in the Night* (1945), and the other a montage compilation documentary, *Hitler Lives* (1945). In the first he got a chance to work outside of the kind of action filming he was used to. In the second he showcased his montage skills on their own, not in the service of a larger narrative. Both films won Academy Awards in their respective categories in the same year, 1945.

From shorts Siegel graduated into feature directing, beginning in 1946 with an exciting Victorian whodunit starring Sidney Greenstreet and Peter Lorre, *The Verdict.* He made only one other film at Warners before his contract expired, the pedestrian and unsuccessful *Night unto Night* (1949), which starred Ronald Reagan and Siegel's future wife, Viveca Lindfors. They married shortly after making the film in 1948. In 1953 they had a son, Kristoffer Tabori, now an actor (who uses the name of his stepfather, the playwright George Tabori). Siegel and Lindfors were divorced in 1953.

As the old studio system began to break up under the impact of television, the antimonopolist Paramount decrees, and HUAC witch hunts, Siegel found himself cast adrift and out of work. For a while he worked under a two-year contract at RKO. The erratic Howard Hughes had taken over the studio and proceeded to ruin it. During this period, Siegel made *The Big Steal* (1949) in Mexico, which first let him show off his action style. The movie was basically one long chase. Here too he met the screenwriter Dan Mainwaring, who was to script three more Siegel films, including *Invasion of the Body Snatchers.* Hughes, however, gave

him few films, so Siegel refused to renew his contract and decided to go free lance instead. In 1952, he made his first film at Universal, *Duel at Silver Creek*. Universal discovered that he could make a good film fast and cheap and that he excelled as an action director.

His big break, however, came from Walter Wanger, who chose him to direct the prison riot movie with a liberal and reformist message, *Riot in Cell Block 11* (1954). Siegel filmed the movie on location at Folsom Prison in California and was able to control vast crowds of men, many of them actual prisoners. The film was an immense success, financially and critically, and lifted Siegel, if not out of low-budget production, at least out of the B-movie stereotype. Big-budget, high-status movies eluded him until the sixties. Nonetheless, he was able to make a distinctive contribution to the movies that followed *Riot*, often shaping them in the screenplay and casting, finding locations for them, and editing them after shooting. As a result, when French critics of *Cahiers de Cinéma* and *Positif* hailed American commercial movies and propounded the auteur theory, Siegel's films became celebrated. British and then American critics began to take another look, too. Among the characteristic Siegel films of this period are *Private Hell 36* (1954), *Crime in the Streets* (1956), *Baby Face Nelson* (1957, another Mainwaring script), *The Lineup* (1958), for which he had done the half-hour TV pilot in 1954, and *Hell Is for Heroes* (1962). There were also a few successful films that strayed from the violent action staple: *Edge of Eternity* (1959), an action film with the Grand Canyon as a setting; *Hound Dog Man* (1959), with the singer Fabian, essentially a nonmusical about a boy's friendship with an unruly mountain man; and *Flaming Star* (1960), with Elvis Presley, another nonmusical, in which Elvis plays a half-Indian subjected to racial prejudice by a mob of townspeople.

Invasion of the Body Snatchers remains the key film of this period, a source of inspiration for Siegel's explorations into his antihero's tensions between instinct and control and the system's formidable assault on the self. The word "pods" entered his vocabulary and still functions there in a lively way. "Don't let the pods get you," he wrote to me recently, encouraging work on this volume.

During the early sixties Siegel did extensive work in television. His move into directing bigger budget films stems indirectly from his work in TV. The 1964 film, *The Killers,* a new version of the Siodmak film of Hemingway's story, was initially intended by Universal as the first 120-minute television movie. Following the assassination of President John F. Kennedy, Universal decided to release this violent film theatrically instead. From that time on, Siegel's fortunes were linked to Universal and only *Dirty Harry* was made outside Universal auspices, on loan-out to Warners.

Even with big budgets, Siegel remained largely committed to the crime film, whether cop or antihero gangster, with occasional forays into other genres and more personal projects. The look, feel, and themes of his crime films became more complex, however. *Madigan* (1968), for instance, introduces a new figure in the moralizing commisioner, Henry Fonda, and the New York it depicts departs in its sleazy, surreal look from the documentary realism of the earlier films.

At the same time, women take on a more important role in Siegel's films, though hardly in a feminist way. In Siegel's favorite film, almost an art film project, *The Beguiled* (1971), Clint Eastwood plays a wounded Union soldier trapped in a Southern women's school, inciting female rivalries and revenge. The film was designed to show that women can be as cruel as men, that the world they inhabit is the same.

Siegel's fortunes have been closely tied to Clint Eastwood since 1969, when Eastwood redefined his spaghetti western persona for American tastes in *Coogan's Bluff.* Here a literal cowboy invades urban America; a prototype for Dirty Harry, Coogan is an Arizona deputy sheriff pursuing criminals in New York. Siegel has been closely associated with Eastwood ever since, making four more movies with him: *Two Mules for Sister Sara* (1970), *The Beguiled* (1971), *Dirty Harry* (1971), and *Escape from Alcatraz* (1979). Siegel also played a small role in the Eastwood-directed *Play Misty for Me* (1971). Increasingly, the antihero themes of his films have been tied to the Eastwood character, which has carried over into the *Dirty Harry* sequels filmed by other directors.

Siegel now lives in Nipomo, California, near San Luis Obispo. In 1957 he married former fashion model and actress Doe Avedon and they subsequently adopted four children. For the past few years he has been writing his memoirs, due to be published shortly by Faber and Faber in England.

Invasion of the Body Snatchers

Invasion of the Body Snatchers

Invasion of the Body Snatchers, then known as *The Body Snatchers,* was shot in the Allied Artists studio on the east side of Hollywood and in locations around it in twenty-three days between 23 March 1955 and 18 April 1955. The cast and technical staff worked a six-day week, with only Sundays off.

Originally Wanger and Siegel hoped to shoot the film on location in Finney's model for Santa Mira, Mill Valley, just north of San Francisco. In the first week of January 1955, Wanger, Siegel, and Mainwaring visited author Jack Finney, who lived there, to talk about the film version and to get a look at the town. When location shooting proved too expensive, Siegel and some of the Allied Artists executives found locations that resembled Mill Valley in nearby Sierra Madre, Chatsworth, Glendale, the Los Feliz neighborhood, and in Bronson and Beachwood Canyons. Much of the film, however, was shot in the studio.

The film was originally budgeted for a twenty-four-day schedule—normal for a low-budget film—at $454,864. However, Allied Artists asked Wanger to cut the budget drastically. Wanger proposed a shooting schedule of twenty days and a budget of $350,000. Before working with the lower budget, Wanger considered a wide range of well-known actors for both leads. For Miles he considered Gig Young, Macdonald Carey, Dick Powell, Joseph Cotten, Steve Cochran, John Hodiak, and Phil Carey. For Becky, he thought of casting Nancy Olsen, Anne Bancroft, Mona Freeman, Donna Reed, Kim Hunter, Joanne Dru, Barbara Hale, Vera Miles, and Diana Lynn. It is likely that the lower budget eliminated many of these choices. Instead, he first chose Richard Kiley, who had just starred in the Mainwaring-scripted *Phenix City Story* at Allied Artists. Reportedly, Kiley turned the role down. Wanger then cast two relative newcomers: Kevin McCarthy, who had played Biff in the London production of *Death of a Salesman* and had just starred in the Siegel-directed *Annapolis Story* at Allied Artists, and for Becky Dana Wynter, who had played in several major TV dramatic roles but had not yet made a film. McCarthy received only $2,500 a week, Wynter, $2,250. Both worked a gruelling schedule that occasionally went into the early hours of the morning. Siegel got $21,668 for directing. The production went over schedule by three days, largely due to night-for-night shooting that Siegel wanted. The final cost was only $382,190.

During the postproduction period, the film was cut and recut extensively. See the "Postproduction File" for a chronology of these changes. These culminated in a late addition of a framing story and voice-over narration by Miles. Mainwaring scripted both and the hospital scene was filmed by Siegel on 16 September 1955, at Allied Artists.

The title *Invasion of the Body Snatchers* was not one the creators of the movie gave it. Allied Artists assigned this title in late 1955 after discarding a number of others. Though the project was called *The Body Snatchers* originally, after Finney's serial, Wanger wanted to avoid confusion with the Val Lewton/Robert Wise 1945 horror movie with a very similar title. Failing to come up with a title, Wanger accepted the Allied Artists title, *They Came from Another World,* assigned to the film in the summer of 1955. Siegel protested vigorously and Wanger sent his complaints on to Harold Mirisch and Steve Broidy, AA executives, in late

September. He also suggested two titles by Siegel, *Better Off Dead* and *Sleep No More,* and two by himself, *Evil in the Night* and *World in Danger.* Allied Artists chose none of these.

In December 1955, when Wanger saw the final cut, he protested about the Superscope format. Although the Superscope format had been part of the early plans for the film, the first Superscope print was not made until December 1955. Wanger felt the film lost sharpness and detail. The film had been shot in a ratio of 1 to 1 : 85. Superscope was a postproduction lab process designed to make the film resemble the popular Cinemascope format. Its ratio was 2 to 1, its image less wide than Cinemascope's. An anamorphic lens was needed both to print and project the image. Some of the original image was obviously lost in this process. Most prints in circulation today and on TV further reduce the image, since they are standard ratio prints (1 to 1 : 33) made from the Superscope image. As a result they lose the image at either end and also magnify the size of the center of the image. Watching a standard ratio print after watching the Superscope image is like seeing a strangely different film.

The following continuity of the film was made from the Criterion Collection laserdisc prepared by Maurice Yacowar. This print is in the original Superscope format. The Criterion Collection is a joint venture of Janus Films and Voyager Press. It can be ordered from The Criterion Collection, 2139 Manning Ave., Los

Angeles, CA 90025. This edition of the film was first released in 1986 and contains a second audio track with a commentary on the film by Yacowar, the original theatrical trailer, a bibliography, and a demonstration of the Superscope format versus standard ratio.

I have tried to produce not only the dialogue and a description of the action and settings, but also a sense of the fluid camera movement that is an important part of the film's style. I have not tried to annotate Carmen Dragon's thunderous music in detail, but I have noted shots in which it seems significant. It has not been possible to suggest the duration of the shots and Siegel's editing style, one of his most noted traits, except by the juxtaposition of shots. Unless otherwise noted, shots are joined to each other by a straight cut.

I have used the standard abbreviations for camera distance: ELS, LS, MLS, MS, MCU, CU, and ECU ranging from extreme long shot through medium shots to extreme close up. POV indicates a shot taken along a character's angle of vision.

The notes to the continuity script show differences between the early scripts and the final shooting script and between Finney's serial and the various scripts. I have also included scenes from the final script that were shot but later cut. Siegel has long complained that the humor was cut from the film due to a policy at Allied Artists not to mix horror and comedy. The restored scenes prove he was correct. With the continuity script and the notes, one can now get a glimpse of what Siegel's original film looked like. Unfortunately, the stills reproduced here are from a 16 mm print. No quality Superscope print was available.

Credits and Cast

Director
Don Siegel

Producer
Walter Wanger

Production Company
Allied Artists

Screenplay
Daniel Mainwaring from the *Collier's* serial by Jack Finney, *The Body Snatchers*

Director of Photography
Ellsworth Fredericks

Cameraman and Assistant Operators
Bud Davidson
Ben Coleman
Phil Rand

Still Man
Fred Morgan

Art Director
Edward "Ted" Haworth

Set Dresser
Joseph Kish

Production Manager
Allen K. Wood

Assistant Directors
Richard Maybery
Bill Beaudine, Jr.

Editor
Robert S. Eisen

Music
Carmen Dragon

Music Editor
Jerry Irvin

Sound Mixer
Ralph Butler

Sound Editor
Del Harris

Boom Man
Bob Quick

Cable Man
John Lister

Grip
Harry Lewis

Special Effects
Milt Rice

Makeup
Emile Lavigne, S.M.A.
Lou LaCava

Hairdresser
Mary Westmoreland

Gaffer
George Satterfield

Best Boy
Claire Sealey

Script Supervisor
Irva Ross

Release Date
February 1956

Length
80 minutes

Cast

Dr. Miles Bennell
Kevin McCarthy

Becky Driscoll
Dana Wynter

Jack Belicec
King Donovan

Teddy Belicec
Caroline Jones

Dr. Danny Kaufman
Larry Gates

Dr. Ed Pursey
Everett Glass

Sally
Jean Willes

Wilma
Virginia Christine

Nick Grivett, the police officer
Ralph Dumke

Dr. Hill
Whitt Bissell

Dr. Harvey Bassett
Richard Deacon

Uncle Ira
Tom Fadden

Mr. Driscoll, Becky's father
Kenneth Patterson

Sam Janzek, the police officer
Guy Way

Proprietor of the Sky Terrace Night Club
Guy Rennie

Grandma Grimaldi
Beatrice Maude

Jimmy Grimaldi
Bobby Clark

Charlie Buckholtz, the gas meter reader
Sam Peckinpah

Mac, the gas station attendant
Dabbs Greer

Martha, his wife
Marie Selland

Aunt Aleda
Jean Andren

Mrs. Grimaldi
Eileen Stevens

Baggage Handler
Pat O'Malley

The Continuity Script

City Street, exterior, night

1. *Fade in.* LS: *a police car, its siren wailing, rushes down a dark street. The camera pans right as the car pulls up before the emergency entrance of a hospital. Dr. Hill and two policemen get out and enter the emergency entrance. Ominous music over.*

Hospital Emergency Room, interior, night

2. LS: *Dr. Hill and the policemen enter. The camera pans left following Dr. Hill as he approaches in* MLS *Dr. Bassett at the reception window.*

    DR. BASSETT: Oh, Doctor Hill.

    DR. HILL: Dr. Bassett? (*Dr. Bassett comes out to Dr. Hill from around the window and the camera tracks left with him.*) Well, where's the patient?

    DR. BASSETT: I hated to drag you out of bed at this time of night.

    They walk across the room. The camera tracks back in front of them and then tracks right as they approach a closed door. From behind it we hear a loud, desperate voice.

    MILES (*off*): Will you let me go while there's still time?

    DR. BASSETT: You'll soon see why I did.

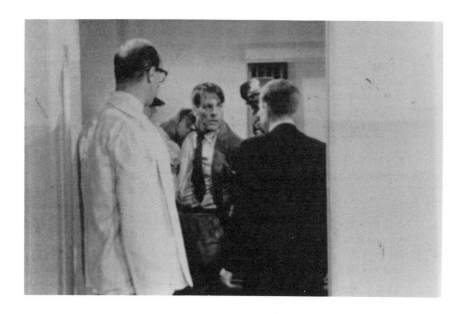

He opens the door to the office. The camera shoots directly into the office from outside the door. A wild Miles, restrained by two cops, lunges at Dr. Bassett and the cops pull him back.

MILES (*screaming*): Doctor, will you tell these fools I'm not crazy? Make them listen to me before it's too late!

DR. HILL: I'll listen to you. (*He enters the office and the camera tracks in with him toward Miles. He talks to the cops restraining Miles.*) Let him go.

3. CU: *Miles is at left in full view, his hair dishevelled, his eyes roving wildly and suspiciously. Dr. Hill is visible in profile at right.*

MILES (*warily*): Who are you?

DR. HILL: I'm Dr. Hill from the State Mental Hospital.

MILES (*putting his hands over his face as the cop on the right again restrains him, screams*): I'm not crazy!

DR. HILL: Let him go! (*The cop steps back from Miles.*)

MILES (*pleading desperately*): Doctor, now you must listen to me, you must understand me. I'm a doctor too. I am not insane! I am not insane!

DR. HILL: All right, all right. Now suppose we just sit down over here, Dr. Bennell, and you tell me what happened.

He leads him over to a couch, the camera tracking forward with them and tilting down, keeping Miles alone in CU.

MILES (*sitting down and trying to calm himself*): Well, it started . . . for me it started last Thursday. In response to an urgent message from my nurse . . .

Slow oil dissolve into the flashback.

Santa Mira Railroad Station, exterior, day[1]

4. ELS: *high view of a train at right leaving a small California railroad station. Miles walks beside the train, then crosses the tracks on the left to the station platform. The camera pans left to reveal the town name on the station, Santa Mira.*

MILES (*continuing his voice-over narration from the previous shot*): . . . I hurried home from the medical convention I had been attending. At first glance everything looked the same. It wasn't. Something evil had taken possession of the town.

5. MLS: *Miles claiming his luggage from a baggage handler who wheels the bags in.*

MILES: These two. (*He gives the baggage handler the claim ticket and then places a tip in his right hand.*) Here you are.

BAGGAGE HANDLER: Thank you, sir. (*He hands Miles the two bags.*)

MILES: Thank you. (*He take his bags and the camera pans left with him as he goes to the bottom of the stairs, then pans right as he goes up to the platform. He passes a man going in the opposite direction.*) Morning, Mr. Fisher.

6. MS: *Sally is walking beside the station, waving to get Miles's attention.*
   SALLY: Doc!

   The camera pans left with her and cranes up to the level of the platform where Miles comes into view carrying his luggage and coat.

   MILES (*approaching Sally*): Hiya, Sally!

   SALLY (*embracing him with her left arm on his shoulder, and getting a quick kiss on the cheek from him*): Hi! Welcome home, I'm glad you're back!

   Together they walk off the platform and in the direction from which Sally came. The camera tracks back with them and pans as they reach the car parked in front of the station. They are now in MLS.

   MILES: How's Mickey and the baby?

   SALLY: Oh, they're fine, but it seems as though everybody else in Santa Mira needs a doctor.

   MILES: Oh?

   SALLY: You've got an office full of patients.

   MILES: Oh, no. On my first day back?

   SALLY: Well, some of them have been waiting for two weeks.

   She opens the rear door and Miles puts his bags in the back seat.

   MILES: Why didn't you send them to Pursey or Carmichael like I told you to?

   SALLY (*opening the front door on the passenger side and getting in*): Most of them wouldn't go—they want to see you!

   MILES: Oh . . . (*He shuts the back door and walks around the back of the car to the driver's side and gets in behind the wheel. He starts the car and begins to drive off.*) What's the matter with them?

   SALLY: They wouldn't say.

The Road to Santa Mira, exterior, day

7. MS: *Sally and Miles in the car with Miles driving, viewed through the front windshield and from directly in front of the car.*

   SALLY: You know, usually people can't talk enough about what's ailing them.

   MILES (*agreeing with her and pondering her information*): Mmmmm.

   SALLY: For instance, Wally Eberhard was in twice and called three times about something, but he wouldn't tell me what it was.

   MILES: That's funny.

   SALLY: Neither would anyone else, from Becky Driscoll down to that fat traffic cop, Sam Janzek.

8. MCU: *Miles.*

   MILES (*with interest*): Becky Driscoll, I thought she was in England.

9. MCU: *Sally.*

   SALLY (*smiling at his reaction*): She got back a few days ago and she wanted to see you.

10. MS: *Sally and Miles seen through the windshield from the driver's side of the car, with Miles closer to the camera.*

    SALLY: Are you still interested?

    MILES: My interest in married women is strictly professional or yours would have been a lost cause long ago.[2]

    SALLY (*laughing, then asking*): How was the convention?

    MILES: Wonderful. (*Then a bit ironically.*) They wept with envy when I read my paper. (*He suddenly looks ahead, alarmed.*)

    Grimaldi's Vegetable Stand, exterior, day[3]

11. ELS: *Miles's car coming down the road from the right background, slightly low angle. A vegetable stand is on the left; a boy runs into the road in front of it. A woman chasing him appears from the side. Miles's car is rapidly approaching him from the background on the right. The horn sounds in warning twice as the boy begins to dash out in front of the car.*

12. MS: *Miles and Sally from the back as seen from the inside of the car over the back seat. Through the windshield between Miles and Sally we see Jimmy Grimaldi running directly in front of the car. Ominous music starts on the soundtrack. The car's brakes squeal.*

13. ELS: *as in 11. The car has stopped in a cloud of dust from the road. The mother chases the boy down the road, while Miles emerges from the stopped car in the background and proceeds to join the chase.*

    MRS. GRIMALDI: Come back here! . . . Jimmy! (*The boy disappears frame left and Miles approaches Mrs. Grimaldi on the right. Heavy chords pound out.*)

    MILES: What's the matter, Mrs. Grimaldi?

    MRS. GRIMALDI: It's nothin', he just don't want to go to school.

14. ELS: *the road ahead of the car and the boy running down it, from Miles's and Mrs. Grimaldi's* POV. *The boy cuts into the woods on the left side.*

15. MS: *Mrs. Grimaldi looking at Miles right, who is closer to the camera and partially turned away from it.*

    MILES (*panting*): Well! . . . (*Lifting his hat with his right hand.*) . . . If I were you, I'd have a talk with his teacher.

    MRS. GRIMALDI (*breathing hard with exhaustion*): Yeah, I will when I get time.

    The music becomes less tense, more mysterious.

    MILES (*looking right, toward the closed vegetable stand, and then turning back to look at her*): What's the matter, has Joe been sick?

16. LS: *Grimaldi's vegetable stand with covers pulled over it.*

    MRS. GRIMALDI (*off*): No, he gave the stand up.

17. LS: *as in 13, low angle, Mrs. Grimaldi and Miles in the foreground.*

    MRS. GRIMALDI: Too much work!

    She looks toward where the boy went and exits frame left.

    MILES: Oh!

    Miles turns around and starts walking back to the car. Sally drives the car up the road to pick him up.

    MILES (*voice-over narration*): The boy's panic should have told me that it was more than school he was afraid of. And that littered, closed-up vegetable stand should have told me something, too. When I last saw it less than a month ago, it was the cleanest and busiest stand on the road.

    Miles gets in the car and they drive off.

The Road to Santa Mira, exterior, day

18. MS: *Miles and Sally inside the car, seen from the right through the windshield, as in 10.*

    SALLY: That's strange. . . She was in to see you too, last Friday, and I tried to get her to go see Doc Pursey but she wouldn't. . . . She said only you could help her.

    MILES: Well, whatever it was, it couldn't have been too serious, I guess. *Dissolve.*

Miles's Office, Santa Mira, interior, day[4]

19. CU *of an X-ray of a skull in front of Miles's face as he holds it up to the light of the open window of his office. At his left, the other half of the*

window is closed and in it can be seen reflections of mountains, the town of Santa Mira, and the X-ray in Miles's hand. The camera pulls back as Miles puts the X-ray down and we see his face in MS, *looking out the window.*

MILES: One minor concussion, two cases of the common cold, and six cancelled appointments. (*Sally crosses left in the background and Miles looks toward her as he talks to her.*) Looks like you rushed me here for nothing. (*He turns and looks out the window again.*)

SALLY (*working on the left, but the drawn shade obscures her upper body*): I don't understand it, Miles. They couldn't wait to see you. But you're still booked up solid for the afternoon.

Through the part of the window below the drawn shade, she can be seen approaching the closed left window.

MILES: Bet they don't show. (*He looks out the window.*) Look, there's Wally Eberhard . . .

Sally pulls the shade up to look out, too.

20. ELS, *slightly high angle: two men talking in front of a bank, a couple with their child passing to the left on the sidewalk.*

MILES (*off*): . . . talking somebody into buying some insurance. . . . There's nothing wrong with him. (*A man and woman enter from the left and cross the street, the camera panning them right slightly.*) And Bill Bittner's taking his secretary to lunch.

21. MS: *Miles and Sally, Miles with his back to the camera and Sally facing him on the right. Behind her we see the reception room through two doors with curtains. The one on the left is open. A bell rings and Sally goes through this door to the reception room. The camera tracks and pans right with Miles as he begins to go to the hall door exit at the right of his inner office.*

MILES: And speaking of lunch, would you tell whoever that is that I'm out having mine? (*Miles goes to the door and stops short of opening it as he hears a voice off-screen in the room.*)

BECKY (*off*): Is Dr. Bennell in?

SALLY (*off*): Uh . . . yes, he's here.

BECKY (*off*): Do you suppose he has time to see me?

SALLY (*off*): Um. Well, if he hasn't there's something wrong with him. Go right in.

Miles walks back from the door and toward the reception room. The camera both tracks and pans left with him, then tracks in as Becky suddenly comes through the open left double door into the inner office, meeting Miles as he comes from the right. She is wearing a very revealing strapless summer dress. Romantic music swells in the background.

MILES (*warmly*): Becky!

22. MCU: *Becky at left, with Miles on the right, his back to the camera. She is smiling radiantly.*

    MILES: Almost five years.

    BECKY: It's wonderful to be home again.

23. MS: *as in 21. Becky and Miles at the door of the inner office with Sally at her desk in the background.*

    BECKY: I've been away so long I feel almost like a stranger in my own country. (*She comes farther into the inner office and turns to look at him as he shuts the door between the offices.*) I hope you don't mind my coming without an appointment.

    The camera tracks back and right with them as they cross the office.

    MILES (*gesturing her to a chair across the room*): Not at all. (*The camera tracks back farther until they are in* MLS. *He stands, arms crossed, leaning against his desk on the left while she seats herself in a chair on the right.*) What'll you have? We're pushing appendectomies this week.

    BECKY (*laughing*): Oh, Miles!

    MILES: Ah, maybe I clown around too much. Pretty soon my patients won't trust me to prescribe aspirin for them. But seriously, what's the trouble?

24. MCU: *Becky. Slight high angle suggests Miles's* POV. *Becky looks down*

*and the romantic music fades and becomes more ominous-sounding. Shots
24–30 are a series of shot–reverse shots.*

BECKY (*seriously*): It's my cousin.

25. MS: *Miles, his arms folded, looking concerned. The low angle suggests
her point of view, but he is filmed slightly from the left.*

MILES: Wilma? What's the matter with her?

26. MCU: *Becky.*

BECKY (*alternately looking up at him, then down seriously*): She has a—
well, I guess you'd call it a delusion. You know her uncle, Uncle Ira?

MILES (*off*): Sure, I'm his doctor.

BECKY (*looking up at him seriously*): Well, Miles, she's got herself
thinking he isn't her uncle.

27. MS: *Miles.*

MILES: How do you mean? That they're not really related?

28. MCU: *Becky.*

BECKY: No, she thinks he's an imposter or something, someone who
only looks like Ira.

MILES (*off*): Have you seen him?

BECKY: I just came from there.

29. MS: *Miles.*

MILES: Well, is he Uncle Ira or isn't he Uncle Ira?

30. MCU: *Becky.*

BECKY: Of course he is. I told Wilma that, but it was no use.

31. MLS: *Becky and Miles, as in the end of 23.*

BECKY: Please, would you stop by and have a talk with her?

MILES: Sally says that I'm booked up for the afternoon, but why don't
you ask her to come in and see me?

BECKY: I'll try.

*She gets up from the chair and Miles escorts her to the exit door of the
inner office with the romantic music swelling up again in the background.
The camera tracks forward, following them.*

MILES: How about some lunch?

BECKY: I can't . . . I'm meeting Dad at the store.

Miles opens the door and they both exit. He is holding her arm.

32. MCU: *Becky and Miles walking down the hallway toward the camera, the
camera accompanying them, both tracking back ahead of them and panning their movements through the narrow hallway. Romantic music
continues.*

MILES (*looking at her romantically*): When did you get back?

BECKY: I came back from London two months ago. I've been in Reno.

MILES: Reno?

BECKY: Reno. (*She manages a slight ironic laugh.*) Dad tells me you
were there too.

MILES: Five months ago.

They turn and go down the stairs away from the camera, which remains stationary at the top of the stairs, tilting down at them and following them to the door to the outside. He is still holding her arm.

BECKY: Oh, I'm sorry.

MILES: So was I. I wanted it to work. Well, I guess that makes us lodge brothers now.

BECKY: Yes.

MILES: Except that I'm paying dues while you collect them.

BECKY (*laughing*): Miles!

Street outside Miles's Office, exterior, day

33. HS: *Officer Sam Janzek is ticketing a parked car in the foreground. Miles and Becky exit at the far right from the office building in the background. They walk to the left, the camera panning left with their movement.*

MILES (*greeting a man who passes by*): Hello, Mr. Gordon.

MAN: How are you?

MILES (*now in* MLS, *walking with Becky around the front of the car Janzek is ticketing*): Sam!

JANZEK: Hello, Doc.

MILES: At it again, hey! (*The camera pans right as Janzek gets on his motorcycle.*) My nurse tells me you were in last week and wanted very much to see me.

JANZEK (*getting on his motorcycle, now visible in the right fore-ground*): It wasn't anything important. (*He rides off on the left.*)

BECKY: Say, didn't he go to college with us?

MILES: Quit his second year to get married. . . . (*They begin to cross the street, the camera tracking back and crossing with them, keeping them in* MS.) . . . like I wanted us to do.

BECKY: Just be thankful I didn't take you seriously.

MILES: You be thankful. I found out that a doctor's wife needs the understanding of an Einstein and the patience of a saint.

The camera pans right as they reach the other side of the street, with their backs to us, then in profile as she stops in front of the store where her father works.

BECKY: And love?

MILES: I wouldn't know about that. (*He removes his hand from her arm and gestures as he speaks.*) I'm just a general practitioner. Love is handled by the specialists.

BECKY (*laughing lightly*): Well, here's where I leave you.

She extends her right hand. He takes it in both of his hands and shakes it. She makes a move toward the door of a store in the background, but he holds onto her and she turns to look at him.

MILES (*coming closer to her*): You know something? This is where you

left me the last time. (*She turns and goes into the store, the camera panning right slightly as she enters. A little boy passes.*) Hi, Johnny. (*Miles pats him on the head.*)
Dissolve.

34. MS: *of the town clock outside Miles's office, reading 4:45, with the windows to Miles's office in the background and a sign affixed beneath the windows, Miles Bennell, M.D.*
Miles's Office, interior, day

35. MS: *Miles is putting on his suitcoat at the closet door in the inner office. Gentle music plays. The camera follows him to the curtained double doors and he addresses Sally at her desk in the reception room through the open left door.*
    MILES (*finishing putting on his coat*): Sally, I'm off. Will you tell the answering service I'll be at home?
    SALLY: Good night, Doc.
    MILES: Good night.
    JIMMY GRIMALDI (*off*): I'm not going in there.
    Miles looks into the reception room from the inner office door.

36. MLS: *silhouettes of Jimmy Grimaldi and his grandmother seen through the glass door that connects the reception room to the hallway, from Miles's POV. The boy is crying.*
    GRANDMA GRIMALDI (*off, but seen as a silhouette*): Stop all this nonsense! (*She opens the door and shoves Jimmy in, while he is trying to break away from her.*) And be a good boy. Come on!
    Jimmy goes quickly out of the frame left and she lunges after him.

37. MS: *Miles steps from his door to Jimmy and his grandmother, the camera panning with him very quickly.*
    MILES: Hey, hey, hey! (*He reaches them and holds the boy; the camera pulls back to show Jimmy with Miles, the grandmother slightly behind them in MLS, with Sally standing at frame right. He tries to calm the boy.*) Hey, take it easy! Isn't this Jimmy Grimaldi?
    GRANDMA GRIMALDI (*nodding*): Yes, Doctor. Can I talk to you a moment?
    MILES (*to her*): Sure. (*To the boy.*) You know I almost ran you down this morning? You've got to be careful when you run out in the road. (*He leads Jimmy and his grandmother to the inner office past Sally, opening the second door, the camera panning right with them.*) Come on, come on! (*For a moment we see the trio in the inner office, but Jimmy breaks loose and runs back into the reception room into Sally's arms, the camera panning with him. She both catches and holds him, as Miles stoops and holds his arms, looks up at him, and talks to him. His grandmother stands at the right.*) Hey, hey, hey, hey, hey, hey, hey. . . . Slow down, now. Look, school's isn't as bad as all that! It can't be.

GRANDMA GRIMALDI: School isn't what upset him . . . it's my daughter-in-law.

Miles is now looking up at the grandmother, as he still holds Jimmy.

38. MS: *Sally holds Jimmy, with Miles's head visible below them, the back of it to the camera and part of the grandmother's upper body visible at frame right.*

GRANDMA GRIMALDI: He's got the crazy idea she isn't his mother.

JIMMY (*crying*): She isn't, she isn't! (*Miles looks up at the grandmother, then back to Jimmy.*) Don't let her get me!

SALLY (*comfortingly*): Nobody's going to get you, Jimmy.

Miles rises.

39. MLS: *from the inner office through the two open doors of Sally, with Jimmy in the reception room, Miles at center rising and ushering the grandmother into the inner office. The camera tracks back and to the right with them as they stop in MS, he on the left, she on the right, before a medical cabinet.*

MILES: How long has this been going on? (*He opens the cabinet.*)

GRANDMA GRIMALDI: An hour ago I found him hiding in the cellar having hysterics. He wouldn't tell me anything, until I started to phone his mother. . . . That's when he said Anna wasn't his mother.

MILES: Could you keep him with you for a day or so?

GRANDMA GRIMALDI: Of course.

MILES: Give him one of these every four hours during the day. (*He gives her the vial he took from the medicine cabinet.*) And call me tomorrow and let me know how he's feeling.

GRANDMA GRIMALDI: Yes, Doctor. Thank you.

Miles walks to the right toward the water cooler; the camera pans with him. He is at the right of the frame alone, getting water from the cooler.

JIMMY (*off*): Don't let her get me!

SALLY (*off*): Nobody's going to get you, Jimmy.

40. MLS: *the reception room. Sally is alone with Jimmy, still holding and comforting him.*

41. MS: *as in 39. Miles walks past the grandmother toward the reception room. The camera pans left with him, and then holds as he approaches Sally and the boy in MLS through the doors. The grandmother is at the door, closest to the camera. Both she and Miles have their backs to the camera, both in MLS, much as at the beginning of shot 39. Miles stoops down to give the boy the water and pill.*

42. MS: *in the reception room, level, but at Jimmy's height. Sally holding Jimmy, Jimmy with his mouth open in the center, and Miles at right giving him medicine. All three are in profile.*

MILES: All right, Jimmy! Open your mouth . . . shut your eyes . . . in the words of the poet, I'll give you something to make you wise.

Jimmy takes the pill and Miles holds the cup of water to his lips.

SALLY (*patting Jimmy on the shoulder*): That's a good boy, Jimmy.

JIMMY (*to Miles*): I'm not going home, ever.

43. MLS: *same setup, but with the grandmother visible at right.*

MILES (*rising*): You're going to stay at your grandmother's house. (*To the grandmother.*) Will you call his mother and tell her . . .

JIMMY (*to Miles*): She's not my mother! Don't tell her where I am!

The grandmother has crossed to the left and has taken the boy's arm in preparation for leaving.

MILES: All right, all right! Run along. Everything's going to be all right! You be a good boy now. (*The camera follows his movements left as he ushers them out of the office, giving Jimmy a slap on the rear.*) Go on!

GRANDMA GRIMALDI: Good night, Doctor.

MILES: Good night. (*He shuts the door, its bell ringing.*) Sally, I've changed my mind. I'm not going directly home. I'm going to stop off and see Wilma Lentz. (*The camera pans his movements right as he crosses in front of Sally.*)

SALLY: Shall I call the boy's mother?

MILES (*turning back to answer her*): Yes, call her and tell her what happened and I suggested it might be a good idea if the boy spent the night at his grandmother's house.

Miles goes into his inner office leaving Sally alone in the frame. The camera tilts down to follow her looking for the phone number in the files on her desk.

Dissolve.

Wilma Lentz's House, exterior, day[5]

44. LS: *Miles crossing Wilma's lawn right, with Uncle Ira mowing the lawn in the center background. The camera pans right with Miles and frames him in* MS.

WILMA (*off, before she comes into view*): Hello, Miles.

MILES: Nice to see you, Wilma. (*Becky and Wilma have both come into view, seated below Miles in a lawn swing.*) Becky. (*Miles puts his left hand on the roof of the swing and leans down to talk to Wilma.*)

WILMA: Let's have it. You talked to him. . . . What do you think?

MILES: It's him. . . . He's your uncle Ira, all right.

45. CU: *Wilma.*

WILMA (*emphatically*): He is not.

Shots 45 through 57 are shot–reverse shots, each suggesting the POV *of the other.*

46. CU: *Miles, Wilma's* POV, *slightly low angle; he turns left to look back at Uncle Ira.*

47. LS: *Uncle Ira at center, Miles's* POV. *He is mowing the lawn and coming in their direction. This interrupts the series of Miles and Wilma shots.*

48. CU, *as in 46. Miles looks back at Wilma.*

49. CU: *Wilma, as in 45.*

    MILES (*off*): How's he different?

    WILMA: That's just it, there is no difference you can actually see. He looks, sounds, acts, and remembers like Uncle Ira.

50. CU: *Miles.*

    MILES: Then he is your Uncle Ira. Can't you see that? No matter how you feel, he is.

51. CU: *Wilma.*

    WILMA (*deliberately and definitively*): But he isn't—there's something missing.

52. CU: *Miles.*

    WILMA (*off*): He's been a father to me since I was a baby.

53. CU: *Wilma.*

    WILMA: Always when he talked to me there was a special look in his eye. . . . (*She puts her hand to her mouth sadly*). That look's gone.

54. CU: *Miles.*

    MILES: What about memories? There must be certain things that only you and he would know about?

55. CU: *Wilma.*

    WILMA (*with anguish*): Oh, there are. . . . I've talked to him about them. He remembers them all down to the last small detail. Just like Uncle Ira would. But Miles, there's—there's no emotion. None!

56. CU: *Miles.*

    WILMA (*off*): Just the pretense of it. The words . . . the gesture . . . the tone of voice . . .

57. CU: *Wilma.*

    WILMA: . . . everything else is the same but not the feeling. (*She sits back and says definitively:*) Memories or not, he isn't my Uncle Ira.

58. MCU: *Miles at first seen from the side, kneels down to be at their level; the camera pans his movement down to Becky and Wilma, who are now at his right.*

    MILES: Wilma, I'm on your side. (*The camera then pulls back a little.*) My business is people in trouble and I'm going to find a way to help you.

59. CU: *Miles.*

    MILES (*looking at Wilma*): Now no one could possibly impersonate your Uncle Ira without you . . .

    Shots 59 through 62 are another series of shot–reverse shots.

60. CU: *Wilma.*

    MILES: (*off*). . . or your Aunt Aleda or even me seeing a million little differences.

61. CU: *Miles.*

    MILES: I want you to realize that . . . think about it . . .

62. CU: *Wilma.*
    MILES (*off*): . . . and then you'll know that the trouble is inside you.
    AUNT ALEDA (*off*): Wilma!
63. MS: *Miles kneeling and Becky and Wilma on the swing, as in 58. All three are looking off to where Aunt Aleda's voice is coming from.*
    AUNT ALEDA (*off*): Where are you?
    WILMA: Out on the lawn. (*To Miles.*) Say nothing to her.
    Miles pats Wilma's knee reassuringly.
64. MLS: *Aunt Aleda walking from the house toward the group. The camera pans her movement right and stops when she reaches frame left. Becky and Wilma are in the swing, Miles is standing at frame right.*
    AUNT ALEDA: Why, Miles! I didn't know you were here. Welcome home.
    MILES: Hello, Mrs. Lentz.
    AUNT ALEDA (*to Wilma*): Did you ask Miles to stay for dinner?
    MILES: I can't tonight.
    AUNT ALEDA: I'm making spoon bread.
    MILES: Please, don't tempt me.
    AUNT ALEDA: Well, maybe next time. . . . Wilma, where are my glasses?
    BECKY: I think I saw them on the mantelpiece. I'll go with you.
    She gets up and the two exit frame left. Miles crosses in front of Wilma and sits down where Becky was. The camera tracks in for a MS.

65. LS: *Uncle Ira is still mowing the lawn.*
66. MCU: *Miles and Wilma from the left, with Miles closer to the camera and looking at Wilma.*
    WILMA: Miles, am I going crazy? Don't spare me, I've got to know.
    MILES (*shaking his head*): No, you're not. Even these days it isn't as easy to go crazy as you might think.
67. MCU: *Miles and Wilma from the right, with Wilma closer to the camera.*
    MILES: But you don't have to be losing your mind to need psychiatric help. I'd like you to see a doctor friend of mine.
68. MCU: *Miles and Wilma, as in 66.*
    WILMA: A psychiatrist?
    MILES: Dan Kaufman. I'll make an appointment for you tomorrow.
    WILMA (*sighing*): All right, but it's a waste of time. There's nothing wrong with me. (*She glances up at Uncle Ira mowing.*)
69. LS: *Uncle Ira still mowing near the house, from Wilma's* POV. *He glances over his shoulder at them.*
70. MCU: *Miles and Wilma, as in 68.*
    WILMA: We better break this up or he'll start wondering. (*She begins to get up and leave frame right.*)
71. MS, *head on: Miles and Wilma get up from the chair. The camera rises with them. Becky reenters frame left.*
    MILES: Wondering what?
    WILMA: If I don't suspect. . . . You've been a big help and I don't want you to worry about me. (*To Becky.*) Or you either. I'll be all right.
    MILES: Sure you will. (*He turns to address Becky on his left.*) Staying here, Becky, or may I drive you home?
    BECKY (*to Wilma*): Would you like me to stay?
    WILMA: Of course not. . . . (*To both.*) Good night.
    MILES: Good night. (*He puts his arm around Becky and then moves forward toward the camera to leave. Becky leaves at frame left.*)
72. MS: *Uncle Ira mowing with a pipe in his mouth. He crosses from frame right and exits frame left. Becky and Miles are leaving Wilma in the far background and are crossing the lawn. They look back and wave to her, then cross the lawn, the camera panning with them, until they reach Uncle Ira on the left. Becky goes on, but Miles stays to chat with Uncle Ira.*
    UNCLE IRA: Nice having Becky back again, eh, boy?
    MILES: Sure is.[6]
    He looks toward Wilma, while Ira looks after Becky going to the car. Miles gives him a strong pat on the shoulder and continues on, the camera panning his movement left to Becky at the front door of the car in the driveway. He opens the door for her, she gets in, and he closes it and starts going around the car.

MILES (*voice-over narration*): In the back of my mind a warning bell was ringing.

73. MS: *Wilma looking after them as they leave.*

MILES (*voice-over narration*): Sick people who couldn't wait to see me . . .

74. LS *of the car pulling back out of the driveway, Uncle Ira watching them at right, then resuming mowing. The camera pans the car left as it backs out of the driveway.*

MILES (*voice-over narration*): . . . then suddenly were perfectly all right. A boy who said his mother wasn't his mother. A woman who said her uncle wasn't her uncle. But I didn't listen. Obviously, the boy's mother was his mother. I had seen her.

75. MCU: *Uncle Ira putting his pipe back in his mouth and watching the car drive away.*

MILES (*voice-over narration*): And Uncle Ira was Uncle Ira. There was no doubt of that after I talked to him.

Streets of Santa Mira, exterior, day

76. MS: *Becky and Miles in the front seat of the car, with Miles nearer the camera. As before, we see them through the windshield.*

BECKY: Miles, he is Ira?

MILES: Of course, he is. . . . What do you mean?

BECKY: It's just that Wilma's so positive. . . . Will she be all right?

MILES: Oh, I think so. I'm a doctor according to my diploma, but I don't really know what Wilma's trouble is. I could start talking psychiatrical jargon but it's out of my line and in Dan Kaufman's. . . . I wish you didn't have to go home for dinner.

BECKY: I don't. Dad's eating out with a friend.

MILES: I could pick you up at seven.

BECKY (*hesitating*): Well. . . .

MILES: It's summer and the moon is full. And "I know a bank where the wild thyme grows."

BECKY (*saying the last part with him*): . . . "where the wild thyme grows."[7] (*She laughs.*) You haven't changed a bit.

Dissolve.

Sky Terrace Night Club, exterior, night[8]

77. ELS *from above: parking lot of the Fireside Inn. The sign for the club, Sky Terrace Night Club, is in* MS *at left near the top of the stairs where the camera is positioned. Miles and Becky emerge from their car in* ELS *and walk right across the lot, the camera panning with them. Dance music from inside the club is heard. As they reach the stairway to the club, an open convertible starts up with a roar and pulls back quickly, nearly hitting them.*

MILES: Whup! whoa! Watch out! *He touches the car to both halt it and brace himself.*

DANNY KAUFMAN (*who is driving the convertible, and looking back*): Sorry! (*Recognizing Miles.*) Hey, Miles, when did you get back?

MILES: This morning.

78. MLS: *Becky and Miles at the side of the car with Ed Pursey and Danny Kaufman in the front seat of the convertible. We see them from over the hood.*

MILES (*reaching in to shake hands with him*): How are you, Danny? This is Miss Driscoll. Dr. Kaufman, our one and only psychiatrist.

BECKY: How do you do.

MILES (*to Becky*): Watch out what you say. (*To Ed.*) Ed, you remember Becky . . .

ED: I should, I brought her into the world.

MILES: You did us all a favor.

BECKY: Hello, Dr. Pursey.

MILES (*to Danny*): This saves me a phone call. I've got a mixed-up kid and a woman who need a witch doctor.

DANNY: The boy says his father isn't his father and the woman says her sister isn't her sister.

79. MS: *Becky and Miles, straight on. Shots 79–86 are a series of shot–reverse shots of the duos.*

MILES: That's pretty close. I knew you'd been studying hypnosis but when did you start reading minds?

80. MS: *Ed and Danny in the car, with Ed looking at Danny and laughing. Ed turns back to Miles.*
    ED: He doesn't have to read them. I've sent him a dozen patients since it started.
81. MS: *Becky and Miles.*
    MILES: Well, what is it? What's going on?
82. MS: *Ed and Danny.*
    DANNY: I don't know, a strange neurosis, evidently contagious, an epidemic mass hysteria. In two weeks, it's spread all over town.[9]
83. MS: *Becky and Miles.*
    MILES: What causes it?
84. MS: *Ed and Danny.*
    DANNY: Worry about what's going on in the world, probably.
85. MS: *Becky and Miles.*
    MILES: Make room for Wilma Lentz tomorrow, will you, Danny?
86. MS: *Ed and Danny.*
    DANNY: Send her in around two.[10]
87. MLS: *the four, as in 78.*
    DANNY: Good night.
    MILES: So long, Danny.
88. ELS: *as in the opening shot of the sequence, 77, with the convertible now pulling out of the lot to the right. Becky and Miles walk to the stairs up to the club.*
89. LS: *they start up the stairs. The camera pans them as they ascend the stairs and stop in MS at its level. On the way they talk.*
    MILES: Well, this is the oddest thing I've ever heard of. (*Seductively.*) Let's hope we don't catch it. (*Jokingly.*) I'd hate to wake up some morning and find out that you weren't you.
    BECKY (*laughing*): I'm not the high school kid you used to romance, so how can you tell?
    MILES: You really want to know?
    BECKY: Ummm.
    Miles kisses her quite passionately. The wind is blowing strongly.
    MILES: Um, you're Becky Driscoll.
    They begin to walk again and the camera pans left with them.
    BECKY (*walking by the nightclub sign, which advertises a singer*): Hey, Santa Mira's looking up!
    MILES: Has, ever since you got back.
    They are walking left along a level walkway to the entrance. They are now in LS and their voices are softer.
    BECKY: Is this an example of your bedtime manner, Doctor?
    MILES: No, ma'am, that comes later.
    They open the door to the club.

Sky Terrace Night Club, interior, night

90. ELS: *the interior of the club, the proprietor and a waiter at the rear. The proprietor moves left to go to the door; the camera pans his movement as he walks behind a stone chimney and a jukebox from which the music we have heard is coming. It then tracks in to* LS *as he greets them at the door.*

    PROPRIETOR: Good evening, Doctor.

    MILES: What happened to the crowd tonight?

    PROPRIETOR: I don't know. It's been this way for two or three weeks now.

91. MS: *Becky and Miles at left, the proprietor at right.*

    MILES (*removing Becky's fur wrap*): Well! At least we don't have to wait for a table.

    PROPRIETOR: Take your pick, here . . . (*He motions left.*) . . . or here. (*He motions right.*)

    MILES: Here, I think. (*He indicates right and hands the proprietor Becky's fur.*) (*To Becky.*) Shall we?

    BECKY: Uh-huh. (*She leads right and he follows, the camera tracking and panning with them until they are in front of the jukebox.*)

    MILES: Where's the band?

    PROPRIETOR: Whole business started falling off, so I had to let them go. There's the jukebox, though.

    MILES: Shall we dance? (*They begin to dance and the proprietor moves to the right.*) I hope you didn't let the bartender go.

    PROPRIETOR (*looking back at them*): I'm the bartender. Martinis?

    MILES (*dancing with Becky in* MS): Two, dry . . . very dry.

    The camera pans right with them as they dance. In the background in LS, *behind the bar, the proprietor is mixing the drinks.*

    BECKY: Miles?

    MILES: Um?

    BECKY: I don't care what Dr. Kaufman says, I'm worried.[11]

    The telephone rings and the proprietor in the background answers it.

    MILES: You are in the capable hands of your personal physician.

    PROPRIETOR: Oh, Doctor!

    MILES: Ah, there's our evening. Sorry.

    They stop dancing and walk toward the bar in the background.

92. MS: *the bar with Miles and Becky in foreground and the proprietor handing the phone to him over the bar. Becky sits on a stool at the right while the proprietor is now in between them on the other side of the bar, mixing their drinks and pouring them.*

    MILES: Dr. Bennell.

    WOMAN'S VOICE (*off, over the phone*): Jack Belicec wants you to come to his house right away, Doctor. He says it's urgent.

MILES (*nodding*): Thank you. (*He hangs the phone up.*) (*To the proprietor.*) Better hold those drinks. (*The proprietor stops pouring the drinks.*) (*To Becky.*) Emergency. Well, at least they called before we ordered dinner. How hungry are you?

BECKY: I can wait.

MILES: It may be quite a while.

BECKY: Then I'll go with you.

MILES (*to the proprietor*): Sorry, we'll be back later.

The proprietor smiles with resignation.

Dissolve.

The Street in front of the Belicecs' House, exterior, night

93. LS: *Becky and Miles in the front seat of the car coming down a dark street. The camera pans left with it as it pulls into the driveway. On a brick pillar at the drive's entrance is a lighted sign, Belicec.*

94. MS: *Miles and Becky seen from the back seat of the car. We see the Belicecs' driveway through the windshield.*

MILES: There's Jack.[12]

Jack comes into view in the light at the top of the drive. He is clearly waiting for Miles; he wears a white sweater and has a pipe in his hand. Miles stops the car and pulls on the brake.

95. LS: *Miles gets out of the car and walks over to Jack; the camera tracks with him. Jack comes toward him from the right.*

MILES: Hello, Jack. What's the matter? . . . Teddy sick?

JACK: No.

TEDDY (*running out to them from the door on the right; she stands between them and holds on to Jack; Miles puts his arm around her for a moment*): Miles, thank heaven! I thought you'd never get here.

MILES: Well, if you're not sick, who is?

The car door slams. Becky is obviously joining them.

JACK: Nobody!

MILES (*indignantly*): Well, then why did you drag me away from my dinner?

JACK: Well, you won't believe it, Miles, but you can see it for yourself. Hello, Becky. (*She enters the frame from the left.*) Good to see you again.

They greet each other with overlapping hellos. Teddy puts her arm around Becky and ushers her to the door.

JACK: C'mon. (*He signals Miles to come in.*)

The Belicecs' House, interior, night

96. LS: *Jack and Miles, with Becky and Teddy behind them, approach the door of the room adjacent to the garage. The camera pans with them until they stop before going into the rec room door, which is off this room on*

*the right. Jack is at the door to the rec room, Miles next to him. Becky
and Teddy are at the left.*

JACK (*standing at the door and turning to Miles*): Would you be able to
forget you're a doctor for a while?

MILES: Why?

JACK: I don't want you to call the police right away.

MILES: Quit acting like a writer; what's going on?

JACK: Maybe you can tell me, you're the doctor. (*He opens the door.*)

97. LS: *the rec room as seen from the side opposite the door. Jack opens the
door in the extreme background. The room is well lighted and there is a
bar on the left. Miles enters, followed by Teddy and Becky. Jack shuts the
door behind them. Miles enters the foreground, which is dark; against the
lighted background, he appears silhouetted. His back is to us as he faces
Jack near the door across the room.*

JACK: Miles . . . uh . . . put the light on over the pool table . . .

*Miles turns and the camera tracks back with him as he enters the dark
area of the pool table, which is now in the foreground. Miles pulls the
cord on the light. A shape covered by a sheet is on the table under the
light. Jack now moves into a dark area at the right front of the bar; he is
now in silhouette. Miles and the shape on the table are lit in chiaroscuro.*

JACK: Go on, pull it down.

*Miles moves left to the head of the table; the camera tracks to the right at
the foot of the table. He pulls the sheet down; a long sustained musical
chord climaxes as he does so. A face is clearly visible from beneath the
sheet. Miles examines the face, body, and arm as loud, ominous music
plays. The others watch in the background.*

98. MLS: *Jack lights his pipe at the bar. Teddy half sits on a stool to the
right. Becky, at her right, stares at the body on the pool table. Jack moves
toward the table and the camera tracks back until we see Jack, the body
on the table, and Miles examining it, all from a very low angle. Becky
comes nearer on the right in the background. Miles continues to examine
the body as the ominous music keeps pounding its chords.*

JACK: Well, what do you make of it?

MILES (*looking up at Jack while examining the body*): Who is he?

JACK: I have no idea.[13]

99. MLS: *Becky is startled by a cuckoo clock at her right striking nine
o'clock. She turns suddenly to look at it, then backs up to where Miles is,
the camera tracking her movement down left and to Miles. She now joins
Jack and Miles at the table in a formation similar to the previous shot;
Teddy looks on from a bar stool in the rear, visible between Jack and
Miles.*

BECKY: Its face, Miles, it's vague.

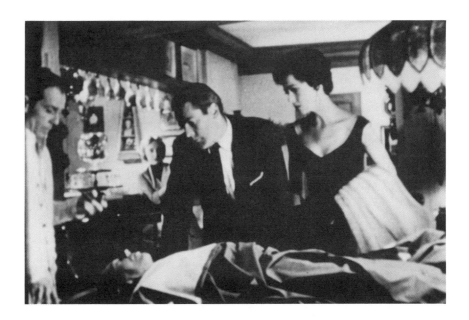

JACK: It's like the first impression that's stamped on a coin . . . it isn't finished.

MILES: You're right . . . it has all the features, but no details, no character, no lines.

JACK: That's no dead man.

MILES (*looking at the body's arm*): Have you got an ink pad around the house?

JACK: Should be one in the desk, why? (*He goes behind them to the desk and the camera pans right to include him in the background.*)

MILES: I want to take the corpse's fingerprints.

BECKY: Of course it's a dead man, what else could it be?

MILES: I don't know. But I've got a feeling that . . . well, this sounds crazy, but if I should do an autopsy, I think I'd find every organ in perfect condition . . . (*Jack comes over to Miles's right with the ink pad and Becky moves behind Miles and then to his left, so she can watch.*) . . . just as perfect as the body is externally. (*He presses the fingers on the ink pad, which Jack holds*) . . . Everything in working order . . . (*To Jack, who is readying the paper to take the fin-gerprints.*) . . . All set to go. Hold that thing. (*He presses the inked fingerprints against the paper.*)

100. CU: *uniform ink smudges, with no detailed fingerprint markings, on a white sheet of paper. Bass chords.*

MILES (*off*): He's blank.

101. MLS: *Becky, Miles, Jack, the body on the table, and Teddy in background, as in 99.*
     JACK: Waiting for the final face to be stamped on it.
102. MS: *Teddy.*
     TEDDY: But whose face? Tell me that.
103. LS *from behind the bar: Teddy with her back to the camera in the foreground in* MLS *and Jack, Miles, and Becky in the background in* LS *looking at her. The body is visible on the table.*
     JACK (*coming over to Teddy and kissing her*): I think we could all use a drink.
     Miles ushers Becky over to the bar, too.
     JACK (*going around the end of the bar*): Bourbon all right?
     MILES (*coming over to the bar, but still looking back at the body*): Fine.
     BECKY (*sitting on the stool to the left and talking to Jack behind the bar*): Nothing, thanks.
     TEDDY (*to Miles as he stands between Becky and her in front of the bar*): Miles, answer me. Whose face?
     MILES (*with his arm around Teddy*): I haven't the slightest idea, Honey, have you?
     TEDDY: How . . . uh . . . how tall would you say that thing is?
     MILES: Oh, five-ten, thereabouts.
     TEDDY: How much does it weigh?
     MILES: Mmm, it's pretty thin . . . maybe a hundred and forty pounds.
     TEDDY: Jack's five-ten and weighs a hundred and forty pounds.
     JACK (*pouring a drink, he drops the bottle. As he reaches for it, it breaks with a loud crash when it hits the sink. He stands up with his left hand exposed; it is obviously cut*): Teddy, will you stop talking nonsense.
     TEDDY: I'm sorry, darling.
     MILES (*hastily going over to the pool table to get his medical bag and quickly returning*): Come on, let's have that hand.
     TEDDY (*insistently*): But it isn't nonsense. (*Jack comes out from behind the bar and goes over to Miles to have his hand looked at. The camera tracks in for a* MS *of the group.*) Becky, you don't think it's nonsense, do you?
     BECKY: Well, of course it is. Jack's standing here in front of you.
     JACK (*as Miles doctors his hand*): Of course I am, bleeding to death.[14] Excuse me. (*He reaches in front of Becky for his drink.*)
     MILES: You know what . . . I'm afraid you may live.
     Miles wipes the cut with cotton and applies a swab with medication; Jack downs his drink.
104. CU *of Jack's hand as Miles swabs the cut in its palm. Jack stifles a chuckle.*
     MILES (*off*): Here, this should fix it.

105. *Becky, Jack, Miles, and Teddy at the bar, as in 103.*

BECKY: Miles, don't you think we should call the police and have them take that dead body out of here?

MILES (*putting an adhesive bandage on Jack's hand*): I'm afraid it isn't just a dead body.

JACK (*taking his hand away as Miles finishes*): Um, thanks.

Creepy music starts as Jack walks over to the body on the pool table. Miles follows him with drink in hand: the camera tracks over until Jack and Miles are in MLS *on either side of the body. The back of Teddy's head is in the right foreground.*

MILES (*to Jack*): I wonder if . . .

JACK: What?

MILES: I wonder if there's any connection.

JACK: What do you mean?

MILES: There's something strange going on in Santa Mira. Dr. Kaufman calls it an epidemic of mass hysteria. Becky's cousin's got it for one. (*Glancing occasionally at Teddy at the bar.*) She thinks that her uncle and her aunt aren't her uncle and her aunt. There're several cases of such delusion. This isn't you yet, but there is a structural likeness. (*Jack leans on the table looking at the body.*) It's fantastic but there must be some reason why this thing is in your house.[15]

106. MS: *Jack at left with Miles's back to the camera at right.*

MILES: Would you be willing to sit up with your strange friend and see what his next move is?

107. MS: *reverse angle, Miles at right with Jack's back to camera.*

MILES: If nothing happens by morning, call the police. If *something* happens, call me, will you?

JACK: You know I will.

They both drink their drinks. Jack moves to the right and Miles follows, the camera tracking with them until they are in LS, *joining Teddy and Becky at the bar. Jack sits down at the bar.*

MILES (*giving Teddy an embrace and a kiss*): Good night. Take it easy.

TEDDY: Sure.

BECKY (*coming over and taking Teddy's hand*): Nothing's going to happen. (*She follows Miles to the door.*)

TEDDY (*to Becky*): Good night, dear.

JACK (*as Becky and Miles exit*): Well, if it does, it'll make a charming, bloodcurdling mystery story. (*He takes Teddy's hand.*)[16]

Dissolve.

Becky's House, exterior, night

108. LS: *Miles and Becky in the car pull into Becky's driveway. Miles gets out of the car and goes around behind it to Becky's side to let her out.*

MILES (*voice-over narration*): I was careful not to let Becky know, but for the first time I was really scared. Dan Kaufman's explanation of what was wrong in town, mass hysteria, couldn't explain away that body on Jack's pool table.

They walk left to the front door, the camera tracking with them. Becky unlocks the door.

Becky's House, interior, night[17]

109. M S: *Becky and Miles enter the dark hallway; they are largely silhouetted by backlighting from outside.*

BECKY: Come in, while I turn the lights on.

MILES (*ironically*): You're a forward wench, dragging me into a dark hallway to be kissed.

The camera pans left with them as they enter the hall and are silhouetted again by outside light entering a room behind them.

BECKY (*turning the lights on*): I'm dragging you into a dark hallway because I'm scared of the dark tonight.

MILES: In that case, I'd better stay and tuck you in.

BECKY (*in almost a whisper*): That way lies madness.

MILES (*turning off the lights again*): What's wrong with madness?

BECKY (*turning on the lights again*): Madness. Good night. (*She puts her gloved fingers to her lips and then touches Miles's face.*)
Off-screen left the sound of a door opening is heard. Miles grabs Becky's arm and they both look left.

110. L S: *the hallway, Miles's and Becky's* P O V. *There are stairs up at left. A shadow is reflected on an open door at the end of the hallway in the right background. Deep disturbing chords herald the arrival of someone coming up from the basement. Becky's father emerges from the cellar door at the end of the hallway. He is rolling down his long-sleeved shirt. The camera tracks back with his advance to where they are standing until all three are in* M S, *Miles and Becky at the left foreground, her father on the right.*

BECKY'S FATHER: Well, it's about time that you two got home.

BECKY: Dad, what are you doing in the basement this time of night?

BECKY'S FATHER: Working in my shop. (*To Miles.*) How about a nightcap, Doc?

MILES: No, thanks. Kinda late. I'll take a rain check. (*He exits frame right.*)

BECKY (*smiling*): Good night. (*She touches her father's hand and begins going upstairs.*)

MILES (*off, as he leaves*): Good night.

BECKY'S FATHER (*looking to the front door*): Good night, Miles.

He follows Becky upstairs and turns the light off.

Dissolve.

The Belicecs' House, interior, night

111. CU, *low angle from the level of the pool table, of the body's head with Teddy and Jack asleep on bar stools in the left background. The cuckoo clock strikes one and Teddy awakens, stretches a bit, and looks around at Jack. Eerie music plays. To deep chords, the body in the foreground opens its eyes. Teddy now approaches the body. The camera tilts up to view her reaction as she looks down at the body; the angle is very low. She is alone in* MS *and caught in the chiaroscuro of the ceiling's crossbeams. She shakes her head and looks at the body's hand.*

112. CU: *the body's hand, which bears a wound like Jack's recent cut and is now pulsing and throbbing, as though the body were awakening.*

113. CU: *Teddy, the camera now level with her. Jack in* LS *in background at the bar. Teddy emits a bloodcurdling scream.*

114. MS: *Teddy starts to run from the body. The camera tilts downward to show the body's head in* CU *in center, much as the sequence began in 111.*

   TEDDY (*grabbing Jack in the background*): Oh, Jack, it's you! It's you!

115. MLS: *Jack and Teddy from a higher angle. Jack rushes to look at the body and Teddy pulls him away from it.*

   TEDDY: No, no, you mustn't go near it. Get out of here please! Please!
   Jack has his arm around her and they run from the house in LS.
   Dissolve.

Miles's House, interior, night[18]

116. LS, *very low angle: a lamp and sofa on the left, Miles at the right answering the rapid knocking at his front door. The only sources of illumination are the table lamp at the left and the overhead hall light near the front door in the rear. Miles lets a sobbing Teddy and Jack in and they come over to sit on the sofa, still in* LS.

MILES: What happened, Jack?

JACK: Teddy says the thing at our place is me right down to the cut on my hand. (*Helps Teddy, who is distraught, to sit down on the sofa.*) Sit down, baby. (*To Miles.*) I didn't wait to look.

TEDDY (*almost hysterically*): It's alive! It's alive! The hand was cut and bleeding and the position of the body had changed.

MILES (*giving her a drink*): Here, here, take this. (*She drinks what he has given her, with Jack putting his hands over hers to guide the glass to her mouth.*) (*To Jack.*) I'll call Danny Kaufman. (*He goes into the hallway in the rear.*)

117. LS: *Miles enters the front hallway from the left, seen from the rear of the hallway opposite the open front door, which he closes as he walks by. A staircase is on the right and in the alcove at its bottom a phone on a small table is in silhouette. Miles approaches the phone and the camera in* MS; *the camera tilts up to keep him in frame and then down as he sits down at the phone, dials a number, and lights a cigarette. He is lit only on the left side by the small hall light inside the entry near the door.*

DANNY (*over the phone, and in a tired tone*): Hello.

MILES: Hello, Danny?

DANNY (*over the phone, without interest*): Yeah.[19]

118. CU: *Miles.*

MILES: Something's happened and I've got to see you right away. Will you get over here as fast as you can? . . . It's important.

DANNY (*after a long pause, with little interest and some irritation*): Aahhh . . . OK.

Miles cracks a slight smile.

119. MS: *Miles, as in 117. He hangs up the phone and gets up and goes to the door on the left which leads to his living room. He calls to Jack and Teddy in the room.*

MILES: He's on his way. I'll make some coffee and be right with you.

JACK (*off*): Good deal, Miles. Thanks.

Miles comes down the hallway toward the phone and the kitchen door.

120. LS: *the back wall of Miles's kitchen, the back door to the left. As Miles opens the inner door to the kitchen, light comes across the wall. Miles's shadow appears on the wall.*

JACK (*off*): Miles, what about Becky? (*Miles enters the frame and goes to the wall in* MS, *about to turn on the light switch. He stops in his tracks.*) Do you think she's all right?[20]

Miles turns around to look back while the orchestra pounds out heavy, strong chords. He walks back across the kitchen and the camera pans his movement until, in MLS, *he looks down the open cellar door in the hallway.*

121. LS: *the basement, the stairs, and the foot of the stairs, from Miles's* POV. *Disquieting violin notes sound through the shot.*

122. MS: *Miles at right looking into basement, then turning right and pondering and recollecting an earlier scene, then looking back to the kitchen.*

    BECKY (*voice-over*): Dad, what are you doing in the basement at this time of night?

    BECKY'S FATHER (*voice-over*): Working in my shop.

123. MLS: *Miles, as in 120; he races across the kitchen and out the back door, the camera panning with his movement.*

    Miles's Driveway and Backyard, exterior, night

124. ELS: *Miles at his kitchen door, right, as seen from his carport with the car in it, left. He races left across the yard, the camera panning and tracking his movements, gets in the car, turns on the headlights, and backs the car out of the driveway.*

    MILES (*voice-over narration*): I don't know what it was . . . call it a premonition, but . . . suddenly I had the feeling that Becky was in danger. I had to get to her as quickly as possible. (*The musical chords pulsate ominously.*)

    Dissolve.

    Becky's House, exterior, night

125. ELS: *Miles's car coming down the street and braking to an angled stop in front of the walk to the house. Miles jumps out on the passenger's side. The car is still moving and comes to a halt as its tires hit the curb. The camera pans left with Miles, then tracks rapidly left as he runs up to the porch and the house door.*

126. MS, *from a low angle: Miles at the door, about to press the buzzer. Then he stops and looks right and left.*

    MILES (*voice-over narration*): I was going to ring the bell, then I had a hunch I had better be careful.

127. LS: *Miles at the door, taken from a low angle, as at the end of 125.*

    MILES (*voice-over narration*): Something was wrong in this house. *The camera tracks back as Miles walks to the left side of the porch and stops at the corner of the house in* MS. *The camera tilts down as he steps down from the low porch onto the ground, then it tracks left with him as he looks in at a couple of first-floor windows. Then he spies a smaller window below him and the camera tilts down with him as he kneels to look through its four small panes. He looks around, then crooks his arm, using his right hand to hold his left. He punches out the lower right pane with his elbow. Quiet, suspenseful music plays throughout this scene.*

128. MS, *from inside the cellar: Miles's elbow comes through the pane of the window as it breaks.*

129. MS: *Miles, as in 127. He is looking up; now he puts his hand through the broken part of the window.*

Becky's House, interior, night

130. MS: *as in 128. Miles's hand picks out a few remaining pieces of glass in the frame, then delicately reaches in to unfasten the lock at the bottom of the window. Miles pushes the window in and, still outside, he peers around the cellar. He lets the window partially close, then enters feet first through it. The camera tracks back a bit and tilts down as he lowers himself to the floor. The camera continues to track back as he moves across the cellar and lights a match. He looks down under a woodworking bench, the camera tilting down with him. He then opens a closet across the way and explores it. The match begins to burn his fingers, so he puts it out and is left in the dark.*

131. LS: *Miles, now half-lighted by the window he came through, but still bathed in shadows and patches of darkness. The camera tracks back and pans right as Miles moves farther into the cellar. A large slanted object is at his right. He lights another match and opens the large lid of what turns out to be a chest. He looks inside.*

132. MS: *Becky's half-formed double in the chest. She is illuminated by his match. The familiar suspenseful chords pound out.*

133. CU: *Miles's face aghast with horror at what he sees. The music pounds. The match goes out as Miles pulls back from what he sees.*

134. MLS: *Miles, as at the end of 131, now shutting the chest furiously and running up the cellar stairs behind the chest. The camera follows his movements by tracking left a bit, then tilting up and panning right as he races up the stairs.*

135. LS: *Miles, seen in a high angle from the top of the stairs to the second floor. The camera pans left with him as he reaches the top of the stairs in* MS, *then tracks forward with him as he goes toward a partly open door at the end of the hallway. In* MLS, *he opens the door and we see Becky's father asleep a few feet into the room. He closes the door and the camera pans right with him as he goes to the last door on the landing. He listens and cautiously begins opening the door.*

136. MS: *Miles seen from inside Becky's room, opening the door. The camera tracks left with him as he quickly goes to Becky's bed and tries to wake her, whispering in her ear.*

MILES: Becky! Becky!

137. CU: *Becky asleep in bed and Miles at her ear, and shaking her a bit. She is unresponsive.*[21]

MILES: Becky!

138. MS: *Becky asleep in bed and Miles at her right, as at the end of 136.*

Miles pulls the covers off and lifts Becky, still asleep, out of the bed and carries her in his arms to the door, the camera panning his movements out of the room.

139. LS: *looking down the hallway from the top of the stairs, toward Becky's father's room, the door ajar, straight ahead, and Miles emerging from Becky's room at the right with her in his arms. He goes left past her father's room, then turns down the hall toward the camera and the head of the stairs. He turns right and begins to descend the stairs.*

140. LS: *Miles with Becky in his arms descending the staircase, as seen at a low angle from the bottom of the stairs.*

141. MS: *reverse shot of Miles carrying Becky, seen from behind as they approach the front door. He opens the door and we see him rush with her down the walk in LS toward his car on the street.*
    Dissolve.

Miles's House, interior, night²²

142. MLS: *Jack standing behind the sofa left, talking to Miles standing right. Teddy sits on the sofa, with Becky in her nightgown sitting on the arm of the sofa to her right and putting her arm around her. Danny Kaufman sits in a chair on the right.*

    JACK: Miles, will you tell me what happened?

    MILES: The same thing—I found another one. (*Teddy puts her hand over her mouth and Becky comforts her.*) In the cellar of Becky's house coming to life while I stood there watching it. It was Becky. (*He puts his arm on her shoulder.*)

    DANNY (*skeptically*): Yeah? I want to see one of these bodies.

    MILES: All right.

    DANNY (*to Teddy*): Now, you're going to bed. (*To Becky.*) And you're staying with her. (*To Miles.*) Put on your clothes. We'll go to Jack's first. (*Miles goes down the hallway to the kitchen, followed by Danny and Jack.*) You got any coffee around here?

    MILES (*off, now in the kitchen*): Yeah, you'll find some in the kitchen.

    TEDDY (*after Jack gives her a kiss and follows them to the kitchen*): He doesn't believe me, Becky.

    BECKY: He will.
    Dissolve.

The Belicecs' House, interior, night

143. LS: *Jack, Miles, and Danny enter the rec room, in the background of the shot taken from the height of the lamp above the pool table. As they enter, the camera tracks back to reveal the pool table. Jack pulls the sheet back but nothing is there.*

    JACK (*looking around wildly*): Somebody's playing games.

    DANNY (*at the head of the table on the left and closest to the camera*): Rough ones. (*He points to a place on the felt.*) There's a blood spot.[23] (*Jack and Miles both look at where he points.*) What you saw was the body of a murdered man. Did you examine it carefully?

MILES: Yes. I don't know what's happened to it. It was not an ordinary body and there wasn't a mark on it.

JACK: I checked it, too, when I put it on the table . . . there wasn't a scratch.

DANNY: You can kill a man by shoving an icepick into the base of his brain and leaving a puncture so small the naked eye can't see it.[24]

Protesting, Miles moves behind Jack and comes over to Danny, the camera tracking in and right on him as he confronts him in MS. *Danny is still closer to the camera and looms larger.*

MILES: Danny, you're ignoring the fact that this was not a normal body and you heard what Teddy said about the hand.

DANNY: I heard lots of things Teddy said and none of them made any sense.

JACK (*coming over between them angrily, the camera tracking further in on the confrontation, with Danny still largest*): All right, now hold onto it, pal. *I* was here too. So was Miles. Now, look. (*He reaches into his pockets and takes out the fingerprints.*) We took his fingerprints. Look at that. Tell me why he didn't have any.

DANNY (*looking at the paper with the smudges*): He didn't want any, so he took them off with acid.

JACK (*grabbing the paper back*): Stop trying to rationalize everything, will you? Let's face it, we have a mystery on our hands.

DANNY: Sure you have, a real one. Whose body was it and where is it now, a completely normal mystery.[25] Whatever it is, it's well within the bounds of human experience and I don't think you ought to make any more of it.

MILES: Well, I wouldn't . . . if I hadn't looked in Becky's cellar. How do you explain away the body I saw there?

DANNY (*leaning forward on the pool table*): I don't think you saw one there.

MILES: You don't think I saw one here either?

DANNY: I know you did because three others saw it, too.

MILES: But I dreamed up the second one?

DANNY: Doctors can have hallucinations too. The mind is a strange and wonderful thing. I'm not sure it'll ever be able to figure itself out. Everything else, maybe. From the atom to the universe, everything except itself. (*He emphasizes his point by pointing his finger at Miles's chest.*)

MILES (*shaking his head*): Nevertheless, I saw Becky's double and the body that we saw here bore an uncomfortable resemblance to Jack.

JACK (*between them, muttering*): Mighty uncomfortable.

DANNY: All right, let's go on to Becky's and have a look.

He gives Miles a shove on the shoulder and the three leave, the camera panning their movements across the room into LS *as they exit.*[26]
Dissolve.

Becky's House, interior, night[27]

144. LS: *Becky's cellar, looking toward the window from the chest. Miles, Danny, and Jack are standing in front of the window and Danny is pointing a flashlight toward the camera.*

DANNY: All right, where's your girlfriend's double?

MILES: OK, skeptic, lift the lid.

Danny leads the way and Miles and Jack follow. In low-angle MS, *standing much as Miles did, he lifts the lid of the chest. He shines the flashlight into it.*

145. MS: *the interior of the chest; the camera pans left quickly over the interior following Danny's flashlight beam; the flashlight is in the upper right of the frame.*

DANNY: There's a body here, all right.

The camera has continued panning left and tilting up, so that Miles and Jack are in MS, *both illuminated by the flashlight.*

MILES: It's Becky's double!

JACK: It sure is.

DANNY (*only partly visible as a dark shape at the right*): Take another look. (*Miles and Jack move toward the chest and the camera retraces its movements, panning right and down. The flashlight once again reveals the interior of the chest, now clearly not containing Becky's double. A rolled-up pillow with a blanket under it are in the chest. Jack's, then Miles's hands reach into the chest and poke around the pillow and blanket.*) Now you see it and now you don't.[28]

146. CU: *Miles and Jack, leaning into the chest, Miles closer to the camera.*

MILES: It was there . . . half hidden by that blanket.

147. MS: *Danny, Miles, and Jack, with Danny closest to the camera. Slightly low angle.*

DANNY: You said you saw it there just now.

MILES: I thought I did.

DANNY (*shutting the lid of the chest*): Why did you come here tonight? You'd seen a dead man at Jack's, an average-sized man; the face in death was smooth and unlined, bland in expression, which often happens . . .

148. MCU: *Miles, with Jack behind him.*

DANNY (*off*): You had just become aware of a curious, unexplainable epidemic mass hysteria . . .

149. CU: *Danny, in right profile.*

DANNY: . . . men, women, and children suddenly convinced themselves that their relatives weren't their relatives at all . . .

150. MS: *the three again, as in 147.*

DANNY: . . . so your mind started playing tricks, and reality became unreality. The dead man became Jack's double in your eyes.[29]

MILES (*still puzzled, but shaking his head*): Come off it, will you, Dan?

DANNY: I know, Miles, this is all hard to believe, but these things happen . . . even to witch doctors like me. (*He points to himself.*)

MILES (*almost yelling*): I saw her here! She was real! (*He opens the chest again and looks in.*)

DANNY: You saw her all right, in every tiny detail, as vividly as anyone has ever seen anything. But only in your mind. (*Miles shakes his head, and closes the chest.*)

JACK: Look, Danny, you can talk all night, but you're not going to convince me.

The cellar light goes on and the three look up toward the stairs off-screen right.

151. MLS: *Becky's father coming down the stairs with a shotgun, seen from a low angle.*

BECKY'S FATHER: What in heaven's name are you doing in my cellar?

The camera tracks back and Danny, Jack, and Miles enter the frame. Danny goes to the left, nearest Becky's father. All are in MS.

DANNY: Using it for an office, Mr. Driscoll. These gentlemen are patients, badly in need of psychiatric treatment. (*A police siren sounds in the distance.*)

BECKY'S FATHER: Oh, stop talking nonsense.

DANNY: I'm not . . . they've been having nightmares.

BECKY'S FATHER (*to Jack and Miles*): If you're drunk, you'd better sober up quick . . . the police are on their way here. (*The siren stops.*)

MILES: Oh, no, no, no, we're not drunk.

DANNY: Nothing as simple as that. Pull up a chair.

BECKY'S FATHER: Why, you're crazy, all of you!

GRIVETT (*off*): Hey! (*They all look left.*) What's going on down there?

152. MS: *Nick Grivett looking in the cellar window with his revolver drawn. Shots 152–159 are shot–reverse shots.*

DANNY (*off*): Hello, Nick, glad to see you.

153. MS: *Danny at left, with Becky's father, Jack, and Miles to his right and behind him in* MLS.

DANNY (*looking toward Grivett, off-screen*): You saved these two characters a trip to the station . . . they want to report finding a body . . . and losing it.

GRIVETT (*off*): Where? When?

JACK: At my place. About seven o'clock.

154. MS: *Grivett at the window, closer than 152.*

GRIVETT: Why'd you wait so long to report it? You know better'n that, Doc.

155. MS: *the four, as in 153.*

MILES: Oh well, yeah, it was a curious sort of a body . . . and then it . . . wasn't there anymore.

GRIVETT (*off*): I have a good mind to throw you both in jail.

MILES: Well, if you'd seen it, you'd understand why we waited.

156. MS: *Grivett, as in 154.*

GRIVETT: Thin man . . . five-ten . . . fingerprints burned off with acid?

157. MS: *the four, as in 155.*

GRIVETT (*off*): I've just seen it on the slab in the morgue. It turned up in a burning haystack on Mike Gesner's south pasture, two hours ago.

158. MS: *Grivett, as in 156.*

GRIVETT (*gruffly*): Now, break it up! Go on home! (*He gestures with his gun and starts to leave the window.*)

159. MS: *the four. Becky's father goes up the stairs, then Jack. Miles comes over to Danny.*

MILES (*still shaking his head in disbelief*): Well, you win. Pick up the marbles.[30]

Fade out.

Miles's House, interior, day

160. *Fade in.* LS: *the kitchen, with Becky preparing breakfast at the stove, a counter in the background. Miles enters a door left in* MS. *Soft romantic music plays.*

MILES: Good morning.

BECKY: Good morning. (*Miles advances toward her, with the camera tracking forward with him. Becky interrupts his kiss.*) Orange juice. (*She makes a motion toward the table.*)

MILES: Thank you. (*He reaches over to the table and picks up a glass.*)

BECKY: How do you like your eggs?

MILES: Oh, any way you'd like.

BECKY: Boiled? two minutes?

MILES: Two minutes?

BECKY: Um-huh.

MILES: OK. (*He puts his hand under her chin.*) You know, dragging you out of bed in the middle of the night was a lot of trouble . . . but it was worth it.

BECKY: Now, seriously, Miles . . .

Loud thumping noises are heard. They both look toward the cellar where the noises seem to be coming from. Miles motions to Becky to keep quiet and he moves left, shutting the door to the stairway upstairs and opening the cellar door. The camera pans his movements. Bass music now rumbles.

MILES (*his back to us, looking down in the cellar, yelling*): Who is it?

161. LS: *Miles's basement and the stairway leading down, as in 121. The bass music still rumbles. After a moment, an ominous large shadow appears on the cellar floor.*

CHARLIE (*off*): The gas man. (*Then he appears at the left of the foot of the stairs.*) Morning, Doc!

162. MS: *Miles and Becky at the door at the top of the stairs, as in 160.*

MILES (*sighing with relief*): Good morning, Charlie. I guess I'm a little jittery.

163. LS: *Charlie, as in 161.*

MILES (*off*): Not getting enough sleep.

CHARLIE: Well, I won't be bothering you anymore . . .

164. MS: *Miles and Becky at the top of the stairs, as in 162.*

CHARLIE (*off*): . . . putting the meter outside in the patio.

MILES: OK.

The romantic music resumes.

BECKY: Oh! (*She jumps.*) Your eggs will be hard-boiled. (*She rushes to the stove, the camera panning right with her.*)

MILES (*moving right to sit at the table, the camera tracking back and tilting down as he sits*): Did you do this for your husband?

BECKY: Um-hmmm. Did your wife do this for you?

MILES: Oh yes, she liked to cook. That's one of the reasons why I'm single. I never was there when dinner was on the table. Well, take my advice and don't get mixed up with a doctor . . . they're seldom at home.

BECKY (*approaching him from behind and putting more juice and a*

*boiled egg on the table. In the process she puts her arms around
him.*): What would you say if I told you I already was mixed up with a
doctor?

MILES (*holding her arms*): I'd say it was too good to be true.

BECKY: Things like this can happen all of a sudden. (*They rock in a
semi-embrace.*)

MILES: What's so all of a sudden about two people who have known
each other most of their lives? (*They look up to the left as the door from
upstairs opens.*)

165. MS: *Jack opens the door and enters the kitchen, the camera panning
right with him. Miles is now bemusedly contemplating the egg which he
holds in his hands in front of him and Becky is back in the center rear at
the stove.*

JACK: Good morning.

MILES (*casually*): Oh, good morning!

JACK (*going over to talk to Becky at the stove*): I thought I smelled some
coffee. . . . Why didn't you give me a call?

BECKY: I didn't want to wake Teddy.

JACK: Oh, she's wide awake. (*Turns to go over to Miles.*) Got a good
sleep. (*He is now standing to Miles's left in the foreground.*)

MILES: Good.

JACK (*to Miles*): But I don't feel that she should go home right away,
Miles. Would you . . . a . . . mind taking in a couple of boarders for a
while? . . . Or do you have . . . a . . . something else in mind?

MILES (*humorously, but looking back to Becky*): Well, I was toying with
an idea . . . but you can stay.[31]

BECKY (*handing Jack a cup of coffee*): Here, Jack.

JACK: Thank you, doll. . . . I'll take it up to Teddy. (*The camera pans
left with him as he exits through the door with the coffee in hand.*)
Dissolve.

Wilma Lentz's Antique Store, exterior, day

166. MS: *Wilma standing behind her store window and looking out with arms
folded, then moving to the left, through the front door, while in the
distance we hear a train whistle. The camera tracks left with her, then
right as she comes down the steps that lead to the sidewalk.*

WILMA: Miles! (*She goes up to him and the camera pans right and
tracks in on the two of them.*) Did you make that appointment for me
with the psychiatrist?

MILES: Yes, two o'clock.

WILMA: I don't need him . . . I feel like such a fool. I woke up this
morning and everything was all right. You don't know how relieved I
am.

MILES: Oh, yes I do. (*He puts his right hand on her shoulder reas-*

suringly.) Listen, will you give Becky a call and tell her about it? She was worried about you.

WILMA: All right.

MILES: She's at my house.

WILMA (*surprised*): At your house? Why?

MILES: Well, it's a long story, but she'll tell you all about it.

He exits toward the camera at the right. Wilma goes back into the store with a worried look; the camera tracks back slightly, then pans left as she goes up the steps. At the door she flips the OPEN sign to its other side, CLOSED, a movement marked by disturbing chords heard through the next shot.

167. MS: *Wilma enters her office and moves slowly left, the camera tracking back and left; she mechanically addresses a man at the desk whose back is to us.*

WILMA: Becky's still at his house.

The man turns around to look at her. It is Becky's father.

BECKY'S FATHER (*also mechanically*): All right.

Dissolve.

Miles's Office, interior, day

168. MS: *Sally is standing at right and arranging some flowers on a shelf in Miles's inner office, in front of a mirror in which she spots Miles entering.*

SALLY: Good morning!

MILES (*seen in the mirror in* LS): Good morning, Sally!

SALLY (*the camera tracking and panning left with her until she reaches Miles near the door*): Take a peek at what's in the reception room

Miles puts his hat down on an examination table and goes left toward the curtained double doors of the reception room, which are closed. The camera tracks left with him.

169. CU: *Miles's hand and head in the foreground as he pulls the curtain back on the right door to the reception room. In* MLS, *seen through the window of the door, Jimmy Grimaldi's mother and Jimmy sit on the couch in the reception room. She is holding a magazine for him to look at.*

JIMMY: Mother, why don't we go home?

MRS. GRIMALDI: In a little while, Jimmy.

She hugs him and starts to look at the magazine with him.

170. MS: *Miles at the curtains, letting them go, as the familiar piano chords pound out. He moves back to the center of the room where Sally is and the camera tracks back until both are in the frame.*

SALLY: He certainly made a quick recovery.

MILES (*walking alone over to the window, the camera tracking his movement, and staring out at the street*): Yeah, I guess we all did.

Dissolve.

Miles's Backyard, exterior, night

171. LS: *Miles's car pulling into the carport.*

    MILES (*voice-over narration*): But driving home I had a lot of questions . . . and no answers. How could Jimmy and Wilma seem so normal now? Surely I had done nothing to cure them. Maybe they wanted me to feel secure, but . . . why?

    Miles gets out of the car and the camera tracks back and right as he joins Becky and Jack on the patio. Jack is in the right foreground, MLS, *at the barbecue grill; Becky preparing food behind him.*

    MILES: Well!

    BECKY: I hope you didn't forget the steaks.

    MILES (*throwing package to Jack*): I never forget anything.

    TEDDY (*coming out of a door in the center background*): Don't worry about him, he's completely housebroken.

    JACK: I need a martini, Beck.

    BECKY: Onion or olive?

    JACK (*turning around to her*): It doesn't matter, I'm going to pour it on the charcoal. (*Working with the grill.*) I can't get this stuff to burn.

    MILES (*taking the martini and carrying it over to Jack, the camera panning right until Jack and he are at the left, with the open greenhouse door behind them to the right*): Oh, a martini isn't dry enough. I'll get you something to start it.[32]

    JACK (*acknowledging the martini, through the pipe in his mouth*): Hmmm.

    MILES (*handing him the drink*): For drinking purposes. (*Jack sips the martini, while Miles moves into the background and encounters Teddy with a tray.*) You're looking shipshape.

    TEDDY: Thank you, sir. (*She puts a potato chip into his mouth.*)

Miles's Greenhouse, interior, night

172. LS: *inside the greenhouse the camera pans right toward the door through which we see Miles approaching. The camera is canted to the left, so that the whole frame appears tilted at about a 45-degree angle. In the left foreground, still quite obscure, are the pods. Quiet, almost romantic music plays as Miles reaches for lighter fluid on a shelf in the left rear.*

173. MS: *one of the pods opens to the sudden intrusion of ominous bass chords. Foam is coming out of the top of the pod.*

174. LS: *as in 172. Miles gets the lighter fluid and steps back out the door into the yard.*

    MILES: Here we are.

175. MS: *another view from overhead of the same pod opening further on the top. Inside is a shape, vaguely human. The ominous music continues.*

176. LS: *Jack and Miles are seen through the greenhouse door, but closer than in 174 and without the tilted frame. Miles is coming back into the green-*

house while the grill now flames in the background. He enters in MLS and
returns the lighter fluid to the shelf on the left.

177. MS: *still another view, overhead, of the pod opening, this time from the
right. A form emerges to the powerful music.*

178. MLS: *as in 176, Miles returning the lighter fluid to the shelf with his back
to the camera; he hears a pop and turns around to see what it is.*

179. MS: *slightly overhead, of the pod opening, this time from the left. There
is a crackling sound.*

180. CU: *low angle of Miles, horrorstruck.*

181. MS: *the pod overhead from the right, as in 177. The head is now emerging from the containing shell.*

182. MS: *Miles as in 178, but advancing into* MS *toward the camera, which is
low angle, slightly above the pods.*
MILES (*calling loudly*): Jack! Jack! (*He leans down and looks out frame
left at the pod.*)

183. MS: *the pod from overhead left, opening. A shape pops out of it. The
music is now intensely loud.*

184. MS: *Jack arrives behind Miles, who is now looking more ahead; same as
in 182. Both lean down to look. Becky and Teddy arrive behind them,
staring too.*[33]
TEDDY (*raising her hand to her mouth in horror*): Oooh!

185. MS: *the pod from overhead right as an arm makes a loud pop and
emerges amid the foam.*

186. CU: *Miles at right with Teddy behind him in* MS, *her hand to her mouth in horror. Low angle. The bass chords pound out.*
187. CU: *slightly low angle of Becky.*
    BECKY (*aghast*): They're like huge seed pods.
188. MS: *slightly high angle view of another pod; it is opening and the head is popping out.*
189. MS: *low angle of the four main characters as in 184.*
    JACK (*pointing toward the pods*): This must be the way that body in my closet was formed.
190. LS: *the group with the emerging pod in the left foreground. The same canted frame as in the first shot of the greenhouse, 172.*
191. MS: *the four, as in 189.*
    JACK: Miles, where do they come from?
    MILES: I don't know.
192. MS: *slightly high angle of the emerging pod.*
    MILES (*off*): If they are seeds or seed pods, they must grow some-place . . . on a plant, probably.
193. MS: *another view of the pod emerging from the right, slightly high angle.*
    MILES (*off*): And somebody or something wants this duplication to take place.
194. CU: *Becky, as in 187, glancing from the pods up to Miles.*
    BECKY: But when they're finished, what happens to our bodies?[34]
195. MS: *low angle of the four, with Jack going into the background and getting a pitchfork.*
    MILES: I don't know. When the process is completed, probably the original is destroyed or disintegrates.
    JACK (*coming up from behind with the pitchfork, saying to Miles*): Stop![35]
    He seems to be asking Miles to stop talking and let his action replace Miles's talk. He is moving forward with the pitchfork to plunge it into one of the pods.
    MILES (*grabbing the pitchfork with his hand and restraining Jack from stabbing the pods*): No, wait!
196. MCU: *Jack and Miles, with Miles restraining him, Teddy in the back-ground right.*
    JACK: Sorry, but I take a dim view of watching my own destruction.
    MILES: Jack, please . . . there isn't any danger until they're completely formed.
    Jack relents.
197. CU: *Becky, as in 187.*
    MILES (*off*): We learned that last night at your house.
198. MCU: *Jack and Miles with Teddy now behind them in* MS.
    MILES: Your blank didn't change right away.

The camera tracks in to a CU *of the two, with Teddy behind and moving between them.*

TEDDY: Not until you fell asleep.[36]

199. LS: *overhead, from high angle, of a pod emerging with the full greenhouse behind it. There is a pop and the upper torso practically sits up.*

200. CU: *Jack leans forward, with Miles now a bit farther in the back and Teddy talking to him, as in 198.*

TEDDY: Miles, when the change does take place, do you suppose there is any difference?

MILES: There must be . . .

201. CU: *Becky, as in 187.*

MILES (*off*): Wilma noticed it. So did little Jimmy.

BECKY (*with a tear coming from her left eye*): So did I.

202. CU, *Jack,* MCU, *Teddy and Miles. All three turn left to look at her, Jack more slowly.*

203. CU: *Becky.*

BECKY (*with a gasping sound*): My father!

204. CU, *Jack, and* MCU, *Miles and Teddy, as in 202. Teddy turns to look at Miles and the camera tracks in and left as Miles goes over to console Becky. Both are in* MCU.

MILES: That must have been what he was doing in the cellar last night, placing one of these. Oh, I'm sorry. (*He holds her.*)

BECKY: I felt something was wrong but I thought it was me because I'd been away for so long.

Miles puts his hand on her head.

205. MS: *the four, low angle, now in a different arrangement. Becky is at the left, held by Miles. Jack kneels in lower right foreground with Teddy behind him.*

TEDDY: They have to be destroyed.

206. LS: *high angle, overhead, of the pods, as in 199.*

TEDDY (*off*): All of them!

MILES: They will be. Every one of them.

207. MS: *the four.*

MILES (*reaching with his left arm and grabbing Jack's shoulder*): Listen, we're going to have to search every building . . . every house in town. (*To all.*) Men, women, and children are going to have to be examined. We've got some phoning to do.

JACK: Well, I'm going to stay right here where I can watch them.

Miles leaves through the door in the background, followed by Becky.

TEDDY: I'm going to stay with you.

JACK (*turning around and talking to Miles and Becky in the doorway, desperately*): And don't call the police. Nick Grivett didn't find any *body* on a burning haystack.

Miles's Backyard, exterior, night

208. MS: *reverse angle, outside the greenhouse door, Miles looking at Becky with the realization of what Jack has said. He turns left and starts walking with Becky a few feet behind him. The camera tracks their movement.*

BECKY: Why don't you call Danny? Maybe he can help.

MILES (*stopping and turning to answer her*): Danny? No, I'm afraid it's too late to call Danny, too.

BECKY: Well, what are you going to do?

MILES (*decisively*): Get help. (*He rushes up onto the porch to go into the house, followed by Becky. The camera pans their movements. On the run, he says loudly.*) I hope that whatever is taking place is confined to Santa Mira. If it isn't . . .[37] (*He opens the porch door.*)

Miles's House, interior, night

209. LS: *Miles, followed by Becky, enters his front hallway and in* MLS *picks up the phone, with Becky at his side. Slightly low angle. Miles dials the operator.*

OPERATOR (*over the phone*): Operator.

MILES: Hello, this is Dr. Bennell. This is an emergency. I want to talk to the Federal Bureau of Investigation in Los Angeles.

BECKY (*to Miles*): Can you make them believe you?

MILES (*his hand over the mouthpiece of the phone*): I've got to.

BECKY: Where do they come from?

MILES: So much has been discovered these past few years that anything is possible. It may be the results of atomic radiation on plant life, or animal life . . . some weird, alien organism . . . a mutation of some kind.[38]

BECKY: So why should they take the form of people? of us?

MILES: I don't know. I don't know. (*He picks the phone up and paces forward toward the camera with it; the camera tilts up as he does, then back as he nervously walks back and forth.*) Whatever it is . . . whatever intelligence or instinct it is that can govern the forming of human flesh and blood out of thin air is . . . well, it's fantastically powerful, beyond any comprehension . . . malignant. All that body in your cellar needed was a mind . . . and it was . . .

BECKY (*off, behind Miles, now looming over the camera in the foreground*): And it was taking my mind . . . (*She comes up beside Miles.*) . . . while I was asleep. . . . I could take that pitchfork myself and . . .

OPERATOR (*over the phone*): On your call to Los Angeles, Doctor, they don't answer.

MILES (*loudly, into the phone*): Well, try again. That office is open day and night. (*To Becky.*) If they've taken over the telephone office, we're dead.

Miles's Greenhouse, interior, night

210. MS: *Jack and Teddy in the greenhouse, with Jack still poised with his pitchfork. Teddy grabs Jack's shoulder.*

211. MS: *overhead view of a pod form covered with light foam, the head at bottom of the frame. The foam blows away to reveal a female shape like Teddy's; the heavy brass chords accompany the revelation.*

212. MLS: *canted frame, Jack and Teddy from a low angle.*

TEDDY: Is that me?[39]

The camera tilts down and pans left as Jack brings his pitchfork to Teddy's pod form. Only the pod at the left, the pitchfork, and Jack's legs at the right are visible. The pitchfork advances to the head of the pod, pauses for a moment, then makes its way to the next pod as Jack moves left. The camera tracks the pitchfork and his feet. He walks to a third pod, pauses again, raises the pitchfork up to the right and looks right; the camera rises to include his body and face in the frame. The camera has been canted to the right throughout.

Miles's House, interior, night

213. MS: *Becky and Miles, with Miles on the phone in his hallway.*

MILES (*furiously, into the phone*): This is an emergency, emergency! Now, look, there's been . . . hup! (*He seems to react to being cut off and clicks the receiver button on the phone in his left hand.*) Operator, get me a better connection.

OPERATOR (*over the phone*): I'll try, Doctor. (*Miles paces back and forth nervously, the camera tilting up and down with his movements.*) It's no use, all the Los Angeles circuits are dead.

MILES (*into the phone*): All right, try Sacramento. Give me the State Capital. I want to talk to the Governor. (*Again he paces back and forth, the camera tilting with him.*)

OPERATOR: (*over the phone*) The Sacramento circuits are busy, Doctor. I'll call you back.

MILES (*looks at Becky knowingly, then calmly, into the phone*): All right. All right. I'll wait for your call. (*He hangs up the phone, saying to Becky.*) I'll take the phone outside.

She leads the way out.

Miles's Backyard, exterior, night

214. LS: *Becky and Miles exit from the porch door into the yard, as seen from the barbecue area with the greenhouse to the right.*

MILES (*yelling, while he is coming down the steps into the yard*): Jack!

JACK (*off, from the greenhouse*): Yeah!

MILES (*running across the yard*): They've got the phone. (*The camera pans right until they are in MS in front of the greenhouse; Jack and Teddy come out. Becky and Miles are in the center, MS, with Jack at the left and Teddy at the right, MS.*) Now you and the girls get in the car and make a run for it. The first town you get to, yell for help.

JACK: Yeah. What about you?

MILES (*pointing to the phone across the yard and talking to Jack*): In a little while that phone is going to ring. If there's nobody here to answer it, they'll know we've gone and block the roads out of town. I'll stall them until you're out of reach. (*He looks at Teddy.*)

JACK: Well then, what are you going to do?

MILES: Try and find out what's in back of this.

BECKY (*to Miles*): I'm staying.

215. MCU: *Becky and Miles.*

MILES: No!

BECKY: Miles, don't ask me to leave you.

MILES (*putting his arm around Becky, they both turn to look at Jack*): Jack, get going!

216. MS: *the four as in 214.*[40]

JACK: Miles, I can't!

MILES (*taking the pitchfork away from Jack*): Somebody's got to go or we don't get any help.

TEDDY (*panicking, and running to the left and grabbing Jack to drag him away*): Please, let's get out of here.

JACK: Well, watch out for yourselves! (*He puts his arm around Teddy and they exit hastily frame left.*)

MILES (*turning briefly toward the greenhouse, then putting his hand on Becky's shoulder*): Go over by the phone. Stay there. If it rings, call me.

She goes back across the yard and he moves right toward the greenhouse,

*with the heavy musical chords beginning again and continuing throughout
the sequence.*

Miles's Greenhouse, interior, night

217. MS: *Miles, in low angle from within the greenhouse. He enters and
comes closer to the camera, almost* MCU, *with his pitchfork poised and
looking downward. The camera pans left and tilts up, much as if this were
a pod's* POV.

218. MCU: *overhead shot, Miles's* POV, *of Becky's double with its head pointing downward at the bottom of the frame. The foam is blowing off the
clearly recognizable face.*

219. MS: *Miles, as in 217. Miles pulls back to strike with his pitchfork. His
face is anguished.*

220. MCU: *Becky's double with the face, more visible, more like hers.*

221. CU: *Miles, with the pitchfork raised to strike. He begins to lean left,
indicating that he can't bring himself to do it.*

222. MS: *Miles, from a low angle, canted slightly left, and seen from behind
some plants. He lowers the pitchfork and moves on to the next pod, the
camera panning left and tilting up with him. He comes closer to the
camera, looks down, and raises the pitchfork once again to strike.*

223. MS: *Miles's double, the face and shoulders almost without foam, seen
from above, Miles's* POV. *The body lies more left to right than Becky's.*

224. MS: *Miles, low angle, raising the pitchfork to strike, all its prongs
visible.*

225. MCU: *Miles's double, high angle, Miles's* POV. *The pitchfork enters the
chest with a rubbery-sounding thud. The phone suddenly rings.*[41]

226. CU: *the phone, with Becky blurred in the background. She rises, her hand in* CU *picking up the receiver. The camera pans up quickly to her face in* CU *and tracks back slightly.*

    BECKY: Hello.

    OPERATOR (*over the phone*): Is Dr. Bennell there?

    BECKY: Yes, I'll get him.

    She starts to put the phone down, but the operator has more to say.

    OPERATOR (*over the phone*): Never mind. Just tell him the Sacramento circuits are still busy, and ask him if he wants me to keep trying.

    BECKY: All right, hold on. (*She puts the phone down a bit and calls out.*) Miles!

227. MS: *Miles, low angle, canted, in the greenhouse, holding the handle of the pitchfork after he has plunged it into his double. Miles has moved back a little from 224.*

    BECKY (*off, from across the yard*): The circuits are still busy!

    MILES: Well, tell her to keep trying! Also try San Francisco and Washington.

    He raises the pitchfork and strikes downward two more times, leaving the pitchfork stuck in the double. He runs toward the rear of the greenhouse in the slightly canted frame, the camera tilting down to follow his movements.

228. LS: *Miles, emerging from the greenhouse, seen once again from the barbecue area.*

    MILES (*as he runs toward Becky*): We're getting out of here right now. *The camera pans left with him as he grabs Becky's arm and ushers her toward the camera and off frame left.*

    BECKY (*as she rushes off*): Well, where are we going?

    MILES: Sally's.

    He lets her hand go and reaches back to take the receiver out of the phone cradle. He then runs off frame left. The camera tracks in to a MS *of the phone on its small table.*

    OPERATOR (*over the phone*): We're still unable to get through to Los Angeles. Do you wish me to keep trying? (*We hear the car door slam.*) Dr. Bennell? (*A little more alarmed.*) Dr. Bennell?

    Dissolve.

Gas Station, exterior, night

229. ELS: *a dark street with Miles's car approaching a gas station from the background. The camera pans left as the car enters the gas station and stops beside a pump.*

    MILES (*voice-over narration*): I needed someone I could trust, and I figured Sally, my nurse, was my best bet. I decided to try to phone her to see if she was at home. Maybe they hadn't taken over the pay phones.

230. MS: *Miles in the car, with Becky in the passenger seat.*
  MILES: I'll try the pay phone. (*He gets out of the car and calls toward the station.*) Hey, Mac!
  MAC (*coming out from the gas station door behind the car*): Oh, hi, Doc! . . . How are you?
  MILES: Listen, will you give me a couple of gallons fast? I'm in a hurry. (*He runs in front of the car and then to a pay phone in the background, the camera panning his movement left.*)
  MAC (*off*): Sure! Martha! Doc's in a hurry. Get the windshield, will you?
  Miles enters the phone booth in the background and shuts the doors.
231. MS: *Becky seen through the window of the driver's side, the camera level with her.*
  MAC (*coming over to the driver's side, and reaching inside to take the keys from the ignition, to Becky*): I have to have the keys to open the gas tank.
  Becky looks at him as he goes behind the car; meanwhile Martha approaches the passenger window and leans in as she wipes the side window.
  MARTHA: Somebody sick out this way?
  BECKY: There's been an accident.
  MARTHA: Funny, we haven't heard about it.
  BECKY: Umm . . . well, it just happened.
232. MCU: *Miles, at right with the phone at his ear, standing inside the phone booth, seen through the glass side of the booth.*
  MILES (*voice-over narration*): Before I could even get her number, I saw Mac closing the trunk of my car. He could have been checking my spare tire . . . (*He hangs up the phone and starts to open the door to the phone booth.*)
233. LS: *Miles, exiting the phone booth. He walks, almost runs, toward the car and the camera.*
  MILES (*voice-over narration*): . . . but I didn't think so.
  MAC (*off, to Becky*): That should do it!
  BECKY (*off, to Mac*): Thank you.
  MILES (*to Mac*): All set?
  MAC (*off*): All set, Doc.
  MILES (*the camera panning right with him as he gets to the car. Becky, Martha, and Mac are now in the frame.*): Fine, thanks. (*He opens the door and gets into the car.*) Put it on my bill, will you?
  MAC (*closing the door for him*): Sure, Doc.
  They pull out left, the camera panning with them. Mac walks into the empty frame, accompanied by quiet disturbing bass music. He watches them pull out, then starts moving toward the station . . . or the phone.

The Streets of Santa Mira, exterior, night

234. LS: *Miles's car driving down a dark street toward the camera; Miles makes a left turn into a side street, the camera panning the moving car right. Heavier chords are played.*

235. MS: *Becky and Miles seen through the windshield. Miles stops the car suddenly.*

    BECKY: But what's the matter?

    Miles gets out of the car.

236. LS: *from the rear of the car, Miles exiting the driver's door and Becky following from hers. Miles opens the trunk and extracts two huge pods; he lays them on the ground. Becky is at his side. He reaches back into the trunk, pulls out a flare, lights it, and sets the two pods aflame. They flare up in a large fire that obscures them and the car. Miles and Becky run back into the car.*

    MILES: We've got to make it to Sally's house.[42]

    The fire crackles and flames brightly as they take off.

237. MS: *Becky and Miles in the car, seen through the windshield. He turns the corner wildly with a screeching sound.*

Sally's House, exterior, night

238. LS: *Miles's car driving down a dark street.*

    MILES (*voice-over narration*): I wasn't sure now there was anyone I could trust, but I took a chance and drove to Sally's anyway. (*The camera pans right as the car turns left and passes two parked cars. Miles parks his car about twenty feet behind them, headed the wrong way for this side of the street.*) When I saw several cars in front of the house, I decided to play it safe.

239. MS: *Becky and Miles inside the car, both looking back at Sally's house. They are seen through the windshield, with the camera on her side.*

    BECKY (*making a move to get out after they have stopped for a moment. Miles pulls her back into the seat*): What's wrong?

    MILES: Probably nothing, but we're not going in there until I'm sure it's safe. Slide over under the wheel and get out of here fast if anybody shows up looking for us.

    He gets out of the car and she slides into the driver's seat.

240. ELS: *Miles crosses the lawn toward Sally's porch, in the left foreground. The camera tracks back as he goes up the porch steps and pans left as he attempts to peep through the bottom of the front window. The shade is obviously drawn. The camera tilts up as in MS, silhouetted, he climbs over the porch railing on the side. The camera tracks down with him as he lowers himself over the rail and crouches beneath the first side window. He rises to look in the window and the camera tracks up; at the same moment Becky's father enters the room in the background with a pod.*

Uncle Ira, Aunt Aleda, and Wilma, among others, are in the room.
Sally sits at the right, closer to the window. Miles ducks down below the
camera level, and the camera stays on the room through the window. The
camera tracks in a bit, to quietly ominous bass music.
BECKY'S FATHER: Is the baby asleep yet, Sally?[43]
SALLY: Not yet, but she will be soon . . . and there'll be no more tears.
The camera tracks back a bit and Miles stands up frame right to look in
the window.
BECKY'S FATHER: Shall I put this in her room?
SALLY: Yes, in her playpen. (*She gets up from the chair.*) No, wait,
  maybe I'd better take it. (*She takes the pod from Becky's father.*)
GRIVETT (*his hand first appearing on Miles's shoulder and startling him;*
  the camera pulls back and pans right to show Miles and Grivett): Why
  don't you go in, Miles . . . we've been waiting for you.
At the window on the left, we can see one of the men in the room coming
to see what is happening. Without hesitation, Miles gives Grivett a strong
left punch to the stomach and a right punch to the jaw. Grivett falls and
Miles jumps back over the porch railing and runs back to the car, as
Becky's father and another man come out the front door, chasing Miles.
The camera pans their movements right a bit.
MILES: Becky, start the car!
241. MLS: *Miles enters the car on the passenger's side since Becky is in the*

driver's seat. Two men pursue them in the background. One of them is Becky's father.
MILES (*opening the car door*): Becky, get going!
She pulls away, as her father and another man stand in frustration on the curb, two women behind them on the lawn; the men turn and run back to the house.
Dissolve.

The Streets of Santa Mira, exterior, night[44]

242. MS: *a parked police car with its right door open. No one is in the car.*
DISPATCHER (*over the radio*): Attention all units! Attention all units! Apprehend and detain Dr. Miles Bennell and Becky Driscoll, now believed heading north in a black and white Ford sedan, . . . (*The camera swish pans right to reveal from a low angle two policeman and two other men seated on stools at a brightly lit outdoor hot dog stand, called "The Hot Dog Show"*) . . . license number 2X37 796. (*The two cops turn around as they hear the radio and get up from their seats.*) All units designated as roadblocks move to your stations. (*The camera pans left with the cops as they move toward the car; the cop on the passenger side appears in MS and gets in the car, then the driver enters at frame left.*) It is urgent. These two persons must be detained and not permitted to leave Santa Mira. Repeat. It is urgent. (*The camera pans right as the police car drives off.*)
There is ominous music throughout this montage sequence, 242–252.
Dissolve.

243. LS: *a busy street with a police officer walking from the left to his parked car right. The camera pans right as he gets in the passenger seat; the driver is already in the car. The lights are turned on and the car takes off.*
DISPATCHER (*over the radio*) Be on the lookout for a 1955 black and white Ford sedan, license number 2X37 7 . . .
Dissolve.

244. LS: *a police car moves left past a lighted building and then down a dark road. Pan left.*
Dissolve.

245. Another LS: *a different police car moves slowly along a deserted residential street toward the camera. The camera pans slowly left with it.*
Dissolve.

246. LS: *at a greater distance, the same car seen from some bushes beside the road. The camera pans right with the car.*
Dissolve.

247. LS: *another police car, perhaps the one in 244, moving right past a deserted building. It stops and a cop gets out on the passenger side, nearest the camera.*

248. ELS: *the cop gets out of the car and moves right.*
Dissolve.

249. LS: *still another police car, a lighter and unmarked one, with two cops, moves right, the camera panning with it, until it stops in a brightly lit gas station. The attendant comes from the pump to talk to the driver. We cannot hear what they say. The car pulls out right with a slight pan right.*

250. MS: *Becky in the driver's seat, Miles at the right, both seen from the rear seat, with Miles looking back out the rear window.*
    MILES: We'll try to make my office. Cut in to that alley on the right.

251. ELS: *the car screeches as it turns in the far background into the alley. It comes down the alley halfway, then turns right into a used car lot. The camera pans right past several used cars for sale until Becky pulls into a vacant place. The car is now facing the camera in MS. Miles and Becky get out of the car. Miles takes a sign from the car on the left, advertising it for sale at $650, and places it on his windshield. He signals to Becky with his head that they should go left, grabs her hand, and they run down the alley from which the car came, the camera panning right to its initial position at the beginning of the shot. Again they are in ELS, as they run and turn in between buildings about halfway down the alley.*

252. ELS: *overhead shot of the two as they round the corner of a building from the right and run in front of it to the right. A police siren sounds nearby. The camera tilts down and pans right with them as they run behind the building, then pans right and tilts up as they ascend some outdoor wooden stairs to the back door of Miles's office building. They are now in MS, level with the camera. Miles pulls the heavy outer door open, struggling with its weight, and they enter the long, narrow, brightly lit hallway, which the camera is now looking directly down.*

Miles's Office, interior, night

253. ELS: *the hallway, reverse angle, with Miles and Becky running toward the camera from the door in the background. They come up to the turn in the hallway in MS, stop by the wall, and Miles looks to the right down the other part of the hallway. The camera pans right and we see the hallway they walked down earlier and the stairs in the background. Miles leads the way to his office on the right; Becky follows. As Miles puts his key in the lock, the stairwell reflects a flashlight and the shadow of a man coming up the stairs is projected on the wall. Miles unlocks the door and they go in.*

254. LS: *Miles's inner office, lit only by the hall light. Miles and Becky enter from the hall door in the background right. Miles opens a closet door to the left of the main door, near the closed double doors to the reception room. They go into the closet.*

255. MS: *Becky and Miles, inside the closet, low angle. A small window with a grille is at their eye level, casting light into the dark closet. Miles holds Becky with his left arm. They hear footsteps and sink down below the level of the grille. A light is turned on in the office and more light shines on Becky's and Miles's faces. Footsteps are louder and a policeman's cap*

and upper face are visible as he glances through the grille. He goes away with the sound of footsteps and muffled drumbeats; the light is turned off and the office door is closed.

BECKY: Do you think he'll come back?

MILES (*shaking his head*): I don't think they'll check again before morning. By then Jack should be here with help.

They start to rise toward the grille.

256. CU: *the grille from office side. Miles's and Becky's heads are seen through it. They open the door, the camera tracking back and left as they enter the office, until they are in* MS.

BECKY: What if Jack doesn't get through?

MILES (*going to a cabinet on the left and opening it*): He's got to get through. (*He closes the cabinet and offers some pills to Becky.*) Here, now take two of these . . . they'll help you to stay awake.

He puts two pills in his own mouth and walks over to the water cooler to the right of the entrance door. Becky follows and the camera pans with them. He gives her a cup and they fill both cups at the cooler. She takes the pills and the water; he drinks his, puts the cup down, and walks left over to the window. He is alone in the frame. He pulls the shade back and looks out, with the camera tracking in on him to a closer MS. *Becky enters the frame from the right and goes to his left by the window.*

MILES (*releasing the shade and turning to address Becky*): We can't close our eyes all night.

BECKY: We may wake up changed . . .

257. MCU: *Becky and Miles in front of the window, the shade pulled halfway down; it is a square of light behind them.*

BECKY: . . . into something evil and inhuman.[45]

MILES: In my practice I see how people have allowed their humanity to drain away . . . only it happens slowly instead of all at once. They didn't seem to mind. (*He meditatively folds his arms, his back to the window.*)

BECKY: Just some people, Miles.

MILES (*looking at her*): All of us . . . a little bit. We harden our hearts . . . grow callous. . . . Only when we have to fight to stay human do we realize how precious it is to us . . . how dear . . . (*Romantic peaceful music starts.*) . . . as you are to me.

The camera tracks in for CU *as they kiss.*

Fade out.

Miles's Office, interior, day

258. *Fade in.* MS: *a telephone ringing, an ashtray with burning cigarettes to its right. The camera pans left and tracks back to reveal Miles half-asleep in his chair and Becky to his right.*

BECKY (*looking from the phone to Miles*): Maybe that's Jack trying to find us.

MILES: He'd know better than to use the phone. (*He puts his arm on her shoulder, consoling her, then looks around nervously and gets up.*) Where is he? Why doesn't he come?

The phone continues to ring. The camera pans right with Miles as he goes to the window and then peers out just above the lower curtains. The shades that were drawn the night before have now been raised.

259. ELS: *high angle of the downtown stores on the left, a triangular park on the right. Many cars are parked and some are moving, with several pedestrians walking. A busy scene. Slow pan right. Although this and all the following shots of downtown Santa Mira are shot at various distances, the high angle is meant to approximate Miles's and Becky's* POV.

260. MS: *Miles, as in 258.*

MILES (*turning to look at Becky*): Just like any Saturday morning. (*He looks back out the window.*)

261. MS: *Becky, sitting in her chair; she rises and comes over to him at the window, the camera tracking up, back and right, until they are in the formation of shot 260. She now stands behind Miles and to his left, also looking out the window.*

MILES: Len Pearlman . . . Bill Bittner . . .

262. ELS: *the triangular park on the left and center, a bus pulling up to it from the right-hand street. Pan left as the bus comes to a stop.*

MILES (*off*): . . . Jim Clark, his wife Shirley and their kids . . . people I've known all my life.

BECKY (*off*): What time is it?

263. MCU: *Becky and Miles at the window, Miles closer to the camera. He looks down at his watch.*

MILES: 7:45. (*Looks at her.*) Yeah, I know. (*Then he looks back out the window.*) It's too early to be so busy.

264. ELS: *high angle of the park and the bus, as in 262. Two people are getting off the bus and two cops appear to receive them.*

BECKY (*off*): What are they doing here?

MILES (*off*): There's the answer . . .

265. MCU: *Becky and Miles, as in 263.*

MILES: . . . must be strangers in town.

266. ELS: *the park and the street to the left along it. High angle but somewhat lower and closer to the action than before. The bus pulls out left. The cops escort the two people to a cruiser at the edge of the park and the two people get in the rear seat.*

MILES: They're waiting for the bus to come and go. There isn't another one through here until eleven.

267. MCU: *Becky and Miles at the window, as in 265. They stare out.*
268. LS: *the police car from a slightly high angle, closer than the other shots, pulling out from the curb with the cops and two people in it. It emits a siren on leaving screen left.*
269. MS: *Becky and Miles at the window, as in 262. The siren from outside wails. The phone rings again and they both look across the room to it, but don't answer it. They resume their looking out the window.*
270. ELS: *high angle of the triangular park, with cars parked in front of stores on the left. Another police car siren sounds as the car pulls up to the left edge of the park. A large number of people from the stores on the left and from the area across the street on the right slowly—and in a very orderly way—walk to the car.*
271. MCU: *Becky and Miles at the window, as in 267.*
272. LS: *the park, closer and lower than in 270. The people are all going onto the two sidewalks of the square. Low rumble of a truck off.*
273. MCU: *Becky and Miles looking, as in 271.*
274. LS: *the park at left and center, same distance and angle as before, but the view is to the right to emphasize a truck coming up to the side of the park nearest Miles's office. The camera pans left as it arrives, until we see the same view as in 272.*
275. ELS: *the same as 274, only higher, the full view, closest to Miles's actual POV. The whole park and downtown are visible. Another truck pulls up to the left side of the park and another pulls in to the apex of the triangle nearest Miles's office. The sound of brakes is heard. Someone goes to the side of the two most recently arrived trucks.*
276. MCU: *Miles and Becky at the window.*
    MILES: Farmers . . .
277. LS: *the two trucks at the left, high angle but lower and closer than previous shots. A tarpaulin is being taken off the trucks and in the rear of the one nearest us, we see a load of pods.*
    MILES (*off*): . . . Grimaldi . . . Pixley . . . Gessner . . .
    GRIVETT (*off, and over a mike*): Crescent City!
278. LS: *high angle of Grivett, standing on a platform with a mike, an officer on the ground below at his left, many people lined up in the rear part of the park.*
    GRIVETT: If you have Crescent City families, step over to truck number one.[46]
279. ELS: *the park and the three trucks, as in 275.*
    GRIVETT: Crescent City. First truck. (*People start going over to the first truck at left rear.*) Redbank. All with Redbank families and contacts, go to truck number two.
280. MCU: *Becky and Miles at the window.*
    GRIVETT (*off*): All with Redbank families and contacts . . .

281. ELS: *the park, trucks, and crowds, as in 279.*
     GRIVETT: . . . truck number two. (*Many people go to the second truck.*) Havenhurst. The first truck. Havenhurst. The first truck.
282. MCU: *Becky and Miles at the window.*
     GRIVETT (*off*): Milltown. The third truck.
283. LS: *the street at the left with the first truck in the background. High angle, but lower and closer than the previous shots. A crowd at the right is receiving pods from the truck off-screen right and the camera pans slowly left as people carry the pods across the street and put them in the trunks of their parked cars.*
     GRIVETT (*off*): Milltown. The third truck. Valley Springs. The third truck. Valley Springs.
284. MCU: *Becky and Miles at the window.*
     MILES: First our town, then all the towns around us. It's a malignant disease spreading through the whole country.
     GRIVETT (*off*): That's all for today
285. LS: *Grivett at the mike, overhead shot. The officer is still beside him but most of the people have disappeared from the background. Same setup and angle as in 278.*
     GRIVETT: Be ready again tomorrow.
     He hands the mike to the officer below him and folds his list of towns.
286. LS: *cars parked in front of the drugstore. Two of the now-empty trucks and the cars leave town, going left.*
287. MS: *Becky and Miles at the window.*
288. ELS: *high angle of the whole area. The truck from the apex of the park exits right.*
289. MCU: *Becky and Miles at the window., same setup as end of 258.*
     MILES (*turning his whole body away from the window and somewhat desperately speaking to Becky*): I can't wait for Jack any longer. (*He holds the bottle of pills up to her to give them to her.*) Stay here!
     BECKY: But you're not going out there!
290. MCU: *Becky and Miles, from reverse angle, the back of Becky's head to camera, Miles's face at right.*
     MILES: I've got to stop them!
     BECKY (*as he rushes away from her*): But wait, we're safe here.
     A door slams just as he rushes right. The camera pans right with him; suddenly he stops as he realizes someone is coming. The camera stops as Miles does. He looks down at the door handle turning a few feet away. The camera swish pans to the turning handle. The door will not open because Miles locked it earlier.
291. MS: *Becky alone at far left, against the wall. She rushes over to Miles, the camera panning her move right.*

JACK (*off, outside the door*): They're not here . . . I hope we're not too late.

MILES (*with relief*): Jack! (*He looks at Becky.*) Thank God! (*He rushes to the door and the camera pans right as he goes to it and hurriedly unlocks it for Jack. He pulls Jack into the room by Jack's left arm.*) Jack, the whole town's been taken over by the pods!

DANNY (*emerging into the doorway behind Jack*): Not quite. There's still you and Becky. (*The camera tracks back as he and Jack come into the room; Miles and Becky walk backwards into the room in front of the camera.*) Miles, it would have been so much easier if you had gone to sleep last night. (*He walks left toward the window.*)

JACK (*walking toward Miles and Becky who are still backing up*): Now relax, we're here to help you.

The camera tracks back and pans left and down as Miles reaches for the phone and takes it off the hook; it tilts up again to include Danny at the window and Jack facing Miles and Becky.

DANNY: You know better than that.

GRIMALDI (*entering the room from the left with Grivett, and going up to Danny*): Where do you want us to put them?

DANNY: Would you like to watch them grow?

MILES (*quietly*): No thanks.

DANNY (*to Grimaldi*): Put them in there. (*Grimaldi goes off screen right.*) (*To Miles and Becky, pleadingly.*) There's nothing to be afraid of. We're not going to hurt you.

292. MS: *Becky and Miles with the right side of the room in the background. Grimaldi can be seen going out of the room in the mirror.*

JACK (*off*): Look, once you understand, you'll be grateful.

293. MS: *Danny to the left by the window, Jack closer to the camera to the right, appealing to Miles and Becky.*

JACK: Remember how Teddy and I fought against it? Well, we were wrong.

294. MS: *Becky and Miles. In the mirror in the background we see Grimaldi and another man carrying two pods into the room.*

BECKY (*to Jack*): You mean Teddy doesn't mind?[47]

JACK (*off*): Of course not . . .

Miles is watching the men bring in the pods.

295. MLS: *Danny at the window and Jack to the right, Miles and Becky in front of them with their backs to the camera, more in* MS. *In the right background, two men pass Grivett with pods and go through the double doors of the reception room with them.*

JACK: . . . she feels exactly the way I do.

BECKY (*in a desperate appeal*): Let us go!

MILES: Look, we'll leave town . . . we won't come back.

DANNY: We can't let you go. You're dangerous to us.

JACK: Don't fight it, Miles, it's no use.

296. MS: *Becky and Miles.*

JACK (*off*): Sooner or later you'll have to go to sleep.

Becky looks at Miles, then at the men leaving the room.

297. MLS: *the group, same setup as end of 291. Grimaldi and the other man are leaving.*

GRIVETT (*in the far background right, to Danny*): I'll wait for you in the hall. (*He leaves the room right.*)

DANNY (*coming over to Jack's left from the window and addressing Miles; the camera pans right and tracks in*): Miles, . . . (*Removing his hat.*) . . . you and I are scientific men. . . . You can understand the wonder of what's happened. Now just think . . .

298. CU: *Becky and Miles. This begins a series of shot–reverse shots, through shot 302.*

DANNY (*off*): . . . less than a month ago, Santa Mira was like any other town. People with nothing but problems.

299. MS: *Jack at left looking up at Danny at right, talking to Miles and Becky.*

DANNY: Then out of the sky came a solution. Seeds, drifting through space for years, took root in a farmer's field. From the seeds came pods which have the power to reproduce themselves in the exact likeness of any form of life.

300. CU: *Becky and Miles. She looks at Miles.*
     MILES: So that's how it began. Out of the sky.
     Becky looks back at Danny; Miles looks at Becky.
301. MS: *Jack and Danny.*
     DANNY (*turning and walking to the open door of the reception
        room*): Your new bodies are growing in there. (*Standing in the door-
        way and looking alternately at the pods and Miles and Becky.*) They're
        taking you over cell for cell, atom for atom. There's no pain. (*He walks
        back to where he was in front of them.*) Suddenly, while you're asleep,
        they'll absorb your minds, your memories . . .[48]
302. CU: *Becky and Miles.*
     DANNY (*off*): . . . and you're reborn into an untroubled world.
     Becky looks up at Miles.
     MILES: Where everyone's the same?
     DANNY: Exactly.
     MILES (*shaking his head*): What a world!
303. MS: *Danny with Jack behind him, their backs to the camera, on the left,
        Becky and Miles in MS at the right in front of them.*
     MILES: We're not the last humans left. They'll destroy you.
     Danny shakes his head.
304. MCU: *Jack glances right up at Danny.*
305. MCU: *Danny.*
     DANNY: Tomorrow you won't want them to. Tomorrow you'll be one of
        us.
306. CU: *Becky and Miles. Becky looks toward him and he presses his face
        against hers. Soft violin music is in the background.*
     MILES: I love Becky. Tomorrow will I feel the same?
307. MCU: *Danny.*
     DANNY (*shaking his head*): There's no need for love.
308. CU: *Becky and Miles.*
     MILES: No emotion? Then you have no feelings, only the instinct to
        survive.
309. MS: *Jack and Danny in the midground left, facing Miles and Becky in the
        foreground right, with their backs to the camera.*
     MILES: You can't love or be loved, am I right?
     DANNY: You say it as if it were terrible. Believe me, it isn't. You've
        been in love before.
310. CU: *Becky and Miles.*
     DANNY (*off*): It didn't last. It never does.
311. MCU: *Danny.*
     DANNY: Love. Desire. Ambition. Faith. Without them life's so simple,
        believe me.

312. CU: *Becky and Miles.*
     MILES (*shaking his head*): I don't want any part of it.
     DANNY (*off*): You're forgetting something, Miles.
     MILES: What's that?
313. MCU: *Danny.*
     DANNY (*solemnly*): You have no choice.
314. CU: *Becky and Miles. The familiar bass notes are heard.*
     MILES (*turning to Becky*): I guess we haven't any choice.
     DANNY (*off*): Good.
315. MS: *Miles close to Becky at the right foreground with their backs to us, with Danny and Jack in the background walking into the reception room in the rear. Romantic music is heard on the track, but with a troubled note. Jack shuts the door.*
316. CU: *Becky and Miles embracing, his face against hers.*
     BECKY (*crying*): I want to love and be loved.[49] (*Miles kisses her to the accompaniment of romantic violin music.*) I want your children. I don't want a world without love or grief or beauty. I'd rather die.
     MILES (*holding his head in his hands, looking at her and shaking his head*): No. No. (*He walks aimlessly toward the rear into* MS.) Not unless there's no other way.
     BECKY (*walking to the rear left into* MS, *with her back to the camera*): Why didn't they just give us a shot or a sleeping pill or something?
     MILES (*puzzled, trying to think of something, he sits down in front of a cabinet of medical tools.*): Drugs dull the mind, maybe that's the reason. (*He opens the cabinet and takes out two knives, then shrugs in disbelief of his plan.*) No, it wouldn't work. I might get one or even two but I couldn't possibly get three of them.
     BECKY (*coming over right to him as the camera tracks in on the two of them and brings them into closer* MS): You're forgetting something, darling . . . me. It isn't three against one, it's three against two. Give me a knife.
     MILES (*turning, he looks again at the medical cabinet*): No.
     The music becomes more suspenseful, as he removes a vial from the cabinet and shows it to her with a look of discovery on his face. The camera pans left with him as he goes to the door to the hallway and locks it. The camera tracks left with him again as he goes to the closed reception room doors. He reaches for the edge of the curtain on the right door.
317. MS: *Jack standing and Danny sitting at Sally's desk in the reception room. Both are staring off into space. We see them through the diaphanous curtain which is being pulled back by Miles's hand at the right. The curtain is then let go.*

318. CU: *Miles letting the curtain go.*
319. MS: *Miles locks the double doors quietly. The camera pans right as he moves right to a medical tray at the right of the doors, takes a syringe, and fills it with the drug in the vial.*
320. MS: *Becky watching what he is doing from across the room.*
321. MS: *Miles, closer than in 319, puts the first syringe down, picks up another and fills it.*
     MILES: Now. (*He holds the needle up and sees that it is working; Becky moves into the frame beside him, right, the camera panning slightly.*) Here. Go over by the desk. (*He points to the other side of the room.*)
322. MS: *Miles and Becky, but further back than in 321. Becky goes out of the frame to the right. Miles picks the needles up from the medical tray. The camera tracks back and left as he slowly eases himself into the closet to the right of the table. It's the same closet he and Becky hid in earlier. As he closes the door of the closet with himself in it, he kicks the medical table in front of the double doors with the curtains and loudly slams the door to the closet.*
323. MS: *Jack standing and Danny sitting, seen from the right side of the reception room desk. Both men suddenly look left at the doors and rush to them, but can't open them. The camera pans left with them as they go to the doors.*
     DANNY: What's going on in there? . . . Miles! Miles!
     JACK: The door's locked. Open the door, Miles.
     DANNY: Unlock the door.
324. MS: *Miles comes out into the reception room from the rear door of the closet they hid in. It connects the two rooms.*
     JACK (*off*): Miles, open the door.
     DANNY (*off*): Open the door, Miles!
     JACK: Miles!
     The camera pans right as he rushes behind the two men who are screaming for him to open the door. He plunges a needle into the lower back of each.[50]
325. MS: *low angle, from inside the office, looking at the doors as they give way from the force of the two men falling onto them and Miles plunging the needles in from behind them. The two men fall into his office on the floor. The camera tilts down to floor level and Miles falls upon them as they struggle.*
326. MS: *Grivett in the hallway outside Miles's door on the left. He tries the door to find out what is happening, but it is locked.*
     GRIVETT: Open the door!
327. MS: *the three men struggling on the floor as in 325. Danny has Miles's head in a stranglehold and Jack is rising from the floor with his arm around Miles's back. Tense music plays.*

328. CU: *Becky, looking on and gasping.*
329. MS: *the three struggling. Miles manages to push Jack's head to the floor, but Danny still grips him.*
330. MS: *Grivett as in 326 forcing the lock.*
331. MS: *the three still struggling on the floor. Miles is getting exhausted in Danny's grip. He is panting.*
332. CU: *Becky, wincing at what is happening to Miles, but not doing anything. There is a crash offscreen caused by the lock to the door giving way and Becky suddenly looks left.*
333. MS: *Nick Grivett comes through the door at the right, Becky's POV. The camera pans left with him as he rushes to the group on the floor and hits Miles hard on the back of his neck. Miles screams out with pain and pulls back. Grivett grabs his throat and starts to strangle him.*
334. MS: *Becky rushes left, the camera panning with her as she comes over to Grivett strangling Miles; she plunges the needle into his neck. Miles gets up, holding his throat in anguish; Grivett rises and goes after Becky, who backs away from him; he collapses on the floor. Miles, still holding his throat, looks at Becky on the other side of Grivett's body.*
    MILES: Our only hope is to make it to the highway.
    Becky reaches toward the desk and picks up her sweater. They run out the door at the right.
335. MS: *Miles and Becky coming out of the office door right and heading left to the turn in the hallway, until Miles alone is in the frame in CU at the turn, the camera panning left. He stops and looks, the familiar bass notes playing quickly. The camera pans left a bit more and we see the long hallway they entered before, leading to the back door of the building. They run down the hallway until they are in LS near the door.*
336. MS: *Miles and Becky at the back door inside. He tries it and can't open it, then sees there is a padlock on it.*
    MILES: Well, that does it. The only other way is out the front door and there's bound to be somebody watching . . . but we'll have to chance it.
    He exits frame right followed by Becky.
337. ELS: *the hallway with them at the end again, as in 335, now rushing toward the camera which is at the turn in the hallway. They reach the turn and stop against the wall in MS as he peers down the next part of the hall where his office is. The camera pans right and looks down the other part of the hall toward the stairs. They run down the hallway until they turn left in ELS by the stairs.*
338. MS: *Miles and Becky at the top of the stairs, slightly low angle. The camera is at the landing at the top of the stairs.*
    MILES (*first looking down the stairs to the left, then to Becky*): Keep your eyes a little wide and blank. . . . Show no interest or excitement.
    She leads the way down the stairs; the camera pans left as they cross in

front of it and we see them descend the stairwell from the high angle of the camera at the top of the stairs, the camera tilting down to follow them. Light pours in the door at the bottom and cars can be seen passing outside.

Street outside Miles's Office, exterior, day

339. LS: *Miles and Becky exit onto the street from a door at the left. Pedestrians walk up the sidewalk on the right and a cop rests against a storefront up the walk. Becky and Miles go down the walk toward the camera, the camera tracking back with them as they walk in a rather robotlike fashion. Sam Janzek enters the frame on the right and stops to talk to them, hands on hips.*

MILES: Well, Sam, we're finally with you.

JANZEK: They were supposed to let me know. The Chief said he'd phone the station, then I'd get the call.

MILES: He phoned, but . . . a . . . the line was busy. He's calling again now.

They walk ahead toward the camera, Janzek staying behind.

340. LS: *a dog crossing the street to the right, from Miles's and Becky's* POV. *The camera pans right with the dog as it crosses the street.*

341. MS: *Becky and Miles walking in the same somber slow fashion, vaguely looking right, to where the dog is crossing. The camera tracks back as they walk.*

BECKY (*suddenly seeing that the dog is in danger, screams in a high-pitched sound*): Oh!

342. ELS: *the dog crossing the street to the right, with a truck entering* MS *from the left and nearly hitting the dog, while slamming on its brakes.*

BECKY (*off*): Watch out!

The dog runs to the right past the truck's right front wheel.

343. CU: *Janzek whirling his head around and looking to the right to see what has occasioned Becky's cry. The dog barks off-screen.*

344. MCU: *Becky and Miles, her head close to his. The dog continues barking for a few seconds.*

BECKY (*softly*): I'm sorry, Miles.

345. CU: *Janzek as in 343, with a more puzzled look on his face.*

346. MS: *Becky and Miles begin to cross the street. Janzek is in the left background near a palm tree watching them. The camera pans right as they cross to mid-street, their backs to us, Janzek now out of the frame.*

347. CU: *Janzek, as in 343, now more troubled, turns his head further to the right to follow them.*

348. MLS: *Miles and Becky in mid-street, their backs to us, walking further across the intersection.*

349. CU: *Janzek, as in 343, now turning his head left and turning around. He walks with his back to us to the door from which Miles and Becky*

emerged. The camera pans slightly left to take in his movement. He goes in the door in MLS *range.*

350. LS: *from the top of the stairs, Janzek enters the stairwell that Miles and Becky just descended. He climbs up the stairs until he is in* CU; *he passes the camera on the landing and the camera pans right, watching him from a low angle, as he mounts to the top of the stairs. He turns left at the top and the camera pans left as he moves down the hallway past the railing of the stairwell, then turns right down a long hallway. He then turns left to enter Miles's office in the background in* LS. *The camera watches him from its position below the stair railing; one post of the railing is missing, so that we can see his actions in the hallway.*

351. ELS: *Becky and Miles in the far left, running across a Richfield gas station with the downtown Santa Mira buildings in the background. They exit frame right, facing the camera, in* MS, *running furiously. Tense chase music starts in this shot.*

352. MS: *Janzek behind the stairwell railing, from a low angle, as before, now reversing his movements hurriedly, as does the camera. The camera pans right to the top of the stairs, he turns and descends, and the camera follows his movements past it; he runs down the stairs out the door and into the street in a high angle* LS.

353. LS: *Janzek exits the front door of the building, with the police car roof in* CU *in foreground. He comes to the car and gets in, in* MS. *The camera tracks down to follow the action through the window. Sitting in the passenger seat with the door open, he picks up the radio mike.*
    JANZEK (*over the mike*): This is Janzek . . . they got away . . . turn the main siren on. (*He hangs up the mike.*)

354. ELS: *overhead high angle, looking down on the town from the top of a hill. A road leads from background to foreground toward the base of the hill. Becky and Miles in* ELS *are running along it toward the hill. A town siren blares.*

355. ELS: *at road level of a part of the road obscured by the hill in the previous shot, with Becky and Miles emerging around a corner, running. The camera pans left with them as they run along this deserted road. The hill rises steeply on the left. In low angle,* MS, *they stop as they start to pass some long steps which climb up the hill.*
    MILES: Here . . . the steps!
    They turn and start climbing the steps in LS. *We see them from the bottom, their backs to us.*

356. LS: *reverse angle of Becky and Miles from a point midway up the steps looking down. They run up the steps until they are in* CU *and pass the camera.*

357. LS: *Becky and Miles in* MLS, *running up the steps and seen from further up, the camera looking down on them and tracking back as they pull*

themselves up the steps by the railing. Police sirens sound and the town siren makes a loud wail. Miles glances back down the steps regularly to see if they are being followed.

358. ELS: *overhead shot of the town as in 354. A crowd starts to make its way down the street Becky and Miles had run down. A police car honks its horn to warn people to get off the road. The camera pans right and down to catch Becky and Miles near the last few stairs as they start to climb them.*

MILES: There's only a few steps more!

They reach a landing in MS *and the camera tracks back and to the right as they climb the last few steps. Then it tracks and pans right as they cross a street with a house behind them. They now face a deep valley in* LS *and, beyond that, a mountain. They run down into the valley to the left.*

359. LS: *the police car at the base of the hill on the road which led to the stairs, as in 355. A crowd is rushing down the road from the right past the camera and exiting left. The police car door opens and we hear the crowd rush past.*

VOICES (*to Janzek, barely audible*): Where are they?

JANZEK (*pointing up the hill*): C'mon, They went this way!

He starts running toward the stairs. The camera pans left to the base of the stairs and Janzek and the crowd push to get up the narrow stairway.

360. ELS: *from overhead, the ridge of a mountain with Miles and Becky two small specks on it, climbing left.*

361. MLS: *Janzek, with the crowd behind him on the stairs, the camera tracking back ahead of him as he climbs the stairs, much as it did with Miles and Becky.*

362. LS, *almost* MLS: *Becky and Miles, seen from the left climbing up the hill, the camera panning right. Miles pulls Becky by the hand.*

363. LS: *Janzek, followed by the crowd, seen from the left at a high angle climbing the stairs. As he emerges into* MS *and passes the camera, it tilts up and pans right. He reaches the top of the stairs and the street. From a low angle the camera watches him and then a few people from the crowd run across the street in* LS.

364. LS: *Janzek at left from a high angle looking out over the valley into which Miles ran. A few members of the crowd get behind him.*

JANZEK (*pointing*): They're over there!

He runs down the path and to the left with the crowd after them.

365. LS, *almost* MLS: *Becky being pulled up the slope by Miles, similar to terrain and camera setup as 362, the camera continuing to pan their uphill movement right.*

366. LS: *the crowd pushing its way onto the path.*

367. ELS: *Becky and Miles on the top of a ridge, from a low angle down below it. They run downwards in* LS *on the right and exit frame right.*

368. ELS: *the two as they run left to right, past a large tree in the foreground, then climb the hill on the right.*

369. MLS: *Becky and Miles climbing with Miles pulling Becky. The camera pans right and tilts up as they climb the steep terrain.*

370. ELS: *the crowd reaching the ridgetop as in 367, seen from the same point down the hill. They descend the same path on the right following Miles and Becky's path and exit right. Janzek in* LS *leads the chase.*

371. MLS: *Miles, reaching a spot near the top, looks back and extends his hand to help Becky up. The camera pans right and tilts up as they make their way over to the top. They stand exhausted for a moment, then Miles decides to go farther. He grabs Becky and disappears in* LS *over the ridge away from the camera's view.*

372. ELS: *the crowd rushing past the tree, as in 368. The camera is a bit farther to the right here. They too climb on the right.*

373. ELS: *Becky and Miles running toward the camera and then to the right on a flat wide dirt road up in the mountains. The camera, slightly overhead, pans right with them as they rush past it. Becky trips and falls. Miles stops and picks her up.*

374. ELS: *the crowd makes their way past the tree and up the hill right where Becky and Miles have climbed.*

375. ELS: *Miles carrying Becky into the entrance of a tunnel, as seen from about twenty-five feet inside it. The camera tilts down as he walks along a board in its middle and puts Becky down. It pans right as they reach the wall of the tunnel, Becky leading their way along the tunnel wall. They rest in* MS. *Miles looks back out the tunnel and Becky is at his right exhausted.*
   BECKY: I can't! I can't . . .

376. MCU: *Miles and Becky against the wall of the tunnel.*
   BECKY (*shaking her head*): Miles, I can't. I can't go on.
   MILES (*also exhausted, but with determination*): Yes, you can!
   He gives her a shove on her left shoulder.

377. ELS: *Becky and Miles, from farther inside the tunnel. Wooden supports hold the tunnel up on the left and right. They make their way along the right wall, supporting each other and holding onto the first wooden support on the right, then stumble to one on the left in* MS. *The camera pans left with them as Miles swings Becky around behind the support. Miles has his hands around Becky's shoulders, holding her up. He looks to the right, then to the left for a place to hide. He spots a place on the ground.*

378. MS: *two boards, slightly high angle, Miles's* POV. *The boards are parted, revealing an area below the tunnel floor.*

379. MS: *Becky and Miles, as in 377. The camera tracks back and tilts down as Miles moves right and throws himself atop the boards. Miles in* LS *pulls the board on the right to the right. Becky enters frame left and starts*

helping in the background. Miles shoves a big board on the left out of the way to the back. Then he lifts up a board it was covering and enters the hole. Becky enters the hole behind him.

380. MS: *from the right and above, Miles helping Becky into the hiding place and holding her as they descend. He starts to pull the board over them as he looks out the tunnel.*

381. MS: *Miles's head sticking out between the two boards, seen from behind. The camera is near the ground. It tracks back and up a bit to reveal both the boards in the center as Miles goes under them and the crowd in* ELS *approaching the opening of the tunnel. We can see Miles's hands adjusting the boards in place and covering him and Becky as the crowd approaches and calls out.*

   JANZEK (*not really visible but among the crowd in the sun at the end of the tunnel*): Here's her sweater. They must be in the tunnel. (*The camera holds as they rush in, led by Janzek with Becky's sweater in his left hand. He stops on the boards and points to another part of the tunnel, directing people that way too.*) Look, Tommy, you go that way . . .

   Some people run to the right. Janzek leads the way ahead, coming in MS *to the camera.*

382. CU: *low angle, the boards as seen from below, with the space between them and people visible, running over Becky and Miles. The camera tilts down to a* CU *of the back of their heads pressed together as they lie in the ground below the boards.*

383. MS: *crowds rushing toward the camera on the boards over Becky and Miles.*

   MAN (*stopping over the boards and yelling*): Give up! You can't get away from us! . . . We're not going to hurt you.

   He runs off-screen left.

384. CU: *the backs of Becky's and Miles's heads, as in the end of 382, as the people rush over them. The camera tilts up and we see the people continue to rush over them. In the bottom foreground, Miles's right arm reaches over to embrace and cover Becky.*

385. MS: *the crowd rushing over the boards.*

386. CU: *the tops of Miles's and Becky's heads beneath the board, as at the beginning of 384, their faces only partly visible.*

   VOICES (*off*): They're not in the tunnel. . . . All right, everybody outside. C'mon. Let's check the hills. . . . Everybody move.

   Miles looks toward Becky as he holds her.
   Dissolve.

387. MLS: *Miles and Becky reflected in a pool of water as they bend over it, put water on their faces, and drink. The camera tilts up to show them at the edge of the pool. They are exhausted.*[51]

BECKY (*resting her head against Miles as if about to collapse*): Miles, I can't stay awake much longer.

MILES: I think they're all gone now. We'd better start or we'll never make it to the highway. (*He holds her arms, then pats her face with his left hand as she rests her head against his shoulder.*)

Suddenly they hear beautiful music and a wordless singing,[52] *and they look more awake. They look right to the outside where it originates. Miles helps Becky up and they move slowly along the left wall of the tunnel, the camera tracking up and right with them. They come to rest behind a part of the wall, still shielded from the outside. They listen and Miles indicates to Becky by looking at her that they should advance outside.*

388. MS: *Becky and Miles step out from behind the left wall and move toward the mouth of the tunnel, seen from behind and a little overhead. The camera tracks with them as they advance toward the entrance. Miles leads Becky by his hand on the right. They move to the tunnel's entrance and Miles looks out as Becky leans against the wooden support on the right. The music continues.*

389. MCU: *Miles and Becky. Miles looks out, then at Becky.*

BECKY: Miles, I never heard anything so beautiful. It means that we're not the only ones left who know what love is.

MILES: Stay here and pray they're as human as they sound. (*He touches her.*) 'Bye, darling.[53]

390. MLS: *Miles leaves the tunnel. The camera tilts up as Miles climbs a small hill on the right, seen through the supports. Becky watches him leave. She turns around and comes into MS silhouetted by the light from the tunnel's entrance. She goes toward the camera as she goes back into the tunnel. She exits frame right into the tunnel's depths.*

391. LS: *Miles makes his way left to right through some brush and trees, a more pastoral landscape, as the music continues.*

392. MLS: *Becky moves right, into the tunnel. The camera pans right with her and tilts down as she kneels at the pool's edge and splashes water on her face and wipes her forehead.*

393. LS: *Miles at the top of a hill, seen from below, making his way down cautiously and looking for the source of the music.*

394. ELS: *Miles's POV, a truck in the foreground, greenhouses behind it, and several men in the fields in the background. One man in the left foreground is carrying a large object. The lovely music is coming to an end.*

395. MCU: *Miles's head peering over some shrubs to get a better view of the scene. The music stops.*

396. LS: *the truck in front of the greenhouses, overhead shot and closer and more detailed than 394 but still Miles's angle of vision. The truck is*

clearly filled with pods and more are being loaded on it. One man brings a pod along the side and gives it to another on the back of the truck.
VOICE OVER THE TRUCK RADIO: This is Station KCAA—the twenty-four-hour platter parade . . . the station of music . . .[54]
The driver enters the truck and clicks the radio off.

397. MCU: *Miles, as in 395. Threatening music quietly comes up. Miles looks to the left and prepares to sneak away.*

398. LS: *Miles, reemerging from the bushes left, as in 393, and starting to go back.*

399. MLS: *Miles, moving left and passing some shrubs. The camera pans left and tilts down as he crosses a ditch.*

400. LS: *Miles, making his way left across the pastoral landscape of 391. This time he puts his hands on the low branch of the tree and pushes himself under it.*

401. LS: *Miles seen through the front right supports of the tunnel, and coming back down the hill he climbed in shot 390. The camera tilts down as he stops in* MLS *in the entrance to the tunnel and looks in.*
MILES: Becky! Becky!
He enters the tunnel and exits frame right.

402. LS: *inside the tunnel, Miles's shadow on a lighted wall. He enters and the camera pans right with him along the wall.*
MILES: Becky! Becky! Where are you?

BECKY (*off, in an odd, soft voice*): I'm here, Miles.
Miles looks to the right and crosses the tunnel, with the entrance in the
background. The camera pans with him as he goes to the other side and
lifts Becky's body up from the ground. She is in a stupor.

403. CU: *Miles and Becky. He lifts her head into frame right.*
     MILES: You didn't go to sleep?
     BECKY (*exhaustedly*): I'm so tired.
     MILES (*holding her neck with both hands and pointing her face directly*
        at his): They weren't people . . . it was more of them. They're grow-
        ing thousands of pods in greenhouses. We've got to get away. (*He puts*
        his right arm under her and starts to lift her up.)

404. MLS: *Miles and Becky with the tunnel entrance in the background.*
     BECKY: I'm exhausted, Miles . . . I can't make it . . .
     With his right arm under her legs he lifts her and starts carrying her out
     of the tunnel over the floorboards. The camera holds on them as they
     make their way in ELS *to the light of the tunnel's entrance.*

405. LS: *reverse angle of Miles carrying Becky in the dark of the tunnel as*
     seen from the tunnel's entrance looking in. The camera tilts down as
     Miles steps off the boards and falls into some shallow water at the
     entrance of the tunnel. They both lie exhausted there.[55]

406. MCU: *Becky lying in the water next to Miles, his arms around her. The*
     camera tilts up a bit as he moves over her and kisses her neck, and then
     embraces her.

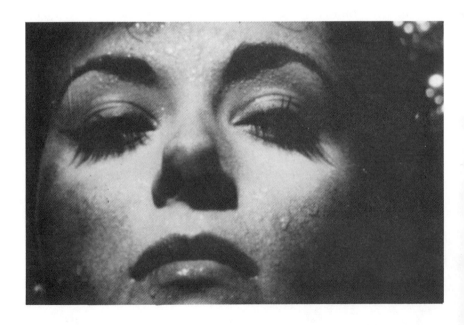

BECKY: We can't make it without sleep. (*She has her left arm around him and draws her to him.*)

MILES: Yes, you can!

He kisses her. A long sustained chord is heard.

407. ECU: *Becky's face, her eyes opening slowly to ominous loud music. Miles's* POV.

408. ECU: *reverse shot, Becky's* POV, *Miles's face pulling away from her, his eyes opening in horror as he realizes she is a pod.*

409. ECU: *Becky's face with the camera pulling back from it, Miles's* POV.

410. ECU: *Miles's face pulling back farther, Becky's* POV. *The loud music continues.*

411. MS: *Miles at right now sitting up, with Becky getting up slowly on the left.*

BECKY: I went to sleep, Miles, and it happened.

412. CU: *Miles, looking at her, not quite able to believe it. This begins a series of shot–reverse shots, 412–421.*

413. CU: *Becky, with hair wet, staring directly at Miles, zombielike.*

MILES (*off, in pain and sighing*): Ohhh . . . Becky!

414. CU: *Miles, shaking his head in disbelief and pain.*

415. CU: *Becky.*

BECKY: They were right.

416. CU: *Miles.*

MILES (*sighing*): Ohhh! I should never have left you.

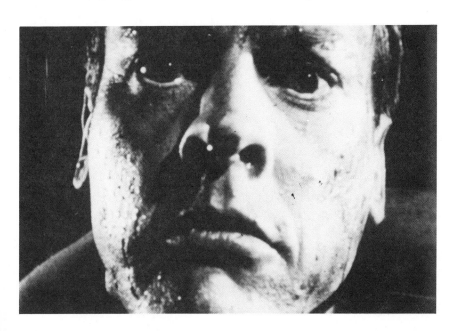

417. CU: *Becky.*
    BECKY (*in a sudden shift of voice, forcefully and scornfully*): Stop acting like a fool, Miles, and accept us!
418. CU: *Miles.*
    MILES (*shaking his head slowly with determination*): No!
419. CU: *Becky staring at him.*
420. CU: *Miles.*
    MILES (*strongly*): Never! (*He starts to stand up.*)
421. CU: *Becky.*
    BECKY (*looking up at him, and screaming*): He's in here!
422. MS: *Becky sitting at left, Miles getting up at right, only his torso visible, as in 411.*
    BECKY (*crying out*): He's in here!
    She turns and looks toward the camera as he rushes out toward it on the right.
423. LS: *the dark tunnel entrance with Miles emerging from it on the right.*
    BECKY (*screaming furiously*): Get him! Get him!
    Miles rushes left past the camera in MS. *The camera pans left and tilts down as we see Miles alone in the frame rush into the wilderness background in* LS.
424. LS: *Becky emerging from the tunnel entrance. She stops against the hill near the tunnel and watches Miles run. The camera pans left and tilts up at her in* MS.

425. ELS: *Miles at the ridge of a mountain pass seen from below and descending down the other side toward the camera.*

  MILES (*voice-over narration*): I've been afraid a lot of times in my life, but I didn't know the real meaning of fear until . . . until I kissed Becky. (*About fifty feet behind him three men appear on the horizon chasing him.*) A moment's sleep and the girl I loved was an inhuman enemy bent on my destruction.

426. LS: *Miles running down the slope, much closer than in the previous shot. He looks back and keeps running toward the camera in* CU.

  MILES (*voice-over narration*): That moment's sleep was death to Becky's soul, just as it had been for Jack and Teddy and Dan . . .

427. ELS: *as in 425, Miles running down the slope with the crowd in pursuit. He's at the bottom and runs right, then out of frame.*

  MILES (*voice-over narration*): . . . Kaufman and all the rest. Their bodies were now hosts harboring an alien . . .

428. ELS: *Miles running toward the camera across a field flanked by trees until he is in* MS.

  MILES (*voice-over narration*): . . . form of life . . . a cosmic form . . . which to survive must take over every human man. So, I ran. I ran . . . I ran as little Jimmy Grimaldi had run the other day.

  The pursuing crowd has emerged in the background. Miles turns to the right and the camera pans with him as he crosses a country road in the hills. It tilts down to follow him as he disappears into a brush-filled slope at the edge of the road.

  MILES (*voice-over narration*): My only hope was to get away from Santa Mira . . . to get to the highway . . . to warn the others of what was happening.

429. ELS: *Miles running down a wooded slope on a path and out onto a street until he is in* MS. *It has suddenly become dark. He stops on the side of the road near the camera, looks both ways, then back; the pursuing crowd emerges down the path he just traveled. He runs right, down the road, the camera panning his movement until he is in* LS. *A busy freeway with an equally busy bridge crossing it is in the background.*[56]

430. MLS: *Janzek and the crowd, seen from the right, coming down the path and out into the road.*

  MAN (*grabbing Janzek's arm*): Wait!

  JANZEK: No. No. We gotta get him!

  MAN: Let him go. They'll never believe him. (*They wait and watch.*)

431. ELS: *Miles, as in 429, but now a distant speck approaching the freeway bridge in the background.*

  MILES: Help! Help! Help! Wait!

432. ELS: *reverse angle, Miles, a small figure running down the road on the right, as seen from the freeway bridge, cars going by in the foreground.*

The camera pans right a bit to keep him in the frame as he nears the
bridge over the freeway. His arm is raised trying to get cars to stop.
MILES: Help! Help! Help!

433. MS: *the same, but Miles has now reached the cars and is desperately*
trying to signal them to stop. As they drive by, he puts his hands on them
to stop them.
MILES: Wait! Wait! Wait! Stop! Stop! Stop and listen to me! (*He goes*
out of frame following a slow car to the right, with his hands on it; the
camera pans right as he raises both arms high to stop the next car.)
Listen to me!

434. MS: *Miles, farther back, stepping into the path of the next oncoming car;*
its brakes screech to a stop.
MILES: Listen! Listen! (*He runs to the window of the passenger side*
with his back to us and leans in.) Those people are coming after me!
(*The car goes on and Miles is already screaming at the next one.*)
They're not human! (*The camera pans left with him as he runs left. He*
is between the two lanes of clogged traffic in the middle of the bridge
with his back to us. The traffic moves slowly. He runs to the car on the
left and leans in.) Listen to me! We're in danger!
VOICES FROM CARS: Get off the street!

435. LS: *overhead shot of Miles from the right lane as he runs left in the*

*foreground over the bridge. One lane of traffic is behind him and we can
see the bridge railing and traffic on the freeway below and behind it.*

MILES: Danger! Do something! (*He puts his hands on a car that passes
in the left lane in the foreground; it goes on.*)

VOICES FROM CARS: Go on, get outta here!

The camera pans left with him as he crosses before a car in the right lane.

MILES (*running up to the passenger side of the car where a man
sits*): You're in danger! Please!

MAN (*shoving him aside as the car goes on*): Get out of here, go on, get
out of here.

*The car goes by, and Miles whirls around and starts to approach the next
one in the same way.*

436. LS: *slightly low angle of the men, Janzek at the right, and others on the
edge of the woods, watching Miles. They look right. Miles's voice can be
heard yelling in the background, but the words are not distinguishable.*

437. LS: *Miles, now seen overhead from the other side of the bridge across
two lanes of traffic. He runs right on the walk, then jumps out in front of a
car which brakes for him, but starts going again right away. Miles leans
in the driver's side.*

MILES: Now, listen, Mister, there isn't a human being left in Santa Mira.
Not one.

The car goes on.

438. MLS: *Miles, seen slightly overhead from an angle as a big truck*

approaches. He is in the middle of the road and he leaps on the running board of the cab and addresses the driver desperately.

MILES: Hey, stop! Pull up, will ya? . . . Pull over to the side of the road. . . . I need your help. Something terrible has happened.

The truck is moving left and the camera pans left with it and Miles on the running board. Miles and the driver are in MS.

DRIVER: Go on, you're drunk!

439. LS: *the same action, Miles being pushed off the truck onto the road by the driver.*

DRIVER: Get out of the street! Get out of here!!

440. MS: *Miles, being whirled around on the side of the truck, which moves on.*

DRIVER (*off*): Go on!

On its side we read in large letters, LOS ANGELES—SAN FRANCISCO—

441. LS: *Miles with his arms outstretched in front of the rear portion of the truck as it passes him by. We can now read the remaining two towns, PORTLAND—SEATTLE, on the side of the truck. Miles's arms are stretched out to halt motorists in the next lane.*

442. MS: *Miles alone in the street. He turns left and the camera pans left; we see the back of the truck he was just pushed off. Miles runs in* LS *with his back to the camera and leaps up on the slats and climbs up to get into the back of the truck.*

443. CU: *Miles, seen from the inside of the truck at the top of the slats. He is holding onto the top board and peering inside the truck. Cars are on the road behind him. The camera tracks in a bit, almost* ECU, *as his eyes register horror and amazement. His mouth is agape.*

444. MS: *pods inside the truck, occasionally lighted by car headlights. Miles's* POV.

445. CU: *as in 443, Miles, preparing to drop off the truck.*

446. LS: *Miles dropping off the truck to the road right in front of the car behind the truck. It slams on its brakes and hits him, bouncing him off the left fender into the middle of the road.*

VOICE: Are you crazy, you big idiot!

447. MS: *Miles, low angle, slightly canted to the right. He waves his arms at the cars and yells out now left, now right.*

MILES: Look! You fools! You're in danger! Can't you see? They're after you! They're after all of us! our wives! . . . our children . . . everyone . . .

448. ECU: *Miles, from a low angle, canted slightly to the right, his face shadowed, sweaty and in anguish, almost addressing the camera.*

MILES: They're here already! You're next! (*He screams with fury and shakes his head up and down.*)

449. MLS: *Miles standing in the middle of the road with his arms outstretched, seen from overhead, cars passing him on both sides.*

    MILES: You're next! You're next![57] (*The voice now echoes as the picture blurs into an oil dissolve back into the frame story.*) You're next! You're next!

    The camera tracks back and up. The same music that signalled the dissolve into the flashback accompanies the transition.[58]

Hospital Emergency Room, interior, night

450. CU: *Miles sitting in the doctor's office; he looks right, then left, then right again, as the camera pulls back and right to reveal Dr. Bassett seated at Miles's left, obviously skeptical. He is chewing on his eyeglasses. Dr. Hill is at the right more intently listening to Miles.*

    MILES: You don't believe a word of this, do you? Sure it's fantastic, but it happened! (*Furiously.*) Don't just sit there and measure me for a straitjacket. Do something! (*Loudly.*) Get on the phone, call for help! (*He looks at the skeptical Bassett, and puts his head in his hands with a loud sigh.*) What's the use . . .

    Bassett looks over at Hill, as Miles holds his head in his hands and sobs between them. Hill and Bassett rise, pass the two cops in the background and go out the door, the camera tracking their movement. Dr. Bassett shuts the door.

451. MS: *Dr. Hill at left, Dr. Bassett shutting the door and moving left to talk to Dr. Hill. They are outside the office door.*

    DR. BASSETT: Well, what do you think? Will psychiatry help? (*He still nibbles on the end of his glasses.*)

    DR. HILL: If all this is a nightmare, yes.

    DR. BASSETT (*with scorn*): Of course it's a nightmare. Plants from another world taking over human beings. (*He casts a glance toward the office door.*) Mad as a March hare. (*He walks in front of Dr. Hill and down the hallway. The camera pans his move and looks down the hall. In* LS *two ambulance drivers wheel an injured man on a hospital table.*) (*To the two men.*) What have we here?

    AMBULANCE DRIVER: Ran his truck through a red light . . . Greyhound bus smacked him broadside and tipped him over . . .

    DR. BASSETT: Put him in the O.R. (*The attendant exits with the driver.*) (*To Dr. Hill.*) Will you take over Bennell for me, Doctor?

    DR. HILL: Certainly. (*He turns right to put his cigarette out in a standing ashtray.*)

    DR. BASSETT (*putting on his glasses*): How badly is he hurt?

    AMBULANCE DRIVER: Both legs, left arm . . . broken all to bits. (*The driver and Dr. Bassett begin to walk left; the camera tracks back and pans right. Dr. Hill is beginning to enter the office on the right but stops short at the ambulance driver's next words.*) We had to dig him out from under the most peculiar things I ever saw.

DR. HILL (*opening the door and revealing Miles sitting in the background inside the office. He stands in the door and asks*): What *things?*

AMBULANCE DRIVER (*standing* MS *left and addressing Hill, who is standing in the doorway to the office. Miles has risen and is coming toward the doorway. The cops are watching him.*): Well, I don't know what they are. I never saw them before. They look like . . . great big *seed pods.*

452. MS: *Dr. Hill in the doorway left, with Miles now at his right* MS, *the officers in the background inside the office.*

DR. BASSETT (*off*): Seed pods?

DR. HILL (*after looking at Miles with a sense of confirmation, he turns left to look at the ambulance driver and asks*): Where was the truck coming from?

453. MS: *the ambulance driver at the left, Dr. Bassett at right.*

AMBULANCE DRIVER: Santa Mira.

He moves out of frame left, while Dr. Bassett looks knowingly at Dr. Hill out of frame.

454. MS: *Miles at the left of the door, seen from behind and inside the office, with Dr. Hill at his right in the doorway, looking left and back at Miles.*

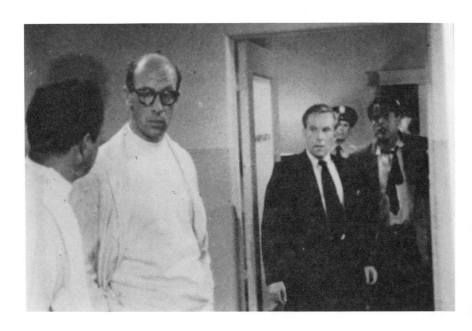

Miles nods and Dr. Hill rushes in, grabs his arm, then goes right, to the two policemen inside the office, the camera panning with him.

DR. HILL: Get on your radio and sound an All Points Alarm! Block all highways and stop all traffic and call in every law enforcement agency in the state!

The two cops leave and the camera pans their exit out the door. Miles is again on the left and rests with relief against the wall near the door.

DR. HILL (*off, into phone*): Operator, get me the Federal Bureau of Investigation! Yes, it's an emergency.

The camera tracks in for a CU *of Miles's face moving from side to side in anguish and relief. He grits his teeth into a half-smile. Strong chords and drums signal a low title at the bottom of the frame: THE END.*

Notes on the
Continuity Script

S cripts of *Invasion of the Body Snatchers* are difficult to find in archives open to the public. None of the major U.S. collections—UCLA, USC, the American Film Institute, the New York Public Library at Lincoln Center, the Academy of Motion Picture Arts and Sciences—have copies. Three scripts can be found at the Walter Wanger Archive at the State Historical Society in Madison, Wisconsin.

All three scripts bear the title *The Body Snatchers* and contain neither voice-over narration by Miles Bennell, the leading character, nor the framing story, both of which were added several months after the film was shot.

The first script is dated 10 February 1955 and is marked *Plus Revisions* in Walter Wanger's handwriting. A second title page bears this additional information: Collier's Magazine Serial by Jack Finney, SCREENPLAY by Daniel Geoffrey Homes Mainwaring. The reference is to the serial just published in *Collier's* in three successive issues, 26 November, 10 December, and 24 December 1954. Finney's revised and expanded version of the serial in book form was not published by Dell Publishers until late February, after Mainwaring had completed his first draft screenplay of 10 February.

This screenplay consists of 124 pages and 282 scenes. The *Plus Revisions,* however, are revisions done after 10 February, nine sequences totalling seventy-five pages, all marked 3/2/55, inserted into the script on blue paper before the earlier scenes. Since Mainwaring was on the payroll into early March, it is reasonable to assume that he is the author of these inserts, although consultation with Siegel and Wanger is also likely. Both the new and the old sequences are given in their entirety, so it's possible to read a scene in the revised version and then look immediately at the original.

The second script in the collection is essentially the revised version of 3/2/55, now standing alone. The only difference between it and the earlier 3/2/55 inserts into the first script is a single page of carbon copy, wherein the real names of the

Marin County towns that the chief of police, Nick Grivett, calls out, in which the first script follows Finney's *Collier's* serial, have been given new fictional names: Milltown, Valley Springs, and so on.

The third and final script is Walter Wanger's copy of the shooting script. It is prefaced by a staff sheet with the production crew and their phone numbers, a list of locations used, a cast sheet with names, addresses, and phone numbers, and a thirty-six-page shooting schedule, broken into twenty days of full shooting and three cover days. The script is marked Final Revised 3/17/55 at the top right corner of the pages. Most pages are so marked. However, there are some pages unmarked and some marked with still later revisions: 3/25/55, 3/26/55, and 3/28/55 (dates during the shooting schedule of the film), all on the top left corner of the page. Since Mainwaring was off the payroll by mid-March and Richard Collins, a regular Wanger writer and a friend of Siegel's, had been hired for ten days of rewrites, it is likely that the later revisions are his. Again Siegel probably had a hand in these and most likely made the changes on the set. In addition to these changes, some shots are crossed out and marked "out," and others have lines drawn through them. There are 291 numbered scenes, with some having subdivisions (A, B, etc.) because of the inserts. All these numbers have been checked off, indicating they were filmed.

The differences among the three scripts are not great. For instance, the order of the scenes in all three scripts is the same. Only one scene has been omitted from the final script. It occurs just *before* Miles and Becky seek refuge at Sally's house; in the early drafts, they attempt to drive out of town and encounter a roadblock. They turn around and are spotted coming back into town by Mac, the owner of the gas station where they have just stopped and where pods had been placed in their trunk. In the final film a montage of patrolling police cars has been substituted for this scene, and placed *after* the escape from Sally's house. This montage does not appear in any script.

The scripts do differ verbally from one another. The first script, for instance, explains things in greater detail, and people talk both at greater length and in a more relaxed way. As the scripts were refined, dialogue was cut and the line of action firmed up. Since the scripts are all rather similar, I have commented in the notes where major changes or significantly different emphases occur. I have also tried to quote the many humorous lines cut by the studio, which Siegel has maintained hurt the film. I have also commented on a few major changes from Finney's serial.

1. Both the first draft and 3/2/55 script begin at the railroad station. But the first opens before the titles with Sally driving to the station and the train arriving under the titles. As Miles picks up his bags, he meets Becky on the platform. She boarded the train at Reno and says she threw her ring in the Truckee River; her dad wants her to stay in Santa Mira. Miles introduces her to Sally and offers her a ride back to town. She says Wilma is

picking her up and says goodbye. Miles says, "For now. You're going to hear from me." Then Miles and Sally leave. In the first draft Wilma actually arrives. Becky has gone into the station and Wilma asks Miles where she is. Miles notes her odd behavior to Sally. "How do you like that? I've been gone a month and she didn't even say hello."

The Hays Office objected to the talk of divorce, especially so early in the film. The solution was to delay Becky's entrance until later in the movie in the final script.

Finney's serial begins at the end of a normal day in Miles's office when Becky arrives with her story of Wilma and Uncle Ira.

2. The line to Sally, Miles saying his interest in married women is strictly professional or hers would be a lost cause, was put in later to indicate that Sally is married. Sally is described in Mainwaring's first draft as "one hundred and fifteen pounds of yellow, wind-blown hair and prime flesh poured into sweater and skirt."

3. This sequence and the characters have no counterpart in Finney's serial. However, the boy who feels his mother has changed is one of several patients who visit Miles's office. The abandoned vegetable stand adumbrates the Finney theme of the pods' listlessness and lack of energy. In Finney's novel Miles and Becky escape from Santa Mira, then return to fight the pods. When they walk through the town, they notice the eerie inactivity, the absence of people working and the town's gradual decay, which before was imperceptible to them. This is probably the cue for this scene.

The scene has been variously interpreted. By those who see the film as anticommunist it furnishes a good example of the death of incentive, old-fashioned American enterprise, and the capitalistic profit motive. Mainwaring, however, may have been having a bit of a joke with the idea. In the final script, though not in the film, the stand bears a sign "Joe Grimaldi— Vegetables and Mushrooms." Mushrooms, like the pods in people's cellars, spring up suddenly. And the vegetable stand may be closed because who can imagine vegetables selling their own kind?

4. The final script includes a shot of Becky entering Miles's office outside. In the film, she is first shown entering Miles's office in shot 21.

5. The scene where Miles visits Wilma and talks with Uncle Ira opens differently in the final scripts and the early drafts.

MED. SHOT AT GARAGE
The garage is untidy, the workbench littered. The family car, unwashed, occupies one side. Miles gets out. Ira moves out into the fading sunshine to meet him.

IRA (*cheerfully*): You're back, Doc, so watch the death rate go up. Kill many today?

MILES (*shaking hands*): Bagged the limit. Your sacroiliac been bothering you again?

IRA: No. Not since you put it back in place.

MILES: Then get busy with that lawnmower.

IRA: More you cut it, the faster it grows. But I suppose it's got to be done some time.

He goes back into the garage. Miles heads for the porch.

The grim opening joke is in the Finney serial. Ira does not mow the lawn in the serial, but stares into space and kicks a pebble listlessly while Wilma and Miles talk.

Siegel has often complained about the humor cut from the final film. Most of that humor is at the beginnings and ends of scenes. Here, however, Siegel himself urged that this encounter with Uncle Ira be cut because he was not happy with the way it played. Unfortunately, the theme of listlessness in Ira and the other pods is lost. Siegel at first tried to retain Miles's urging of Uncle Ira to mow the lawn, but that eventually got cut, too.

6. Miles's reply to Uncle Ira, "Sure is," is wild sound recorded and added later and not in the script. This was Siegel's suggestion.

7. The line, slightly misquoted, is from *A Midsummer Night's Dream* II.i.249. It is the beginning of a famous lyrical and romantic speech by Oberon, a favorite in the past for high school study.

8. All the scripts refer to the club as the Fireside Inn. The only name we see on the sign, however, is the Sky Terrace. Perhaps it is an entertainment room at the inn. In Finney's serial, Miles has a similar conversation with Kaufman (in the serial, Manny), Pursey, and Carmichael at a weekly town medical meeting.

9. In the conversation between Danny Kaufman and Miles outside the Fireside Inn, shot 82, Kaufman likens the epidemic of mass hysteria to seeing flying saucers. "Instead of seeing flying saucers, everybody and his brother are deluding themselves that their cousins and their uncles and their aunts . . . aren't." These lines were cut.

10. Another bit of humor cut from the film is at the end of Danny Kaufman's exchange with Miles in the parking lot. He says to Becky in shot 86, after making Wilma's appointment for around two, "Are you quite sure this gentleman you're with is what he seems?" and Becky answers "soberly": "Suddenly I'm not sure of anything." Then they part and Miles and Becky go into the club. Siegel fought strongly for restoring these lines.

This scene has no counterpart in the serial, where they go to a movie. Jack summons them from the movie, promising something better—probably a reason why the scene was changed in an era when movies were losing audiences to television.

11. In the early drafts, after expressing her worry in shot 91, Becky adds that these things don't happen anymore. Miles cites an epidemic of dancing sickness that swept Europe two hundred years ago and Orson Welles's famous *War of the Worlds* broadcast of 1938.
12. The line "There's Jack" is wild sound, not in the script, and added later at Siegel's suggestion.
13. In the final script, after this question in shot 98, Miles asks Jack how the body got here. Jack tells Miles he has no idea how it got in his house. He then tells how he found it and put in on the table. "It was in the closet where I keep my old manuscripts. A while ago I came down to look through them, and there it was, lying on top of the cartons stark naked. I put it here. . . . Want to call the cops, Miles?" Miles says no and Jack suggests it's not just a body. Miles says it looks "unused."
14. In the final script, the bandaging scene reads:

> JACK (*feigning lightness*): Bleeding to death.
> BECKY: Miles—don't you think we should call the police and have them take that dead man out of here before we all go stark, staring mad?
> MILES: What could they do? This isn't just a body and you know it.
> *Jack goes around the bar, glancing at the table as he does so.*
> JACK (*to body*): Come to think of it, old thing, we do have a lot in common.
> MILES: But why, that's what I'd like to know. I wonder if there's any connection.

Again Siegel fought to restore these lines.
15. In the final script, Jack adds, "Whatever it is, I don't like it."
16. When Miles and Becky leave in shot 107, Jack is again more humorous. "I half hope something does happen. It'll make a lovely, bloodcurdling mystery story."
17. This is another scene that caused particular trouble with the Hays Office.
18. When Jack and Teddy come running to Miles's house, the final screenplay suggests that he has been up reading the books on his coffee table. "On the coffee table are four books dealing with hypnosis, mass hysteria, and unexplained phenomena." Miles is so sleepy that he confuses the ringing doorbell with the phone and even thinks he is in bed before putting on his slippers to answer the door. This opening to the scene was cut. In the script Teddy is also more hysterical when she arrives.
19. When Miles calls Danny Kaufman in shot 117, in the final script Danny "curses like a wild man" over the phone, language that the script suggests is "filtered" out. Miles says, "Why, Doctor, where in the world did you learn such language? From your patients' foul and slimy subconscious, I suppose." And Danny responds rather angrily, "I'll hang up and leave the

phone off the . . ." which dissolves into another "tirade." This is another example of a darkly humorous joke that is cut.

20. In the final script, Jack does not trigger Miles's worry about Becky in shot 120. The glance down the stairwell to the basement does this by itself. The wild line of Jack's was added later at Siegel's suggestion.

21. In the final script, Becky is described as being in a "drugged sleep." Nevertheless, she wakes up as Miles carries her down the stairs, screams, and he covers her mouth. She asks where he is taking her. Some of this was clearly changed on the set, as several lines are crossed out and others substituted.

22. In the final script the next scene opens with Teddy telling Danny Kaufman that the body was Jack's. Danny says he believes her. Miles is not yet back from Becky's. Miles enters with Becky on Danny's line and says, "And so do I." Miles then tells all of them that he found another body coming to life and that it was Becky's. Teddy sobs and wonders, "What are we going to do?" Some of this appears to have been cut on the set, since there are various lines crossed out.

23. In Jack's rec room when Miles, Danny, and Jack look for the body, in shot 143, there are some more lines, probably cut on the set.

> JACK: And what's this stuff? (*on the pool table, after Danny has noted the blood spot*).
> DANNY: Ordinary dust.
> MILES (*picking up some of the fluff*): It doesn't look ordinary to me. Feels like some type of vegetable matter. Fibrous . . .
> DANNY (*picking up some fluff, putting it in his wallet*): If it makes you happy, I'll run a lab test on it.

The script also suggests that since the transformation did not take place, the body has disappeared. "Where the head and shoulders were is a pile of thick, grey fluff, like the dust one finds under a bed in an unswept bedroom." This failure at transformation is described in greater detail in Finney's novel. William K. Everson, an early reader of the script for Allied Artists' foreign distributor, suggested this would be difficult to film. It was probably not only difficult visually, but too complex to follow and would have added to the confusion. The comment can be found in an interesting letter he wrote to Allied Artists, in the Wanger Collection.

24. After Danny makes the suggestion about killing with an icepick in shot 143, Miles says, "I guess I should have turned it over. But you heard what Teddy said about the hand." The Hays Office complained about detailing this method of killing, but it was shot anyway.

25. In Danny's lines about the normality of the mystery in shot 143, he suggests that it was "a gangster murder, probably."

26. The final script suggests that the last shot of this rec room sequence is a

view of the pool table. "A gust of wind comes through the open door and stirs the heaps of dust on the green felt. As it swirls up . . . *Dissolve*."

27. In the final script this scene begins with all three lowering themselves through the window of the cellar Miles entered earlier. In Finney's serial, Miles checks out the cellar alone on the way home and finds no body of Becky. He agrees that Manny, who has been lecturing him and Jack on the normality of the mystery, is right.

28. In the woodbin in Becky's house, they also find a "pile of fluffy dust at one end" in the final script. Again the film omits any reference to the disintegration of the pod forms.

29. In the shooting script, Danny adds more to his explanation of what caused Miles to see the doubles. "The dead man became Jack's double in your eyes. You left here holding on to that delusion. You came out of a deep sleep to face an hysterical, fear-crazed woman, and became fear-crazed yourself . . ." Miles then motions to the bin and says, "She was so very real." And Danny adds, "Yes, but only in your mind. You saw her all right . . . etc." These lines were probably cut because the scene they refer to, of Teddy's hysteria, had also been cut.

30. After Miles's remark Danny Kaufman adds in the final script, "You pick them up—you need them more than I do."—another humorous line that was cut and that Siegel tried to restore.

31. In the final shooting script, Miles explains further the idea he was toying with after Jack leaves and he and Becky are alone in the kitchen over breakfast. This exchange is largely from Finney's *Collier's* serial, except for the last line, which is handwritten in.

MILES: Don't you want to know what the idea is?
BECKY: Your breakfast's getting cold.
MILES: All right. But would you mind sitting over here at my left, instead of at my right?
BECKY (*puzzledly*): No. But why? (*She goes and sits at his left. Miles smiles at her*).
MILES: Because I kiss left-handed, if you know what I mean.
BECKY (*smiling back*): No, I don't.
MILES: Well, a girl at my right . . .(*Demonstrates, curving his arms around the empty space at his right side.*) . . . is uncomfortable for me. It just doesn't feel right somehow; it's something like trying to write with the wrong hand. I just don't kiss well, except to my left. (*He lifts his arms around her shoulders and, meeting no resistance, kisses her.*)
BECKY: Oh, a southpaw . . . [*handwritten in*]

These pages have above them the notation "Revised 3/28/55" during the time the movie was being shot. Even after the movie was finished, Siegel was urging Wanger to have this scene restored.

32. In the barbecue scene on Miles's patio, Miles suggests he will get kerosene to light the fire. Jack wants to use a martini to ignite it. The final script also describes more fully the use of the kerosene in lighting the barbecue. In Finney's serial, there is no outdoor barbecue scene or greenhouse. Jack discovers the pods in the coal bin while searching the house to placate Teddy, who is too fearful to go to sleep.

33. The final script has all of them using hurricane lamps inside the greenhouse to view the pods opening. As the pods open, they not only crackle, but emit a "faint whispering noise, like wind in dry leaves."

34. When Becky asks Miles what happens to the bodies when the duplicates are finished, Miles answers, "They must be destroyed somehow and revert to that dust we found." Again the reference to dust is cut.

35. Jack's strange, confusing, and not altogether clear utterance of "Stop" before Miles halts him from destroying the pods is not in the script and does not make very much sense in the film.

36. In shot 198, after Teddy notes that Jack's double did not change until he fell asleep, Jack jokes, "I have a feeling it'll be a long time before I sleep again." This is another example of a humorous line that was cut.

37. In shot 208, when Miles tells Becky he is going to get help, he adds, "I'm going on the theory that it's too big to be handled by anyone here."

38. When Miles is phoning and speculating about the origin of the pods, he adds to atomic radiation and mutation, "or someone may be experimenting with synthetic life."

39. In shot 213, when Teddy asks Jack if the double is hers, he jokes, "You've got good company, kid. We're all there." Another joke that was cut.

40. In shot 216, when Jack and Teddy leave, the screenplay and film begin to diverge significantly from Finney's serial. In the serial, all four leave town to get help from the FBI in San Francisco. Becky starts to fall asleep and Miles discovers two pods in the trunk. They stop and Miles destroys the pods by stomping on them. However, they suddenly decide to return to Santa Mira. "But now we knew that we had a duty to go back to Santa Mira and do something, to make a move at least, against whatever was threatening us and our town—or maybe our country, or even all life on our planet." Back in town, the couples split up with a new plan. Jack and Teddy go home, to escape later in the day and get help. Miles and Becky decide to stay and find out more about the pods in order to fight them. As they walk through town, they note the gradual decay and abnormal inac- tivity of the town. They then go to Sally's house where they discover Sally and others are pods. They run through the hills seeking Professor Budlong, a local college biology teacher who has commented on strange seed pods, possibly from outer space, in a news story Jack had saved. They talk with Budlong and discover he is a pod. Budlong explains the pods' transforma-

tion and taking over of human bodies in a pseudoscientific manner. They then run from Budlong's house, see Jack and Teddy escaping from the police, and hide in Miles's office.

41. When Miles stabs his double in shot 225, "we hear a tiny whimpering, like that made by baby mice when you step on them." In the film, it's a thud. Siegel complained about the double in this shot, claiming it looked fake and rubbery.

42. This line is wild sound added later, at Siegel's suggestion, to clarify the plot.

43. The scene begins differently in the final script.
    The shade is partially drawn. Miles, flat against the house, sidles up to the window as Sally speaks.
    SALLY (*off*): Not so loud—I want the baby to get to sleep.
    The familiar voice reassures Miles and boldly he steps into CLOSE F.G. to look through the window, camera panning with him. The back of his head partially blocks out the room. Then, as he ducks down out of sight, we see what he saw—Sally, her husband Micky, in slippers, pants, and shirt-sleeves, Wilma Lentz and her uncle and aunt, sitting in the living room, and entering the room from the hall, Becky's father, carrying a seed pod.
    DRISCOLL: Baby asleep yet, Sally?

    The camera follows these surprisingly detailed directions, but omits the early line, apparently a reference to the sound of the radio. Siegel urged the cut to omit the radio sound.

44. The final script does not include the montage of police cars. It does contain a cancelled scene after the scenes at the gas station and the burning of the pods, and *before* they seek refuge at Sally's, where Becky says no one is following them, but Miles suggests Mac has alerted people who will. Earlier drafts of the script contain a scene prior to the visit to Sally, of Miles and Becky trying to get out of town and finding the road barricaded by the police. As they drive back into town, "the thing that was a nice guy called Mac" spots them and alerts others. In the serial, they simply see the barricades masquerading as road repairs from the window of the office where they have gone to hide and know that escape is hopeless.

45. The final script has these lines for Becky: "We were made in God's image. (*She shudders*). But these *things* that look like us . . . they're evil."

46. The shooting script has Crescent City, Redbank, Havenhurst, Mill Town. Following Finney, the first draft and the 3/2/55 script have real Marin County places: Sausalito, Marin City, Mill Valley (the model for Santa Mira), San Rafael, and so forth. Actually, Crescent City is also a real place, the northernmost town in California. Much has been made of the various new names. Maurice Yacowar in his commentary on the Criterion

laserdisc feels there are communist implications to Crescent City and Red-bank. Many have noted that Milltown is the name of a popular tranquilizer of the fifties.

47. In shot 294, after Danny Kaufman tells Miles and Becky that they'll be thankful and Jack says he's right, Jack adds: "Well, Teddy and I were wrong. Yesterday we were all mixed up—always upset about something or other. . . . Now all that's changed." And when Becky asks, "Teddy doesn't mind?" Jack replies, "For the first time in her life, Teddy's well-adjusted." This is one of a number of remarks about Teddy's hysterical temperament, all cut. In the files of script fragments, there is an insert scene, not filmed, in which Jack and Teddy try to escape from the police. Jack is knocked unconscious by them and Teddy runs, only to be killed by the police car. A cop flings her body in a ditch.

48. In shot 301, when Danny Kaufman describes the takeover process to Miles, he adds after "There's no pain," "Suddenly the duplicate absorbs your minds, your memories—and you're born into an untroubled world." Miles then says, "Becky and I are trapped—I know it. But we're not the last humans left—they'll destroy you."

49. Crossed out in the final script after Becky says she wants to love and be loved is Miles's reply: You do love . . . you are loved." And Becky's next lines: "I want your children. I want to hear them cry. I want to console them. I don't want a world without love or grief or beauty."

   Both the first draft and the 3/2/55 script contain clearer proposals by Becky for suicide, which the Hays Office objected to vehemently. In the first draft, Becky suggests, "We can sleep forever. Shall we?" and Miles replies "No—that's too easy. And they wouldn't care if we did—they want us dead, one way or another. I tell you there's no use. So take this and go to sleep." In the revision of 3/2/55 Becky simply suggests that we can sleep forever and Miles says, "Not unless there's no other way." In contrast to this defeatism, Finney's serial uses a romantic moment between Becky and Miles to fire them up for one last try at freedom and their eventual marriage, which they feel is their due.

50. The scene with the hypodermic needles seems to have been worked out at the last minute. The first draft, following the serial, has a considerably more complex kind of transformation ruse, substituting male and female skeletons from Miles's closet to act as models for the blanks and thereby use them up. Miles even draws blood from himself and Becky to pour on the blanks and complete the deception. In the final script we still see the blanks, but their "skulls are hairless, faces expressionless, resembling no one—like mannikins in a store window." Miles, who has previously un-locked the double doors, causes a crash that brings Danny and Jack into the inner office, and appears to them to be giving himself an injection to go to sleep. Next to him Becky feigns sleep, as though she has already had the

injection. Jack goes to Becky and she stabs him in the stomach with the hypodermic needle; Miles locks his arm around Danny's throat and jabs him in the neck. There is really no fight, only mild resistance before Jack and Danny collapse. Miles also has less trouble with Nick Grivett; they let him in and Miles grabs him around the throat and stabs him in the neck. Violence is a characteristic Siegel trademark; in addition, Stuart M. Kaminsky points out that several of his films feature major confrontational scenes in which doors are initially shattered and protagonists crash through them. See *American Film Genres,* pp. 218–226 (also reprinted in this volume). The Hays Office had warned against too graphic violence in this scene, particularly with the use of hypodermic needles.

51. The shot of the reflections in the pool (387) and the tilt up to the main characters is set up this way in the final shooting script.

52. The music Becky and Miles hear from the tunnel is described as "the chords of a guitar and the sound of a soft Mexican voice." It was also to have lyrics, which are simply listed as lines from a Mexican love song that Miles translates. This give more resonance to Becky's next remark: "I've never heard anything more beautiful. It means we're not the only ones left who know what love means." It appears that the lyrics were dropped late in postproduction. But some vocalization without words was retained.

53. In shot 389, after Miles says goodbye and prepares to investigate the source of the song, Becky adds: "No, don't say that. Don't ever say goodbye."

54. In shot 396 the voice on the radio is "in rapid Spanish."

55. In shot 405, near the entrance to the tunnel, when Miles is carrying Becky, she says to him: "You're too tired, Miles. Put me down." He continues to carry her and falls.

56. The scene on the freeway bridge, which ends the final script, is somewhat different. "In the third car in the line there is a middle-aged lady sitting in the car looking at Miles, fascinated and horrified. Miles comes to her window." He yells: "Get help." The camera moves in on the woman as her eyes widen and she quickly rolls up her window. ". . . Miles is standing next to the woman's car, his hands on the door, pleading with her." This scene is omitted. The scene of Miles's confrontation with the truck driver, however, is not in the script, nor is his leap onto the truck and his viewing of the pods in the back. Many of Kevin McCarthy's lines in this sequence are wild lines made after shooting.

57. The end to Finney's serial is more upbeat than the original ending of the film—and even of the framing story. Becky is not turned into a pod while Miles leaves her in the tunnel. Together they attempt to make their way to Highway 101, but Miles, recalling a World War II Churchill speech about fighting the enemy everywhere, decides to make a last-ditch stand against the pods, despite certain capture, not by a wild pursuing mob but by a listless gathering of people in the woods between them and the highway.

Pouring gasoline into irrigation ditches, Miles sets the pods aflame. Many burn, but the fire goes out. Nonetheless, as he and Becky are captured, the pod people all turn to watch the pods fly away, leaving an inhospitable planet. "This planet and race would never receive them." Jack arrives with FBI agents who take control. The surviving pod people lose all energy and give themselves up to the authorities. None of them survives beyond a few years. Santa Mira returns to normal.

58. Shot 449. The final script ends on a much more subdued note.
The car jerks away from him (Miles) and Miles falls to the ground, the camera moving in on him as he lies exhausted. We hear the shriek of brakes again. Miles moans and moves. Cars surround the area in which he lies.
WOMAN'S VOICE (*with sympathy*): Poor man! Is he ill—was he hit?
MILES: Go wherever they are . . . kill them! Find the field where they grow.
During this, we hear footsteps, Camera pulls back and we see that two or three men from surrounding cars are coming toward Miles. Camera moves in as the men bend over Miles and gently lift him up. The camera moves into CLOSEUP *of Miles.*
MILES: . . . And burn them. Burn them! There's no escape . . . no time to waste. Unless you do, you'll be next.
THE END

Postproduction File

Postproduction File

The Walter Wanger archive in Madison, Wisconsin, contains extensive material on the production and postproduction process of *Invasion of the Body Snatchers*.

What happened to the film in postproduction is complex and important. Although only a small portion of the postproduction file is reprinted here, it should give a sense of what happened to the film after shooting was completed.

Two long memos from Don Siegel to Walter Wanger, reprinted almost in their entirety, testify to Siegel's work on the film after shooting. One is written after seeing the first complete edit of the film several times, 19 May 1955. Siegel wrote the second after seeing the new version of the film with the framing story and voice-over narration, 21 September 1955. In both, Siegel's extraordinary care with the editing process is abundantly evident. Siegel throughout shows satisfaction with the movie he originally shot and confines himself to fine-tuning it. In the first letter, writ-

ten while he still had some control over the editing, most of his suggestions were followed. By the time of the final edit and the addition of the material demanded by Allied Artists, however, Siegel's suggestions were less heeded. Many of them are probably last-ditch efforts to restore material that had been cut by others; some simply try to minimize the damage done by the voice-over narration. When Siegel tells Wanger that "what we have done for the picture has helped it" and "I think we've got a good picture," he may simply be reining in his dissatisfaction; he is certainly on record many times elsewhere for opposing the cuts and the late additions. I have annotated the suggestions, showing which were followed and keying them to the numbers of the shots in the continuity when necessary.

If Siegel was satisfied with the film as shot, Wanger was not. He immediately began tampering with it, adding a variety of speeches and prefaces. Wanger was the first to conceive a voice-over introduction for Miles. Even before that, while the film was being shot, he was trying to get permission in England to use a Churchill quotation as a preface.

The Wanger files contain an extensive, elaborate, and sometimes funny correspondence with Lee Katz, Orson Welles's agent in England, attempting to get Welles to do a preface and tag for the film. Wanger began writing speeches for Welles's opening as early as 15 June. He spent much of the time up until the shooting of the framing story on 16 September chasing the elusive Welles, bargaining with him about a price (finally settled at 10,000 pounds), and making preparations for filming the preface. For reasons that are not documented, the sequence seems not to have been shot, despite all the preparations. A few days before the filming of the framing story, Wanger was thinking about using Ray Bradbury as a substitute. Again, this does not seem to have been filmed.

The studio scheduled three previews for the film on the last days of June and the first day of July. Wanger's memos indicate these previews were successful. Later reports from Siegel and Mainwaring suggest otherwise, that audiences could not follow the film and laughed in the wrong places. Some of this must be true, because Wanger had enough doubts about the film to schedule another preview on his own in mid-August. This he found disastrous, as his memo of 24/26 August to himself reveals. Apparently, even before this, Allied Artists had become disturbed about the film. They had announced they were changing the title to *They Came from Another World,* a conventional science fiction title. At this point Wanger did not protest. And when Wanger showed the film in the mid-August preview, it had already been subjected to what he calls "sharp so-called B cutting" and had lost some of its "laughs," "humanity," and "quality." The "B cutting" was most likely cutting to streamline the film and remove any idiosyncratic departures from genre formulas. Here is most likely where the beginnings and endings of scenes were cut and where the humor disappeared. As Siegel has frequently pointed out, Allied Artists had a policy of not mixing humor with horror.

Wanger speaks about the organization, Allied Artists, panicking when he asks to take the film out for a bit longer. Thereafter the files are silent on the next major transformation, the new framing story and voice-over narration. There is no reason to doubt that Allied Artists demanded these changes and that Wanger persuaded Siegel and Mainwaring to do them. But there is nothing in the files to substantiate this important matter. The new beginning and ending make their appearance on 12 September in several versions. The one that is filmed contains many changes in dialogue in pencil in Siegel's handwriting.

The frame story was shot 16 September 1955. On 21 September, Siegel wrote Wanger saying—probably out of politeness—that he was satisfied with the picture. He protested the title *They Came from Another World* as belonging too much to cheap science fiction and suggested two of his own, *Sleep No More* and *Better Off Dead*. He appended a long list of notes, again minutely tightening up the edits and minimizing the problems of the voice-over.

Wanger sent the titles and notes to the Allied Artists executives and also argued against *They Came from Another World*. Later Wanger was to fire a few more salvos at Steve Broidy and Harold Mirisch about the bad quality of the Superscope prints. The movie by this time seems to have been largely out of his hands, even though he strongly promoted it. One of the most interesting aspects of this promotion can be seen in a speech given 12 October 1955 to the regional American Booksellers Convention in Los Angeles. Here Wanger spells out his liberal, anticonformist interpretation of the film and makes a strong plea against censorship and for critical thinking.

Letter to Walter Wanger

Don Siegel

May 19, 1955

Dear Walter,

Having seen our picture quite a few times I feel sanguine about the result. I think, for what it is and for what has been put in it, "Body Snatchers" is about as good as we could hope it to be. The rest is up to you and there is no one better qualified to carry on for the good of the picture.

The last running I had with Heermance was on the whole a good one.[1] Most of the things he had the cutter do I liked but there were some things I did not approve or understand. I'll try to remember everything but there are sequences he still has to change and other things left undone. I hope he will use the scissors himself instead of just telling the cutter what to do.

The Churchill foreword was not in.

After the commentation is finished SALLY'S running up the ramp is to be cut just before she greets MILES. (This means cutting in the middle of a PAN and alas we shall no longer see Sally's bosom joggling up and down.) [This cut was made to shot 6.—Ed.]

When MILES gets back into the car following the near accident with the BOY I would like to cut to PROCESS[2] just as the car has started to leave. As Dick now has it we are in PROCESS before the car starts to leave which looks fakey. [Miles now gets into the car and they drive off; see shot 17.—Ed.]

The SHOT of Sierra Madre background with the X-ray lifted up into the SHOT is now eliminated. I thought it smoother to leave it in and CUT to the X-ray being dropped out of the SHOT revealing MILES at the window. [This was done; see shot 19.—Ed.]

The opening of the IRA LENTZ is much better now. We don't CUT to any individuals of Ira. However I wanted to play Ira's line: "But I suppose it's got to be done sometime," over MILES walking over to BECKY and WILMA at the swing. Dick is going to cut it so that you remain on Ira as he gets up to start mowing the lawn and then shorten Miles' entrance to the swing. It's all right but I don't like Ira and wanted to leave him as quickly as possible. [All this opening with Ira was later cut; see shot 44 and note 5.—Ed.]

I wanted to CUT to a CLOSEUP of WILMA when she says her line: "he is

---

1. Dick Heermance was the head of Allied Artists editing department. Although uncredited on the film, he worked closely on it with Siegel from the beginning and did much of the cutting.

2. In this period, a process shot was one made on the set with foreground characters, often in cars or trains, in front of a projected background. We now call this rear projection.

not." This is when the music starts in this sequence and is the keynote of our story. As it is now played we are in MASTER THREE SHOT. Dick didn't want to cut to a CLOSEUP of Wilma as it is in his opinion difficult to get back into the MASTER but I think it will work and the line needs punctuation. [The closeups are there, but while Siegel seems to refer to shot 45, the music does not begin until shot 57, where Wilma says more definitively, "He isn't my Uncle Ira."—Ed.]

Several CLOSEUPS of BECKY are cut out of this sequence which I think is good. [There are no closeups of Becky in this sequence.—Ed.]

The ending of the sequence is now much better as we end on a CLOSE SHOT of IRA. [This shot, 75, is one of the most memorably disturbing shots of the film.—Ed.]

The exterior of the FIRESIDE INN is better now as we are in a TWO SHOT of MILES and BECKY when she says: "Suddenly I'm not sure of anything." However I'd like to make a wild line of that as I can get a better reading.[3] [This line is not in the movie.—Ed.]

The car in PROCESS up Belicec's lane is shortened which is good. I'd like to make a wild line of MILES': "There's Jack now." [This wild line was added to the shot.—Ed.]

The INSERT of the fingerprints is terrible and must be done over.[4] Although it will have no lines, no whorls, it still must not be too fakey. [Shot 100 still looks fakey, but perhaps it was done over.—Ed.]

Dick cut in an extra OVER-THE-SHOULDER SHOT of MILES and JACK at the billiard table when MILES says: "It's fantastic . . ." It didn't work and should be put back as it was which Dick promised to do. [There are now only two over-the-shoulder shots, 106 and 107, in this sequence.—Ed.]

After Theodora screams at seeing the hand and tries to pull Jack out with her Dick CUT to a CLOSER SHOT of Jack and Theodora as they leave thus eliminating too much footage on the fake head on the table. I think this is wise as it insures that no one will be aware of what we did. [The closer shot, 114, is in the film. In shot 111, Jack obviously played his awakening double on the pool table. A stand-in for Jack sat on the barstool with his back to the camera in the background. But 114 substitutes a fake head with its eyes closed, since Jack is active in the shot.—Ed.]

When MILES hears BECKY'S voice it is to be played over the SHOT of the basement with the last of it over MILES' CLOSEUP. This is much better but I don't like the SHOT of the basement—too much light. It is true that the one I used was too dark but we need one in between the two. [Becky's voice-over in

3. A wild line is a line recorded after shooting and inserted either to replace an existing line or to add a line clarifying the plot or a character.
4. An insert is a shot, usually a closeup, cut into the principal shot and usually designed to clarify an object important to the action.

Miles's memory does not begin until the CU of Miles, shot 122. The basement is still very light.—Ed.]

. . . The next change we come to is the greenhouse. This is very difficult for me to describe. I'm sorry to report that what I saw I didn't like as well as what we had. Dick promises to work on the sequence and I hope that what you will see you will like. However I can only go by what I saw. The beginning up to MILES' discovery of the pods is better the way Dick cut it but after that it seems to go to pods—if you'll forgive me. For example—he cut out the SHOT of the rake falling against one of the pods which I liked. There are too many CLOSEUPS of the pods and almost none of the reverse FOUR SHOTS and no reverse TWO SHOTS of the pods. I can't remember all the cuts but my overall impression was not good. If you don't like what Dick has now done—which I haven't seen—I suggest we go back to what we had. [In the final print, there are six shots of the four people watching the pods open and still no two-shots of the pods. There are, however, two overhead LSs of three pods opening.—Ed.]

When we go with MILES and BECKY to the telephone we stay with them until Miles says: ". . . we're dead." This is better than cutting away as I did. However the transference is no way near as good. Dick eliminated the FOUR SHOT of the BODIES which I thought was good to follow the line: "Dead." He made the transference happen too quickly and I didn't like it nearly as well as before. He used his SHOT of the fork entering the body of Miles which is all right with me although frankly I still like my PAN SHOT with the fork into the body. [The cut is now to a MS of Jack and Teddy (210). Heermance's cut of the fork going into the body (225) remains.—Ed.]

At the gas station Dick eliminated the operator's voice in the telephone booth. I approve of this cut. [We do not hear the operator in 232.—Ed.]

. . . We took out the line: "Not so loud—I want the baby to get to sleep" as by doing so we don't have to hear the radio playing in Sally's house. [The scene opened with these lines, now eliminated. See shot 240 and note 43.—Ed.]

In Miles' Office when he is standing in front of the window with the curtain drawn and Becky comes over to him Dick is going to make a better match cut. [In shot 261 Becky, in MS, rises from a chair and walks over to Miles, who is looking out the window. The end of this shot is now the same as the end of shot 260, with Miles looking out alone.—Ed.]

When people get off the bus and the police hustle them into the police car Dick cut out the line: "They must be strangers in town," which worked well. [This line has been restored to shot 265.—Ed.]

After GRIVETT crosses to the platform in the square Dick tried to CUT to GRIVETT'S CLOSE SHOT and then to the LONG SHOT of the trucks entering the square which didn't work. He is now going to try to CUT to the CLOSE SHOT of the truck entering which should work. It's about what we had before. Several of the cuts of the pods being put into cars are shortened and Grivett's lines come over Miles and Becky which I think is okay. [In the final print, we do not see

Grivett cross to the platform. In several shots we see the trucks arrive. A closer shot of the trucks precedes a closer one of Grivett on the platform with the mike.—Ed.]

. . . The dog is seen scurrying past the truck which is actually better than my trying to kill the dog. [The dog can be seen running away frame right in shot 342.—Ed.]

During the chase, I would like a SHOT or several SHOTS of the pursuers before we see BECKY and MILES going under the tree and up the steep hill. If we follow the cut of Becky and Miles coming down the hill and immediately cut to them going up the hill we geographically narrow the chase. Then I would like one shot of the pursuers scrambling to the top of the hill just before Miles sees the excavation in the tunnel. I think Dick is going to do this. What I did wrong before was to cut too many times to the pursuers coming up the hill. [Several shots of the pursuers were inserted and shot 374 shows them climbing the hill as Miles and Becky enter the tunnel.—Ed.]

Dick has cut to the HUGE CLOSEUP of the girl in the mud before cutting to the one of Miles. This seems good but has to be retimed which I think Dick is doing. [Becky is shown first in ECU, shot 407.—Ed.]

Dick used the shot of the pursuers coming down the hill after Miles which I don't like. [The pursuers are there, shots 427–429, but only with Miles in the foreground.—Ed.]

. . . AND that's that. I hope you can make some sense out of my very bad typewriting. My excuse is—my typewriter is old, I'm old and I don't have Daphne.[5]

---

5. Daphne Timewell was Wanger's secretary.

Suggestions for Additions to the Film

Walter Wanger

Wanger's first suggestion is a Churchill quotation he wanted to use as a preface. Attached to the page in the files is a small card with a quotation from Alfred North Whitehead. These items are undated, but Wanger wrote an Allied Artists executive in England on 28 March, while the film was being shot, about using the Churchill quotation, which was from a recent speech to the House of Commons.

"The day may dawn when fair play, love for one's fellow men, respect for justice and freedom, will enable tormented generations to march forth serene and triumphant from the hideous epoch in which we have to dwell. Meanwhile, *never flinch, never weary, never despair.*"—Winston Churchill

"Today the notion of a Master Race is being revived, and most of us agree that it means the moral degradation of mankind."—Alfred North Whitehead

The next item is a short introductory voice-over for Miles, the beginnings of the voice-over narration added to the film:

"THE BODY SNATCHERS"

May 3rd, 1955.

My name is Miles Bennell.

Little did I realize what I was to encounter on my return from a medical meeting in New York—I am a normal sort of fellow and I tried to meet these unusual happenings the best I could—being a doctor, I was aware of the progress of this Atomic Age, but I was not prepared to grasp the horrible significance of what the world was facing, and, especially, what was going to happen to the human race. And, last of all, I never would have believed anything like this could start in a nice little town like Santa Mira.

It was a problem to piece the strange manifestations together—a nightmare, in fact—

I warn you, there were many loose ends to be tied up.

Wanger's introduction was rewritten by Richard Collins:

"THE BODY SNATCHERS"
May 5th—Opening Dialogue—Dick Collins.

My name is Miles Bennell.

I'm an ordinary sort of fellow, and nothing much out of the ordinary ever happened to me—not until this day, the day I'm telling you about.

It started much like any other . . . a few rumors, a frightened boy, an

uneasy feeling, then, as I put the pieces together, I saw—not clearly at
first—just what the world was facing—something just as terrible as the atom
bomb—more terrible, because the world didn't realise—or care . . .

It was a long time before I was able to tie all the ends together. I couldn't
believe anything like this could start in a nice little town like Santa Mira. But
I'm running ahead of my story . . .

Wanger felt some clearer direction was needed near the beginning of the film,
to indicate where the action was going. On 30 June he wrote a speech for Sally to
make just after the near accident with Jimmy Grimaldi:

Don't think I'm crazy Doc, and, if you do, send me away—because I
can't stand it here in Santa Mira any more.
Something terrible is happening, [and, *crossed out. Handwritten in above,*
I know] it isn't obvious, and I can't put my finger on it.
It's like a jig-saw puzzle, and you've got to put it together. Don't let
anybody convince you that things are all right here. Things are really terrible, and it's serious.

Again to clarify the action, Wanger wrote a speech for Danny Kaufman, undated, and appended notes about other problematic sections of dialogue:

DANNY
It's too late to do anything about it. You just can't wait until the last minute.
The whole place is undermined. We've brought it on ourselves. I don't
know—maybe our behavior, maybe our ideas, maybe our lack of intestinal
fortitude. Self-propelling, we subvert ourselves. Maybe this is what happened to the Roman Empire. Maybe we didn't care enough. But you can't
escape it—your ship is sinking. We're taking over.
The final speech of the picture has got to be rewritten, and the relationship
between the girl and boy must be heightened. The last decent thing on earth
is love, love can't thrive under these conditions, can't exist. Mob rule. No
standards are the guide for this catastrophe. Perhaps it is the lack of leadership directing this movement.

Wanger wrote another speech on 1 July, again to make the message more
explicit. It is not clear who was supposed to deliver it, but it is obviously a pod
referring to Miles:

I told you he was dangerous to us. He won't give up. Someone will listen
to him. One honest man can ruin us. That's how we have always been
beaten.

"The Body Snatchers"— Memorandum

Walter Wanger

July 8th, 1955.

I believe that the three previews we have had made it evident that we have a very powerful piece of entertainment and a very unusual box office attraction in THE BODY SNATCHERS. There are still some spots I would like to see re-edited and cleared up—some call for minor retakes. But I believe this picture, if it is refined and well balanced, and made a little more clear, with the proposed Foreword, a new title, and the right kind of a sensational campaign, might be an outstanding moneymaker.

1. Regarding the title—the best that I have been able to come up with is WORLD IN DANGER.
2. Regarding the Foreword—Naturally, if Orson Welles agrees to do it, that will be fine. I believe there should be some changes made in my suggestions of June 15th, which I am sure he will rewrite in any event. I propose these corrections:

"I am Orson Welles. A few years ago, people were frightened by my "War of the Worlds" broadcast, which, I must say, seems pretty tame considering what has happened to our world since. When I think of the A-bombs, the H-bombs, the fall-outs, the changing climates, the unprecedented number of earthquakes, cyclones, tornadoes, and the floods that have occurred all over the world; and the space ships, the 'flying saucers,' the supersonic flights, and more flaming volcanoes than ever, surely even Nature is behaving strangely, and no phenomenon seems impossible today.

Strange things are happening all around us, some visible, and some not. I'm not surprised that Dr. Bennell didn't recognise what he was about to encounter when he was called back to Santa Mira, that small town in California, which, surely, was the last place he would expect to discover what he did. But there is no doubt our world was in danger!"

Optional Tag:—

"This is Orson Welles again. I don't know how you feel about all this, but I know how I do—we've got to stop them!"

If Welles does not give us an immediate answer, I agree with Walter Mirisch that we should get somebody else, and try to finish up the picture as quickly as possible. The three best people would be, in the following order: 1. Edward Murrow. 2. Lowell Thomas. 3. Quentin Reynolds.[1]

Naturally, Murrow would be best and if he would agree to it, and agree to use his 'Person to Person' technique, this would be excellent because we could show him bringing in his equipment, into a dark room, where Dr. Bennell is recovering from the shock, and commence as if he had been covering the Santa Mira mystery and now had the opportunity to interview the man who escaped and saved the world. At the end, Murrow could thank Dr. Bennell and say that, as long as people believed in faith, decency, and the dignity of man, the world would be safe—or some such sentence that would give hope, and show that Bennell saved the situation. The 'Person to Person' technique would be a stunning thing to use, if we could get permission. I will make every effort, when I get to New York, to do what I can in this direction.

I am personally very anxious to get the picture finished because if we can get it in shape by the end of July, or rather one print over to Edinburgh, we are entered in the Festival. I think that would be a wonderful send off, and they'd accept the picture as a very important one, and give us good international publicity. Naturally, with this foreword, we will not need Bennell's speeches over the opening scene at the station. That sound track can be eliminated.

In view of the light manner in which the opening sequence is played, I suggest Process re-take a close up of Sally, in the car, immediately after the near-accident with the little boy, containing this sort of dialogue:—[There follows Sally's speech reprinted above, which Wanger says "would give a little more direction to the coming impact of horror." Then follow suggestions for Jack's wild line to Miles about Becky's safety, and a whole series of other wild lines and additional speeches for the scenes before and after the one at Sally's house.—Ed.]

. . . We should have some scene, or some wild lines, of the pods plotting. I've discussed with Don Siegel some telephone conversations—maybe after the mechanic fills the car, he calls the chief of police, and the chief says:—"We've got everything covered. There are road blocks out." Then, after they escape from Sally's house, there might be another message of some sort. Certainly, after they have given the needle to the three pods, when Janzek telephones the alarm in and says to turn on the siren, there should be a speech from him to the effect that—"They've killed the Chief and Dr. Kaufman, and Jack, and everybody must get out on a manhunt to get 'em and shoot to kill, and they mustn't get away. . ." so the chase looks less like a cross country relay—but really a matter of life and death.

I've discussed with Carmen Dragon, changing the music for the chase. He has some other music, that I believe he can substitute, that will be far more effective as I think this music is too rhythmic and melodic to have any menace. We are also discussing eliminating the song and just putting in instrumental.

Wild lines can also be superimposed at the greenhouses, where Miles dis-

---

1. All three were popular newsmen of the period.

covers all the pods being put in the trucks at the end of the picture—we might be able to improve this by having some sort of orders given.

I believe definitely that, after Becky turns, there are several things wrong:—

1. If we could have one more line from Becky, just to give the audience a little more chance to absorb what has happened, and then steal a line from earlier in the picture, over Miles, where he says: "I've got to go out and stop this!", so you get the feeling that he's going out to stop it more than ever because he's lost his girl, rather than the feeling that he jumps up and runs from the girl he loves. Also, instead of having him pursued the minute he gets out there, as if the chase is continuing in waltz time, let him get away, and don't let the people get after him till he's on his way to get help. We should feel he's really going to get help and it's all been intensified by the girl turning. I think this will change the end quite a bit and give the audience a better understanding.

2. I don't think there's any doubt that the end should be slowed up; that the end title comes in too soon after he has made his big speech. We should put the stuff through an echo chamber and have, "You're next, you're next!", and all the wild sounds we can, reverbed to be as effective as possible.

3. There is also the question to be considered, as to whether we should eliminate the truck from the last scene. Because, if the truck is eliminated, and we give the impression that his warning gets over, it'll be much easier for the audience to absorb the idea that he was successful in reaching the outside world before the malignant cancer had spread too far. On the other hand, it must be considered that this is quite a shock, and from the horror standpoint makes it a more terrifying picture.

I feel that the audience enjoys this picture enormously, and it plays very much like the old type of big attraction, such as 'The Bat,'[2] used to play, and if we do that kind of business, everything will be all right.

Of course, we must have a stunning campaign for it. We have to have a Horror Campaign, a Science Fiction Campaign, and a lot of accessories, like buttons saying: "I don't want to be a pod." "I'm not a pod." "Are you a pod?"—a whole pod series of buttons to give out and to try to get the pod concept as popular as the Sally concept was in 'Private Worlds'[3] when we put that out. This is one of those attractions where one minute you scream, one minute you laugh.

There is also the possibility of doing something about the second pod scene at the Freeway, if we still need clarification, but I believe that the suggested rearrangements, as set out above, would do the trick if we had the right kind of foreword.

2. *The Bat* (1920) was a play by Mary Roberts Rinehart and Avery Hopwood, an old-fashioned thriller mixing humor and horror that was still regularly revived by stock companies in this period.
3. *Private Worlds* (1935) was a pioneering movie produced by Wanger that explored the problem of mental illness. In a famous sequence, Sally, a doctor's wife, played by Joan Bennett, hallucinates that she is going mad like the patients.

Starring Orson Welles

Walter Wanger

wo versions of opening and ending sequences for Orson Welles are reprinted here. The first is not dated, but Wanger started drafting these sequences as early as June of 1955. It is interesting because it places Welles on the scene where Miles has collapsed. Welles plays an interviewer, much like the radio newscasters in his "War of the Worlds" broadcast, which this is obviously designed to recall. The 13 September version is the final one, as it was to be filmed. Apparently filming was cancelled by the substitution of the framing story on 16 September.

Early Draft

NEW OPENING, THE BODY SNATCHERS
Fade in
Ext. Broadcasting Truck, night
The truck is parked on a dirt road up against a hillside. Lights from o.s. cars speeding around a turn in the o.s. highway sweep across it now and then and there is the steady roar of o.s. traffic and the steady wail of sirens. Waiting beside the truck is the operator, holding a microphone and looking off anxiously. ORSON WELLES *hurries out of the darkness. As he moves f.g., the light of a passing car sweeps across him.*
WELLES: Let's get on the air.
He takes the microphone from the operator who hurries around inside the truck.
CLOSE SHOT: *Welles at microphone. As he speaks into it, the roar of traffic and the wail of o.s. sirens continues.*
WELLES: This is Orson Welles. I am standing just off Highway 101 where it intersects the road to Santa Mira, California, the town on which the eyes of the whole world are focused tonight. For the past hour I have been listening to the strangest and most frightening story I ever heard in my life—a story that in any other time than this one would be unbelievable. Not all of those who heard the story with me are convinced. There are those who insist Dr. Miles Bennell is mad— that what has happened couldn't happen in this world of ours. I say it could and did. This is no ordinary world we are living in. We have A-bombs and H-bombs, space ships and atom-powered submarines. We send men and machines hurtling through the skies faster than the speed of sound. We plan space stations in the stratosphere to launch ships to

explore celestial seas. We look up in the night and, seeing flaming balls streak across the sky, are no longer sure as we once were that they are shooting stars. We are not sure of anything, and can you blame us? Even the weather has become unpredictable. Climates change suddenly. The once stable earth trembles and volcanoes belch flame and smoke. Cyclones, tornadoes, and floods rage with a fury hitherto unknown. Now we know that there are undreamed-of forces in our strange and changing universe. Now we know there is life on another world. What has happened and is happening right now proves it.

Dissolve

Present opening of picture. Orson Welles' voice comes over the shot of the train and Bennell getting off.

WELLES' VOICE: It all started the day a streamliner paused at a whistle-stop and a passenger got off. He was Dr. Bennell and he had cut short his vacation to hurry home to Santa Mira where a strange epidemic had broken out.

End Narration

TAG, THE BODY SNATCHERS

As the picture ends, quick dissolve

Ext. Broadcasting Truck, night

CLOSE SHOT: *Welles at microphone.*

ORSON WELLES: Now do you wonder why they wouldn't listen to him—why his cries for help went unanswered while time slipped away until it was almost too late to stop this strange invasion from the skies? Luckily for all of us, there were people who would listen. Let's hope that what went on here will stand as an object lesson to every human man. In this day and age anything can happen and if you're asleep when it does, you're next!

Final Draft

As the main title ends,

Fade in

Ext. Cloudy Night Sky

UP ANGLE SHOT: *There is a thunderclap, then lightning rips through the clouds.*

Int. Orson Welles Study

CLOSE SHOT: *Welles at window. He stands in the dimly lighted room, back to camera. O.S. there is another thunderclap and as a flash of lightning follows, he turns from the window.*

WELLES: This is Orson Welles. I warn you that this is a strange story, full of unanswered questions—a story that cannot be neatly tied up at the end, everything resolved and satisfactorily explained. Because I don't fully know what happened, or why, how it began, how it ended, or if it has ended. Since the time of man, the world has been full of unexplained oddities—(*As he speaks, he moves to the writing desk where a student's lamp illuminates a pad covered with pencilled notes, and piles of books, magazines and newspapers beside it. Indicating notes.*) Blood red rains in Cochin, China in 1887 and again in 1921—a shower of eels in Alabama in 1892—a fall of small frogs on London in 1921—a flight of nine huge whirling disks over Mount Rainier in 1947—flying glaciers over Texas in 1949—a shower of grain on the Empire State building in 1951. History is replete with verified reports of such phenomena. Now from Santa Mira, California, comes one of the strangest of them all.

O.S. there is another thunderclap followed by a great flash of lightning. As the flash lights up the storm,

Dissolve

Ext. Small Emergency Hospital, night

FULL SHOT: *This is a small hospital on a quiet street in a suburban community. In close f.g. is a lighted sign telling us this is an emergency hospital. In front of the hospital are several state police cars and an ambulance. Approaching fast, with siren going, is another police car. Welles' voice continues over the shot.*

WELLES' VOICE (*over shot*): The world first learned about it in a small wayside emergency hospital from a young doctor Miles Bennell, who was being held for observation.

As the narration ends, the police car, its siren dying, slams to a stop.

TAG

WELLES: Orson Welles again. That is the story. So if a man comes running toward you in the night, babbling obvious nonsense, will you listen to him? You'd better, because it might not be nonsense. In this day and age, anything can happen and if it does—(*pointing finger at camera*) you may be next!

For Theatre Trailer

When Kevin McCarthy is struggling in the arms of the two policemen and speaks to the Doctor, "Make them listen to me before it's too late," have him turn to the camera in a CLOSE UP.

KEVIN: Make them listen to me! If you don't . . . if you won't . . . if you can't make them understand . . . then the same terror that's happening to me . . . will strike at you. And you, too, will be threatened with the most incredible menace that has ever struck this earth of ours!

Alternative Trailer

CLOSE UP: *Kevin, as he turns to camera.*

KEVIN: Make them listen to me! If you don't . . . if you won't . . . if you can't make them understand . . . then the same incredible terror that's menacing me . . . will strike at you!

Memorandum to Myself

Walter Wanger

August 24th, 1955.

The Preview, at the Bay Theatre, of BODY SNATCHERS, which was the fourth preview of this film, in my opinion—and in the opinion of most of the people I spoke to who had seen all the previews—was our least effective preview. Although some of the laughs were eliminated, also a great deal of the humanity and quality of the picture was eliminated by sharp, so-called 'B' cutting. The big thrills, which always got great gasps from the theatre audiences at the prior three previews, did not receive the reaction.

The cards were the least complimentary, and I would say, with the exception of a half-dozen tightening cuts, which were made by Heermance, the quality of the picture and its chance of success have been lessened by the unsympathetic treatment.

I still stand by the memorandum which I sent to Mr. Mirisch and Mr. Broidy, to which I have never had any official answer, in a great deal of conversation.

The 3 sneak previews were held at my suggestion. When we left the projection room after a showing for Mr. Broidy and other executives, everybody was elated with the picture, and thought it was a great thriller, with the exception of the possibility that the end was too abrupt and not clear and that there should be something done about that. Otherwise, everybody was highly satisfied. I was the one that said I had some doubts about audience reaction, and would like to take it out and study the picture a little bit. I did not know that the organization would be panicked by going through such a realistic and normal treatment.

In no previews did we have so many walkouts and so much unrest.

Memorandum to Walter Wanger

Don Siegel

September 21, 1955.

Dear Walter,

Following are my notes after seeing the picture with the new opening and ending, plus the narration. I think what we have done for the picture has helped it and, if my notes please you and Dick and Walter, I think we've got a good picture.

One more thing, the title as now suggested is stupid if for no other reason than a great segment of those who might see the picture will have thought that they have already seen it. I've yet to find anyone, including the sales organization, publicity, who likes this title THEY COME FROM ANOTHER WORLD. I suggest two titles, both of which fit the picture like a glove, or, if you prefer, a pod, and they are: SLEEP NO MORE, and BETTER OFF DEAD.

I've had my say, the rest is up to you.

Oh, yes. I still am against the Orson Welles opening.

Regards,
Don

ENCL:

. . . In the sequence where they find the BODY in JACK'S BAR the following lines of Jack's should be put back:

"Come to think of it, old Buddy, we do have a lot in common."

"Whatever it is I don't like it."

"I was just going to suggest it." (Approx.)

". . . It'll make a lovely, bloodcurdling mystery story. . . . I hope I'm around to write it!" [Siegel tried in vain to restore the humor.—Ed.]

OVER the EXT. BECKY'S HOUSE when MILES and BECKY return, start NARRATION so that it ends just before, or as, BECKY enters her house. [This was not done. See shot 108. The narration stops as they get out of the car; they cross the lawn in silence. Siegel was obviously trying to tighten up the film.—Ed.]

. . . The NARRATION which covers MILES running to his car should start later than it now does.

(NOTE: The MUSIC in this whole sequence should be held down. Also the MUSIC should continue after he breaks the window and *particularly* continue through the sequence in the basement up to the time that he discovers the body of Becky in the box. The MUSIC should reach a high crescendo at the exact moment we see the body—similar to the time when we first see the body on the billiard table in the BELICEKS' PLAYROOM.). [In shot 124, the narration starts at the beginning of the shot. Again Siegel's suggestion went unheeded. In shots 132–133, however, his suggestions about the music were followed.—Ed.]

. . . INT. BASEMENT. Sc. 97. After MILES says, "You win, pick up the marbles," have DANNY say: "You pick 'em up. You need 'em more than I do." [Once again Siegel tried to restore a humorous line from the original, to no avail.—Ed.]

. . . Inasmuch as we are short on footage, and also I *like* the sequence, put back the tag between MILES and BECKY concerning the left-handed kissing. The way it is now cut, it is much too abrupt when we go to WILMA'S ANTIQUE SHOP. [Another attempt by Siegel to restore humor from the original script.—Ed.]

. . . I don't quite know what to do with the NARRATION that covers the time when MILES, at NIGHT, drives up to his BACKYARD. Somehow, the way it is now, it doesn't seem to fit. Maybe we don't need this narration. [The narration begins during the dissolve between shots 170 and 171.—Ed.]

. . . Having seen the pod sequence, as it is now cut, for the umpteenth time, I am more than ever convinced that the most dramatic way to cut this sequence is never to see the pods until after the LARGE C.U. of MILES when he calls for JACK. Prior to this, without seeing the pods, we will hear the ominous offstage crackling, etc. [There are four MSS of the pods opening before the large CU of Miles. In the fourth shot, he spots them. Siegel's suggestion was not followed.—Ed.]

Sc. 124. INT. LATH HOUSE. Following the DOLLY with JACK, pitchfork in hand, PAST the bodies lying on the ground, put back in, his line: "You got good company. We're all there!" [Again, Siegel tried to put back a grimly funny line. It is not in the film.—Ed.]

Sc. 133. When MILES plunges his pitchfork into the "body" of himself, the shot that is now in definitely looks like rubber as the double body's chest starts to cave in. The shot that I made which PANS DOWN with the PITCHFORK into the "body" is perfect.

Notwithstanding Mr. Heermance's objection to it, I—not as a director but as a fellow half-arsed cutter, insist it is perfectly okay cutting-wise. And, even if Mr. Heermance were right, which I insist he isn't, the shot he has cut in is technically not good. [Shot 225 stayed as it was. This is Siegel's second objection to it. The body does not appear rubbery; however, when the pitchfork prongs enter the body we hear a rubbery thud. This is obviously intentional, since any kind of sound could have been dubbed in. The shock cut to the phone ringing also deflects our attention.—Ed.]

. . . Sc. 136. As MILES and BECKY run off to his CAR and the CAMERA DOLLIES into the INSERT of the TELEPHONE, OVER the OPERATOR'S VOICE, put in the NOISE of MILES' CAR ENGINE starting up and taking off. [In shot 228 we only hear the car door slam, not the motor starting.—Ed.]

In the TELEPHONE BOOTH, be sure, when the NARRATION starts, that MILES' HEAD is not facing the telephone mouthpiece, otherwise it will look like he is talking into the telephone. Start the NARRATION later and continue it OVER the shot as MILES runs back towards his car. [The narration in shot 232 unfortunately does begin just as Miles turns to talk into the telephone.—Ed.]

. . . Following MILES' running away from BECKY, after he has kissed her, I would like to time the NARRATION so that it ends as MILES appears out of the RAVINE onto the ROAD LEADING TO THE FREEWAY. Take out from the NARRATION the reference to his kissing Becky. [The line about kissing Becky and learning the true meaning of fear is probably, unintentionally, the funniest in the film.—Ed.]

In one version, we had MILES falling down in the ROAD when he was being chased, which I thought looked pretty good, and I would like to see it recut as it was. [The narration now stops in the previous shot, 428, before the one where Miles runs onto the road leading to the freeway, 429. Again, Siegel was trying to tighten up the movie.—Ed.]

After MILES says: "Thank God!", it is not necessary that we hear too clearly the offstage lines of DR. HILL getting the Operator and asking for the F.B.I. The MUSIC should start to swell up following the "Thank God!" [Perhaps Miles is muttering "Thank God," but we don't hear it. Dr. Hill's lines certainly can be heard. Since the Hays Office objected earlier to the use of God's name, perhaps it was thought wise to delete it here, too.—Ed.]

Excerpts from a Speech to the American Booksellers Convention

Walter Wanger

War has lost much of its glamour and fanfare. The war of the future is accepted by all as a horrible, scientific disaster. Most people realise that it can be won by those who have the most bombs and the biggest armies but all agree that the peace and the rebuilding will be achieved by the best informed and most capable. So, if this is true, it is obvious how much more important the bookstore in the community becomes, and you, the bookseller. Yours is the key to the future.

Many of us fear conformity. Wisdom and reason based on education will allow us to have individual judgment and character like the founders of this nation hoped that we would have. I have just finished a picture based on this subject of conformity. The film shows how easy it is for people to be taken over and to lose their souls if they are not alert and determined in their character to be free, otherwise they will become mere vegetables—just pods. By the way, the film is called THE INVASION OF BODY SNATCHERS and is based on a book I found at Martindale's. We show invasion of these pods in an American community where they would least expect this horror to take place. Well, there are some communities in the country where there are pods because there are not enough bookstores or enough books. I always judge a community by its bookstores, and whenever I meet a man or woman who says: "I'm too busy to read," I know I am talking to somebody that is a *pod* and can be taken over by an enemy because there is no intelligent resistance. In this atomic world, adult education, and the continuing desire to improve oneself, are as necessary as eating. We are not living in days of frustration. We are living in days of great opportunity, contrary to the thoughts of some.

It is no easy thing to keep up with this world today, and without coming to your bookstores, I don't know how people are going to be able to do it. You have taken on an intensified importance. I believe that television is going to send you more readers—just as motion pictures helped the public to take an interest in the rest of the world. We cannot afford to have pods who say: "I am too busy to read."

With aviation opening the world—as it has, for instance, in my own business, motion pictures—where we used to be restricted to California, today we meet our Hollywood associates who have just finished a picture in India, or Africa, or Hongkong, or London, and fly back and forth with the grace and ease of coming in from Stage 2 at Paramount.

This forces us, even in our little world, to accept the fact that things are different. There is no doubt that this is a new world and we must orient ourselves and keep ourselves as alert as possible. This is obligatory. The bookstore is the pivot of community enlightenment. Of course, we all know that books are dangerous and that, in totalitarian countries (or wherever there is totalitarian thinking) the bookseller is regarded with suspicion, and book burning becomes a popular sport. This is readily understandable because that horrible little thing, the book, can make you think, and there's no invention as yet—no lie-detector, no electronic machine—that can tell what effect a good book will have on a man's soul. This is indeed dangerous because you enjoy perfect freedom when you are alone with a book, with an idea.

We must fight those who believe in censorship, as they are the enemies of a free press. There are also those pompous individuals who think that we are superior to our allies and that we shouldn't export pictures or books or plays that show us in an unbecoming light because they won't understand that this is not representative of the whole nation. This, of course, is one of the silliest things that anyone can do. Why should our allies be second-class citizens and we first-class citizens, and then we ask them to trust us? If you have a friend, you shouldn't be ashamed to tell your troubles to your friend and perhaps it will bring him closer to you. As a matter of fact, speaking for films that have been made under a system of free enterprise and have been successful at the box office, and that are critical of America, I am sure they do us a great deal more good than the films that try to paint America as a Utopia. That glorification was what the Italians and Germans used to attempt under totalitarian regimes, and we, quite rightly, used to deplore it. So, it seems altogether inconsistent for us to copy totalitarian methods when we are trying to prove to the world that we have enough understanding to allow us a great share in world leadership.

The sooner we recognise our obligations, the sooner we will impress the rest of the world with our sincerity, and by the shedding of our adolescence become an adult and truly civilised nation. All the ammunition and reinforcements that the soul needs to face this new world—the ethics, standards, character, integrity, forthrightness, imagination, courage, charity, vision, warmth and decency and faith—can be found in your priceless and impregnable arsenal, the world's literature. Consequently, you, my friends, are going to play a tremendous part in this era of enlightenment. It is a serious challenge to keep abreast of the times. I, for one, will look to you to help me lessen my ignorance and become a humble and informed citizen of this new world.

Interviews, Reviews, and Commentaries

Interviews

Don Siegel is an articulate, voluble, and entertaining interviewee and lecturer about films, especially his own films. A frequent guest at universities and film festivals, and a subject of lengthy interviews in most of the major film journals, he can hold forth on the subject of filmmaking for hours with a seemingly inexhaustible and rich supply of ideas. Perhaps the best place to sample his views on his career is Stuart M. Kaminsky's *Don Siegel, Director* (1974), virtually a running interview with Siegel on each of his productions. Siegel is presently writing a very long autobiography, which is soon to be published.

Stuart M. Kaminsky and Guy Braucourt get Siegel to concentrate on *Invasion of the Body Snatchers,* a key film for Siegel enthusiasts in both America and France. Here one can find all the familiar stories about the studio and the ending, the editing out of the humor, the previews, and the nature of pod-ism that I have already drawn upon in my introduction and notes. Perhaps most surprising about the interview with Kaminsky is its fatalistic tone—Siegel admits that "there's a very strong case for being a pod." Siegel also seems to open up psychological themes which no one has yet explored in depth when he links the fear the characters have of sleeping with his own chronic insomnia and fear that if he falls asleep he won't wake up. With Guy Braucourt, he touches interestingly on the theme of fascism and its relation to pod-ism.

Don Siegel on the Pod Society

Stuart M. Kaminsky

Kaminsky: It has been reported that Sam Peckinpah wrote a script for or part of *Invasion of the Body Snatchers*. Is that true?

Siegel: No. Sam was my assistant on that picture, as he was on several of my pictures including *Riot in Cell Block 11* and *Private Hell 36*. Sam may have made suggestions, but he didn't write any of the film. Sam did act in the film, however. He was one of the pods, the meter reader in Dana Wynter's basement.[1]

Kaminsky: The film has a frame, a prologue and epilogue which shows Kevin McCarthy being brought into a hospital to tell his story and then later, at the end, getting the doctor to believe him when some pods are found. According to Daniel Mainwaring you were very much against the frame.

Siegel: Very much against it. Danny wrote it because they told him he had to.

Kaminsky: "They?"

Siegel: The studio.

Kaminsky: Did you direct the prologue and epilogue?

Siegel: Yes. They were going to shoot it anyway and I decided that since it would be in the picture, I might as well do it as well as I could.

Kaminsky: What don't you like about the prologue and epilogue?

Siegel: First of all, it lets you know right away that something unusual is going on. If you start, as I wanted to, with McCarthy arriving in the town of Santa Mira, it reveals itself slowly, we understand why McCarthy can't readily accept the terrible thing that appears to be happening. And the dramatic impact of the ending is reduced with the epilogue. I wanted to end it with McCarthy on the highway turning to the camera and saying, "You're next!" Then, boom, the lights go up. In the final version, however, we go back to the hospital . . . and that's after the fact.

Kaminsky: The film is still extremely popular. According to NTA, which distributes it, it is among the most requested films on television. Can't the opening and close be cut or is my question naive?

Siegel: Many people do cut that frame, those sequences, when they show it.

From *Science Fiction Films*, ed. Thomas R. Atkins, Monarch Film Studies (New York: Simon and Schuster, 1976), pp. 73–82.

1. Sam Peckinpah also appears in the forefront of Miles's pursuers near the bridge at the end of the movie. He is the man with the moustache in shot 430, an approximation of which can be found in the publicity still reproduced near the description of that shot in this book.—Ed.

Every few days the picture is run somewhere, some underground theater. And the tacked on opening and closing are removed.

Kaminsky: Do you think anything else hurt the film?

Siegel: Yes. Allied Artists had an old-fashioned credo that horror pictures couldn't have humor. I had a great deal of humor in the picture and though they cut out a lot, they didn't totally succeed.

Kaminsky: What was the basis of the humor they cut out?

Siegel: I felt the idea of pods growing into a likeness of a person would strike the characters as preposterous. I wanted to play it that way, with the characters not taking the threat seriously. For example, if you told me now that there was a pod in my likeness in the other room, I would joke about it. However, when I opened the door and saw the pod, the full shock and horror would hit me and the fun would be gone. I wanted the people in the film to behave like normal people. That does come through in the film.

Kaminsky: As in the barbecue scene. King Donovan, Carolyn Jones, McCarthy, and Dana Wynter have an outdoor barbecue even after they have accepted mentally that something is terribly wrong. Only when they see the pod do they panic.

Siegel: Precisely.

Kaminsky: The film contains surprisingly few special effects, surprising because your background at Warner Brothers was in montage and effects.

Siegel: Well, special effects were relatively unimportant in *Invasion of the Body Snatchers.* We spent about $15,000 on special effects, a very small amount. Instead of doing what so many science fiction and horror films do—spend all their money on special effects and put poor actors on the screen—we concentrated on the performers. The main thing about the picture, however, was that it was about something and that's rare.

Kaminsky: It's about . . .

Siegel: Pods. Not those that come from outer space, vegetables from outer space. People are pods. Many of my associates are certainly pods. They have no feelings. They exist, breathe, sleep. To be a pod means that you have no passion, no anger, the spark has left you.

Kaminsky: Your spokesman for the pods is a psychiatrist played by Larry Gates. A psychiatrist in the real world usually represents sanity and . . .

Siegel: Having the psychiatrist as spokesman for the pods was a conscious choice. Once you become a pod you believe in it and he really believes in it, is able to speak with authority, knowledge about how it is preferable to be a pod instead of a human.

Kaminsky: Yes, you allow him to make a frighteningly strong case for accepting pod-ism.

Siegel: Well, I think there's a very strong case for being a pod. These pods, who get rid of pain, ill health, and mental disturbance are, in a sense, doing good. It happens to leave you with a very dull world, but that, by the way, my dear friend, is the world that most of us live in. It's the same as people who welcome going into the army or prison. There's regimentation, a lack of having to make up your mind, face decisions.

Kaminsky: So one point of the picture is that being a pod relieves you but gives you no challenge. To be a pod is the same as not existing.

Siegel: That's right.

Kaminsky: In *Invasion of the Body Snatchers,* there is no real physical threat from the pods. The threat is from sleep. Sleep is the villain. To fall asleep is to allow the pods to take your mind.

Siegel: Yes. It's a very frightening thing to face, the physical challenge of keeping someone awake. The suspense created is very great because, obviously, we'll all have to sleep. It's like when people suffer from chronic insomnia as I do. They are afraid to go to sleep. One reason for this is that they fear they won't wake up. There is a parallel to this in the film.

Kaminsky: When McCarthy meets Dana Wynter on his return to Santa Mira, he invites her to go somewhere with him. He jokingly says, "It's summer, the moon is full and I know a bank where the wild thyme grows." It is one of many motifs picked up and played with from more traditional horror films. When McCarthy does encounter the pods, he tries all the traditional ways to kill them, though it is not underscored. In the greenhouse, you made a special point of having the camera down low when he plunges a pitchfork into the pod, like driving a stake through the heart. And later he tries to burn the pods placed in his trunk.

Siegel: But more appear.

Kaminsky: The only thing he can do is run and even that . . .

Siegel: . . . he can't do. He tries to get the police on his side but he discovers that the police are pods. He tries to call Washington but discovers the telephone operator is a pod. He can only try to escape.

Kaminsky: We get quite far into the film before we and McCarthy are absolutely sure the pods exist.

Siegel: That's right. We delayed it as long as we could because from that moment on, it was just an out-and-out chase, the whole town against this one person who isn't a pod and this girl who isn't one but will be. What I thought was quite delicious was the fact that pods feel no passion. So after he comes back to her in the cave and kisses her to keep her awake, a delicious, non-pod kiss, he knows she's a pod because she's a limp fish.

Kaminsky: By the way, do you like the title of the picture?

Siegel: No. *Invasion of the Body Snatchers* was the idea of some studio pod. The title I wanted was *Sleep No More.*

Kaminsky: Referring to Hamlet's soliloquy on suicide?[2]

Siegel: Yes.

2. The line is really from *Macbeth* II.2.36; although Kaminsky may be thinking of: "To die; to sleep;/No' more; and, by a sleep to say we end/The heart-ache and the thousand natural shocks/That flesh is heir to, 'tis a consumation/Devoutly to be wish'd." *Hamlet* III.i.56.—Ed.

Kaminsky: The reason McCarthy leaves her in the cave is because he hears music, Brahms I believe, although the script originally called for Mexican music. In any case, it makes him think it is being played by real people because pods have no need for music.

Siegel: And he finds they are pods waiting for the weather forecast while they load more pods on a truck. I frequently try to mislead the audience a little.

Kaminsky: That's especially jarring since the doctor, McCarthy, has gotten to the point where he trusts almost no one. At the end, this distrust pushes him to the brink of madness.

Siegel: Well, there he is on the highway, trying to get someone to listen to his warning and no one will listen. It would probably drive you crazy. Remember he spins against a truck, tries to climb in and sees that it is filled with pods going to all the different cities marked on the sides of the truck. That's when he wheels around and yells "You're next!" Because you are next. I don't care where you are, whether you're sitting in a theater or reading a magazine, whether you are in the United States or another country. There are pods and they are going to get you.

Kaminsky: At one point when the pods are being disbursed from trucks in the town square, we hear that one is for the people of Milltown. Was this one of the jokes, a comment of some kind on tranquilizing one's self into pod-ism?

Siegel: Well, that was in the script. It's possible we meant it as a gag, but I don't remember.[3]

Kaminsky: Everything about the film is constricting, closed in on itself. We see little Jimmy Grimaldi running down the road away from his pod mother at the beginning of the picture and later we see McCarthy running in the same kind of panic down the same road when he is pursued by the pods.

Siegel: That was done quite deliberately. I like that. In many of my pictures, I'll start with some action and later end with a related action, an action related in style.

Kaminsky: Then there are some intangible things that make the film particularly chilling. For example, Uncle Ira, played by Tom Fadden, is particularly frightening although he does nothing but mow the lawn while the girl whispers that he is not her Uncle Ira. Now the camera position and lighting are important, but there's something else.

Siegel: Perhaps his face. The fact that he's older than he looks might have done something. I remember working with him on the scene and being very pleased with the way it came off. Part of it was a strange little smile he gave.

Kaminsky: Yes. It is normal and yet something is wrong. People are not who you

---

3. Siegel is correct that Milltown is in the script, but it was not added until a very late date, when generic town names replaced real Marin County places. It may be a joke, but it may also be simply a variation on Mill Valley, where the author of the serial, Finney, lived, and which he used as a basis for his fictional Santa Mira.—Ed.

think them to be and, ultimately, your greatest enemy is your own pod self. There are many references to fear of one's self. It is especially striking when King Donovan goes off with Carolyn Jones and says to McCarthy "Look out for yourself." It is a bit of commonplace banter, but we know that it is chillingly literal. Ultimately it is our own tendency toward pod-ism which we must overcome.

Siegel: Yes, I don't think you're reading anything that isn't there.

Kaminsky: As far as McCarthy being a doctor . . .

Siegel: The town is like a cancer growth. The town, like a section of your body, is ill, and it's going to spread, the way, many times, political ideas spread.

Kaminsky: There are some parallels in the film to Howard Hawks's *The Thing,* which came before *Invasion of the Body Snatchers* and dealt with an emotionless vegetable creature from outer space that lived off humans and, more recently, to *Night of the Living Dead* in which the metaphor becomes most stark and those who die become pods consuming the living and . . .

Siegel: . . . there was a television series, *The Invaders,* which was along the same lines.

Kaminsky: That's right. Creatures from outer space replacing humans, and if I might add, it's the theme of Godard's *Alphaville* in which people become podlike and give themselves over to a computer. Have you seen the film?

Siegel: No.

Kaminsky: What we come back to is that there is no hope in your film.

Siegel: People without being vegetables are becoming vegetables. I don't know what the answer is except an awareness of it. That's what makes a picture like *Invasion of the Body Snatchers* important.

Interview with Don Siegel

Guy Braucourt

raucourt: . . . Invasion of the Body Snatchers, which wasn't discovered in France until a dozen years after it was made, is one of the greatest science fiction films.

Siegel: It is in fact my favorite film, which doesn't mean that it's my best work but that it's the most interesting subject I've ever filmed. I had a lot of difficulties at the time because the studio was against the film, while producer Walter Wanger, scriptwriter Daniel Mainwaring, the actors, and I all firmly believed in it, as we saw how well the shooting was going. I remember a joke I played on the leading lady, Dana Wynter, while we were shooting. We were all living in separate bungalows, and Dana's was more isolated than the rest. One day I went and tapped at her window, and when she came out to see what was happening I slipped into her bedroom with one of the pods used in the film and left it there. A moment later we saw her come running out, white-faced and speechless—that's how much she believed in the film!

What happened in the States at that time was that if a film didn't have a big budget or impressive credits with top stars, the critics ignored it. Since then things have changed a little, but not much. Anyway, no one took any notice of the film when it was first released, especially as the studio had inflicted a ridiculous title on it, over my objections. I wanted to call it simply *Sleep No More.* But little by little movie lovers and student groups began to take an interest in the film and give it a reputation, so that it has ended up being very well known.

Braucourt: I believe the studio added the prologue and epilogue, which put the main action in a frame and opened up the possibility of a happy ending.

Siegel: There were three previews of the film the way I'd made it, and the audiences reacted in an extraordinary way, just as I'd hoped. They started out laughing, but then the tension increased and they ended up thoroughly scared. The final scene was the one where the hero runs out into the highway, trying to stop a car, and he points his finger at one of the drivers—in reality, at the audience—shouting, "You're next!" like in a trial. But having heard the audiences laugh, the studio thought that the public was reacting against the film, and didn't realize what the laughter really meant. I was opposed to making any changes, but Walter Wanger, who was on my side, persuaded me that it was better to do them myself, in the same style and spirit as the rest of the film, because someone was going to make the changes anyway and they might very well compromise what

From *Focus on the Science Fiction Film,* ed. William Johnson (Englewood Cliffs, N.J.: Prentice-Hall, 1972), pp. 74–76. Originally published in *Image et Son* (April 1970):80–84.

we'd already planned and shot. So I decided to add the prologue and epilogue. But let me repeat that all of us who worked on the film believed in what it said— that the majority of people in the world unfortunately are pods, existing without any intellectual aspirations and incapable of love.

Braucourt: Some critics have seen the film as a parable about the spread of fascism. Is that too farfetched an interpretation?

Siegel: At the outset, neither the scriptwriter nor I had that in mind. What we wanted to attack was much more a general state of mind that is found in everyday life. As the director I found it much more exciting, instead of seeing the story as a fascist plot, to show how a very ordinary state of mind could start out in a very quiet small town and spread to a whole country. But it's certainly possible to make the interpretation you mention; I've no objection to it at all. In any case, I think it arises quite naturally because the aim of fascism is that people under its rule should be like that, having no emotions or personality, like vegetables.

Braucourt: Why have you never made any other science fiction films?

Siegel: First of all, because the special-effects side of them frightens me off a bit. I worked on special effects for seven years, and I did an enormous amount of second unit work on action sequences, and when I started out as a director there were attempts to lock me into action and special-effects films. I refused to be typecast that way, and when I found myself with a science fiction subject, I decided right from the start to take the opposite approach to what's usually done in the genre—lots of trick shots, sets, and machinery, and, stuck in front of them, some wooden actors whose faces show no expression except a bit of terror now and then! So I said to the producer, "Don't worry, there's no need to set aside 90 percent of the budget for special effects, we're going to give priority to the action and characters." . . . It's not that I'm categorically opposed to special effects, it's just that I'm not interested in seeing them get more attention than the story. . . .

Reviews

ike many B-films of the period, *Invasion of the Body Snatchers* was not widely reviewed in the major media. *The Reader's Guide to Periodical Literature* for 1956 does not list a single review of it in the many magazines that it indexes. The *New York Times* did not review the film: In this period the *Times* ignored many citywide chain openings, particularly if the movies seemed to be sensational or frivolous. The science fiction film was also the most derogated genre of the period, often thought to be intended only for teenagers.

This section opens not with a review from the *New York Times,* but with a letter to its chief film critic, Bosley Crowther, a friend of Walter Wanger's. Trying to sell Crowther on seeing the film—and perhaps writing a Sunday article on it similar to a recent one on monsters—Wanger argues that the film has a serious idea, a "plea against conformity," and praises the work of the young stars in it. Interestingly, he faults Allied Art-

ists' distribution for not exploiting the film sufficiently. Understandably he could be angry about sharing a double bill with *The Atomic Man* and about the silly ad campaign that made it look like a routine science fiction thriller. But the "exploitation picture" label that Wanger affixes to it would not have helped it get reviews in the *Times,* nor other prestigious publications.

The failure of the *Times* and major magazines to review *Invasion* probably stems from a combination of all three factors: its lowly science fiction status, its overtones of an "exploitation picture," and its offhanded distribution. It is not true that B-movies were always ignored in major journals and papers. *Riot in Cell Block 11,* with a strong social message, was critically acclaimed. Further, Wanger was associated with major features, so that it is surprising that his name alone didn't attract reviewers. Siegel had also achieved a measure of fame with *Riot.*

The movie was reviewed in many

local newspapers and all major trade journals, however, always with approbation and some excitement. Most of the reviews praise the startling premise and the taut direction; only a few hint at deeper themes like creeping conformity and the dangers of atomic energy. Reviewing was not the sophisticated art then that it can be today. Plot summaries and a few notes of strengths and weaknesses were good enough for the majority of reviewers.

Wanger was particularly pleased with two reviews from England that Dana Wynter sent him (one is re-printed here). With some education as a child in England and a long stint there during World War II, he was an Anglophile and began to muse about moving there, where he was better appreciated.

Finally, though he complained about the lack of exploitation Allied Artists gave the picture—probably a result of their puzzlement with it and weariness with its many complications—the picture did good business. Wanger, always impressed with that, uses it as a final lure to get Crowther to see the film.

Letter to Bosley Crowther, Film Critic of the *New York Times*

Walter Wanger

May 7, 1956

Dear Bosley,

Enjoyed your story on "Monsters" again, and would like to ask you, if you have time, to have Allied Artists send you a print of *Invasion of the Body Snatchers,* which I made. I tried to make it a plea against conformity, and apparently the exhibitors didn't think it was right to have an idea in a picture of this sort, and instead of a Broadway showing, it opened in Brooklyn at the Albee, I think, or the RKO Circuit. However, I know some friends of mine tried to get in and they couldn't because the line was so great. The picture has been doing very well, and was ranked by *Variety* the 9th picture in the nation, and then 10th picture in the nation, which pleases me very much. It was Dana Wynter's first film, and while Fox was trying to make up its mind whether to test her or not, I took her without ever having seen a foot of film. I have great faith in the girl, and she has a leading man, an excellent man you know well, Kevin McCarthy. No doubt you will see what I'm after in this picture, and apparently the public agrees with us. However, the ever-loving, complaining distributor and exhibitor has missed the chance to really exploit this picture. It's definitely an exploitation picture which they didn't exploit, which is not inconsistent.

I hope to see you when you get out here. I have stupidly indulged myself in a heart attack, and have been home reading for the last six weeks, and have really had a chance to catch up with such things as *Inside Africa, Girl with the Swansdown Seat,* which I loved, also *Good Behavior,* by Nicolson, which I think you will enjoy very much.

With every good wish,

As always,

From the Walter Wanger Collection, Center for Film and Theater Research, State Historical Society of Wisconsin.

Los Angeles Examiner

Sara Hamilton

Watch out there! You too may become a potted plant. Or at least a hollyhock.

Neighbors of yours and mine did, you know. In a California town not too far away practically the entire population turned into a vegetable salad of sorts and the results—well, see this picture, *Invasion of the Body Snatchers,* this almost terrifying science-fiction yarn. And see what can happen to innocent people when least they suspect it.

And while you're shivering, give it some thought, too, for lurking close to the story surface is the suggestion that maybe, in these hectic times, we have subconsciously been hoping for some way out. Some escape from worry and fear. And the unspoken but united mass thought has produced the answer. A VEGETABLE! Scary, isn't it?

Based on a slightly familiar theme (remember *The Thing*?), that of man becoming a plant monster, the tale has been wisely placed by Walter Wanger in a normal, everyday sort of town with normal everyday citizens as victims.

Victims of what? A plant. A dreadful sort of vegetable matter, supposedly dropped from the skies and hopped up into full growth by a cosmic atomic ray. From its giant pod there finally emerges a human form in the exact likeness of a man, woman or child living within its reach. And while his twin victim sleeps, his vegetable prototype absorbs his mind but none of his emotions. He wants no part of love, fear, kindness or thought for the future.

The slowly creeping plague is fairly under way when young Doctor Kevin McCarthy returns to his practice in the town to meet and fall in love with the beauteous Dana Wynter.

Together they sense some eerie thing is happening to their fellow townsmen when victims face their own friends and even relatives without recognition.

And this alone should crowd the theaters. How to face Aunt Hortense with no recognition? People will come from off the hills to learn this secret.

Anyway, it gets more and more fantastic and more and more fright-wiggy as the entire town slowly becomes vegetablized, with only young Doctor McCarthy left to flee the town and warn the country.

The climax is horrific, and if I don't stop looking over my shoulder right now I'll never get through this.

Dan Mainwaring wrote the screenplay and Don Siegel directed. Both lads did an outstanding job. . .

From the *Los Angeles Examiner,* 1 March 1956, sec. 2, p. 6.

Weekly Variety

"Whit."

Walter Wanger comes up with a tense, offbeat piece of science fiction here that looks headed for stout box-office returns, particularly in view of the present market leanings in this field. Occasionally difficult to follow due to the strangeness of its scientific premise, action nevertheless is increasingly exciting as it builds to a strong climax. With its exploitation potential, film is suitable for either top or bottom spot of double bills.

Adapted by Daniel Mainwaring from Jack Finney's *Collier's* serial, characterizations and situations are sharp as audience interest is enlisted from opening scene. Don Siegel's taut direction is fast-paced generally, although in his efforts to spark the climax he permits his leading character, Kevin McCarthy, to overact in several sequences. Film would have benefited through more explanatory matter to fully illuminate the scientific premise, but all in all the topic has been developed along lines to hold the spectator.

Plotwise, narrative opens on a strange hysteria that is spreading among the populace of a small California town. Townspeople appear as strangers to their relatives and friends, while retaining their outward appearances. McCarthy, a doctor recalled from a business trip by his nurse when this epidemic starts, is confronted with solving these mysterious happenings, and helping him is Dana Wynter, with whom he's in love. Gradually they learn the explanation.

A weird form of plant life has descended upon the town from the skies. Tiny, this ripens into great pods and opens, from each of which emerges a "blank," the form of each man, woman, and child in the town. During their sleep, the blank drains them of their normal emotions, all but their impulse to survive. Windup shows the townspeople now all but McCarthy and his girlfriend afflicted, trying to halt the two from escaping to warn the rest of the world. McCarthy finally is able to get away, after femme during a sleep of sheer exhaustion becomes a "pod person," and broadcasts his fantastic story.

McCarthy delivers a persuasive account of himself, and Miss Wynter, a pretty newcomer, shows fine promise. Strong support is provided by King Donovan, Larry Gates, Carolyn Jones, and Jean Willes.

Technical credits are only registered by Ellsworth Fredricks with his cameras, Carmen Dragon for an atmospheric music score, and Robert S. Eisen for tight editing.

From *Weekly Variety,* 29 February 1956, p. 112.

The Hollywood Reporter
Jack Moffitt

Walter Wanger has introduced an element of timely philosophy into this science-fiction drama which, if properly exploited, may have a boxoffice appeal similar to that of *The Thing*.

The basic premise is that some form of cosmic atomic action has caused a noxious type of vegetable matter to take root upon the earth. From the pods of these evil plants emerges a human-like being which captures the mind and assumes the identity of any sleeping human that is near it. Then apparently the human body disappears or wastes away while the vegetable human takes its place. The only difference is that the vegetables feel neither love nor mercy, fear nor worry for the future—none of the emotions that give man a touch of divinity.

Behind the fantasy, Daniel Mainwaring, in his script, and Jack Finney, in his original story (serialized in *Collier's*) seem to be saying that modern man, tired of facing the mental problems of our intricate age, is prone to welcome the irresponsible life of a human vegetable. This is a sobering and shocking thought.

While the mechanics of the plot gimmick are rather sketchily handled in the movie, the actual telling of the story, by virtue of Don Siegel's direction, contains a great deal of solid emotion and suspense. The horror is intensified by being played against scenes that are seemingly matter of fact and commonplace. . . .

From *The Hollywood Reporter*, 16 February 1956.

Boxoffice

E ver since atomic explosions posed the possibilities of mutations to animal life because of radioactive fallout, the concocters of science-fiction screenplays have been enjoying a field day, what with giant ants, outsize tarantulas—and what gives you goose pimples? Herein the same line of imaginative thinking is carried to one further step of extremity by treating with colossal seed pods that hatch out personality-less humans which absorb the brains and memories of the contemporary individuals they resemble. While the chills are a trifle tardy in developing, because too much of the early footage is devoted to establishing the yarn's rather complicated plot, when they ultimately begin they are sufficiently numerous and fantastic to satisfy the ticket buyers who enjoy having their spines titillated; and there is an action-laden climax that partially compensates for the initial leisurely pace.

As is true in many films of its ilk; the picture leaves as many loose ends as are to be found in a bowl of spaghetti. Nonetheless, an over-all appraisal indicates that it is amply qualified to serve profitably and popularly as a supporting piece on any dual program. While devoid of well-established names, with the possible exception of Dana Wynter, the sincere cast records satisfactory performances under able direction by Don Siegel. It's a Walter Wanger production, and is substantially mounted. . . .

From *Boxoffice*, 25 February 1956.

Daily Film Reviewer [London]

"F. J."

Brilliant and unusual science shocker for the countless thousands who enjoy being chilled to the marrow. . . .
. . . . . . The horrors and build-up of tension are extraordinarily well done in this film. But what gives it an added value is its explicit warning of the ever-present danger of losing our own humanity and turning into a passionless automaton with the mere outward semblance of a human being. "Humanity is never more precious than when you are in danger of losing it" is the moral of the story—and a very worthwhile one, too.

On the "X" level, this movie will satisfy the most rabid horror fans. But, because the horrors are not senseless sensationalism but have a real value, the film will also give entertainment, and food for thought to audiences which cannot take the normal run of science shockers.

Kevin McCarthy is excellent in the main role. The others have less to do, but Dana Wynter is decorative, and the supporting cast convincing.

An outstanding product of its kind.

From *Daily Film Reviewer* [London], 23 August 1956.

Commentaries

One major critical stance toward the film and Siegel has been to celebrate him as an auteurist within the narrow confines of the Poverty Row film. Peter Bogdanovich's article on B-movies from 1972 catches the mixture of personal expression and craft he finds in three B directors: Siegel, Budd Boetticher, and Samuel Fuller. Bogdanovich, who had recently begun making films himself after a successful career as a film historian, follows up on the excitement French critics first found in Siegel in the fifties and celebrated in *Cahiers de Cinéma* and *Positif*. Bogdanovich—along with Andrew Sarris and Manny Farber—was quick to praise the creativity he found here. Bogdanovich noted in particular the freedom these directors found in the smaller studios. Along with the tight constraints of budgets and short shooting schedules came a freedom from ideological constraints and the opportunity for more personal expression than could be found under the major studios. Hence derive the distinctive personal qualities of their films and their direct, almost visceral relationship to American life.

Of those who have celebrated Siegel as an auteurist, Stuart M. Kaminsky has been the most loyal and energetic. The author of a book-length series of interviews and numerous articles on Siegel, he has summarized Siegel's main themes in the article reprinted here. Not only does he find a thematic consistency in Siegel's works but also a kind of battleground, a dialectic that each film engages in a slightly different way, a war between control and instinct that is never fully won. For Kaminsky, *Invasion* is central to Siegel's canon.

Another major strand of criticism focuses less on Siegel and more on the film and its ideology. Ernesto G. Laura, writing in the Italian journal *Bianco e Nero* in 1957, must surely have been the first to suggest in print that the film is a parable about American fear of Soviet invasion. Since that time, ideological and social criticism has had a major resurgence, with the result that this view of *Invasion* is now the dominant one. It can easily be found in the sections on the film in Peter Biskind's investigation into the ideology of fifties films, *Seeing Is Believing* (1983) and Nora Sayre's analysis of Cold War films, *Running Time* (1982).

Neither Sayre nor Biskind is concerned with the stated intentions of the film's creators. Peter Biskind—in an article "Pods, Blobs, and Ideology in American Films of the Fifties"—suggests that the ideological meaning of *Invasion* can be determined by its structure and tone, its conception of the hero and his results, and the use of important social mechanisms like the army and doctors. From this perspective he reads the film as a radical film, but unlike my reading in the Introduction, as one from the radical right, not the left. Paranoia, a distrust of all institutions, a refusal to believe in cops or docs, a lone wolf hero convincing us that in his madness he alone is right, are all hallmarks of the radical right-wing film. Nora Sayre's article focuses on the invaders as alien monsters; she too underscores the paranoid politics and its Soviet invasion fantasy.

A third strand of criticism, which is also important for contemporary critics, is unfortunately not reflected in the selections here. Stuart Samuels, in an article "The Age of Conspiracy and Conformity" in *American History/American Film* (1979), bypasses the auteurist issue and reads the film as a kind of Rorschach of American concerns in the fifties, an uneasy mixture of malaise and belief in the new

bureaucracies. For him the film reflects three major concerns that can be found in influential books of the period as well, David Riesman's *The Lonely Crowd* and William H. Whyte's *The Organization Man*. These are alienation, conformity, and paranoia. Maurice Yacowar on the 1986 Criterion laserdisc uses this method to analyze the film, modifying it with some respect for Siegel's auteurism. In these analyses, the film can be anti-communist, although it is primarily an expression of the paranoia and fear dominant in American society in the mid-fifties.

Two other strands of criticism seek to locate the meaning of *Invasion* at a deeper level beyond either the auteurist statement or the political parable. Increasingly *Invasion* and other science fiction films of the fifties have been placed within the genre of horror, largely because of their monsters and the fears they represent. Because of its psychological basis in the unconscious and gender warfare, the horror genre offers a fertile ground for contemporary speculation.

The horror/science fiction writer Stephen King does not abandon a concern with the way the social intersects with deeper meanings, but he is more concerned with subterranean meanings and the way both the older and newer versions of the film open them up. King finds the main meaning of both versions in the fear of death. Michael Paul Rogin analyzes the science fiction and horror movies of the fifties in his book *Ronald Reagan the Movie* as indicators of political and social meanings, but only as they are controlled by unconscious forces. Noting the fear of sleep in the film, Rogin suggests the monster comes from within—"the dream wish of the 1950's was to escape from the anxiety of separate identity and to merge with society." The political consciousness of *Invasion* is subordinate to its "sexual unconsciousness." It "united deceit with bodily invasion and located both in female influence."

An even more explicit feminist reading by Nancy Steffen-Fluhr, "Women and the Inner Game of Don Siegel's Invasion of the Body Snatchers," suggests like Rogin that a fear of sex underlies and controls the overt political meaning of the film. The pods are ambiguous; while they represent nonlife and the lack of emotion, a kind of death, they also represent fecundity and passionate feelings that are repressed. In form they are vaginal and connected to Becky, who naturally becomes one of them. In Steffen-Fluhr's view,

Invasion "is a film which substitutes a physical *invasion* for an intra-psychic *evasion*. It is a *psychomachia* by and for beleaguered males of the mid-1950's. . . . The principal evader is Miles, or, more precisely, the macho authorial consciousness for which he is the voice. His alliance with Becky, his 'other half,' is a powerful, life-enhancing configuration. So long as it lasts, it protects him against the forces of depression. . . . In the end, Miles (and the film for which he speaks) turns against intimacy and androgyny and reasserts the simpler, though more sterile values of the American patriarchy."

Once one goes beyond an auteurist reading, it is clear that *Invasion* contains enough material to suggest a variety of psycho-social fears both of the period and the present, that keep it a lively source for reflection. The mining of meaning by critics will undoubtedly continue.

B-Movies

Peter Bogdanovich

They say television has replaced the B-movie, but it's not true. The reason why the "second feature" was so often able to achieve such vigor and interest is that it was made, so to speak, while no one was looking. Never taken very seriously by critics, and even less so by the studios (as long as costs and schedules were closely observed), the B-movie director could many times work in a freer atmosphere than some of his higher-budgeted contemporaries. TV production is so closely supervised by networks, sponsors, advertising executives, and producers that any sort of personal expression becomes almost impossible. Actually, the only relation between television films and the old B-movies lies in their similar budgets—whence the B-picture acquired its name in the first place.

However, even an exceptional TV film like Tom Gries's and Truman Capote's *The Glass House* was budgeted at over twice what the average B-movie director usually had to work with. That's one of the main reasons why they were required to be far more resourceful and imaginative in achieving their effects than the fellows with A-budgets. In need of an exotic location, they'd have to find a way to shoot it in Griffith Park. Want a city block, a small-town square, a western street? Check the back lot. Sam Fuller, making a New York story like *Pickup on South Street,* had to figure out a way of disguising downtown L.A. to look like Manhattan and Brooklyn. Allan Dwan once did a whole film in ten days on the sets left standing from Orson Welles's *The Magnificent Ambersons.* That was the other thing—they had to work fast. Ten-, fifteen-day schedules. I can't imagine how they did it and made the films look so good. One of the most absurd questions I've heard—and several producers, in discussing one or another man who has only worked under those circumstances, have asked it: "But do you think he can handle a big budget?" I never could figure out why time and money should be considered more difficult to deal with than speed and poverty. If you want a particular kind of sunset and you can afford to wait till it comes along—they say David Lean has been known to do that—where is the problem?

The fact that several of these directors not only did their films "at a price," but also made a series of movies that form a cohesive personal vision is nothing less than remarkable. Sam Fuller, Don Siegel, Budd Boetticher come to mind. Also men like Edgar G. Ulmer, Joseph H. Lewis, André de Toth, Phil Karlson, Allan Dwan (in his sound period). If they were sometimes defeated by their assignments or their casts—Siegel with *Spanish Affair* or *No Time for Flowers,* Fuller with *Hell and High Water,* Boetticher with almost everything before 1955—they

From *Pieces of Time* (New York: Arbor House, 1973), pp. 148–153.

nonetheless brought their considerable craft and distinctive styles to even the most lamentable material. Almost all the work falls into the action genre—westerns, gangster films, thrillers (though Dwan made a delightful group of low-budget comedies in the forties: *Brewster's Millions, Up in Mabel's Room, Getting Gertie's Garter, Rendezvous with Annie*); these are things American directors have consistently distinguished through the years and for which little critical recognition is ever received.

Don Siegel, for example, has managed, often against stifling odds, to bring a disquieting ambiguity as well as a unified viewpoint to assignments which, in other hands, could easily have been routine. Schooled in the tough no-nonsense Warner Brothers tradition of Raoul Walsh and Howard Hawks, his films are unpretentious and as precisely executed as they are unconventional in their implications. (His recent escalation to sizable budgets has not dimmed his energy nor diminished his bite.) *Invasion of the Body Snatchers*, despite its pulp title and its tacked-on opening and close (studio cold feet) is, along with Hawks's *The Thing*, the best and most terrifying science-fiction movie ever made. A cautionary fable about the world's relentless movement toward a lack of feeling, it retains a special meaning today, even though it was made while America was still reeling from the McCarthy era's assault on sensitivity. *Riot in Cell Block 11* is still the finest prison picture to come out of the U.S. (the best from Europe is probably Jacques Becker's eloquent and little-known *Le Trou*), just as *Hell Is for Heroes* remains one of the only war films to examine the inherent psychosis of a man who is brave in battle, whose most antisocial behavior actually becomes heroic in the abnormal circumstances of war. Siegel's best police movie, *Madigan* (he has made at least two others), is particularly interesting in its examination of the easy corruptibility of lawmen, at the same time as it reveals the squalor and misery of their daily life. On the other hand, he has looked at the underside of the underworld with chilling incisiveness in *Baby Face Nelson, The Lineup*, and *The Killers* (1964 version); as Andrew Sarris has pointed out, his hero—whether within the law or not—has always been "the antisocial outcast" in a world of pervasive corruption. A bleak vision perhaps, but free of cant in its depiction and marked by a vigorous gift for visual storytelling.

Even a casual look at the final chase sequence in *The Lineup* puts to shame some of the more publicized recent examples of the form, and the fatal shootout at the end of *Madigan* is among the most brilliantly shot and cut pieces of action I've ever seen. It never fails to move me, not simply because of the poignancy of its outcome in the story, but even more for the excellence and clarity of its direction. Howard Hawks, a master of action, has summed it up: "That stuff's hard to do," and indeed it is something not to be taken for granted in a medium that has, for twenty years, been steadily losing its sense of craft.

Having himself been a bullfighter, it is not surprising that Budd Boetticher has made the best pictures on that subject: *The Bullfighter and the Lady, The Magnifi-*

cent Matador (he dislikes those B-movie titles as much as anyone would), and his latest, *Arruza,* which took him fourteen years to complete and an incredible series of disasters to overcome, at least two of which almost cost him his life. The story of the making of *Arruza* is, in fact, a testament to the dedication and indestructibility of the B-movie director at his best, often having little at his command but guts and determination. Between a disquieting little thriller called *The Killer Is Loose* in 1956 and an effectively perverse gangster film, *The Rise and Fall of Legs Diamond* in 1960, Boetticher made an extraordinarily consistent and evocative series of seven Randolph Scott westerns that forms one of the high points in the history of that much-maligned genre. Even less well known than the comparable, though higher-budgeted, series of five that Anthony Mann did with James Stewart during roughly the same period (*Winchester 73, Bend of the River, The Naked Spur, The Far Country, The Man from Laramie*), Boetticher's films were never noticed by critics—except in France and, later, in England—but taken separately, or as a whole, they are far more beautifully directed and considerably richer in their implications than Sam Peckinpah's much-acclaimed *Ride the High Country* (with Scott and Joel McCrea) which actually concluded the cycle, and which Boetticher was not free to do because of his involvement with *Arruza.*

Beginning with *Seven Men from Now* and ending with *Comanche Station,* the Boetticher-Scott westerns, all made very quickly and inexpensively, explore, without pretense but with considerable humor and energy, the often ambiguous relations between heroes and villains, as Scott is pitted against such imposing adversaries as Lee Marvin (*Seven Men from Now*), Pernell Roberts (*Ride Lonesome*), Richard Boone (*The Tall T*), Claude Akins (*Comanche Station*). If *Decision at Sundown, Buchanan Rides Alone,* and *Westbound* are less memorable, it is mainly because the casting of the "heavies" was not on as interesting a level—just one of a B-film director's many limitations. That Boetticher was able to transcend these more often than not is just another indication of his ability.

Sam Fuller is probably the most explosive talent ever to blast its way through Poverty Row. Eccentric, iconoclastic and in the tradition of tabloid journalism (Fuller began as a reporter and one of his most personal films, *Park Row,* deals with early New York newspapering), his pictures all bear the same vibrant individualistic stamp. One of the only low-budget American directors who has consistently written and produced most of his films, he has had to compromise on his material less often than any of his contemporaries, though still having to be content frequently with inadequate actors or schedules. In Fuller's case, however, he has generally been able to turn even the most crippling restrictions into an amazingly consistent, exciting style. His films abound with meaningfully inventive camera work and unusual, complex cutting patterns that are nothing if not bold, as well as being uniquely his own. Several books have been written about his work in France, England, and Germany, but American recognition is

long overdue. His westerns—*I Shot Jesse James, Run of the Arrow, Forty Guns*
—are as different and against the grain as they are filled with a kind of pug-
nacious authenticity. Similarly, he has made the only war films that look like they
were made by a man who lived through a war, which he did as a member of the
1st Infantry ("The Big Red One") during World War II. *The Steel Helmet, Fixed
Bayonets, China Gate, Merrill's Marauders, Verboten!* are completely free of
the sentimentality or piousness that informs most films about men at war; you get
the feeling that this is really the way it was—amoral, totally destructive, un-
bearably intense and claustrophobic.

Similarly unnerving are Fuller's crime pictures, the best of which, *Pickup on
South Street* and *Underworld, U.S.A.,* are riveting classics in the genre, and
reveal, along with the others, *The Crimson Kimono, Shock Corridor, The Naked
Kiss,* a decidedly unglamorous, often scabrous side of modern American life.
(*House of Bamboo* took his seamy Americans to Japan for a similarly relentless
view.) Often extreme, his vision of the world is reflected in broad, expressionistic
strokes, and belongs entirely to the movies; he has brought his feisty, uncom-
promising zest for pictures into every frame he has ever shot.

A good-sized book could be written chronicling the impressive accomplish-
ments of these men and others in this largely unheralded tradition (and now just
about defunct in the new boom-or-bust movie industry). Classics in the field like
Fritz Lang's *The Big Heat,* Robert Aldrich's *Kiss Me Deadly,* Joseph Losey's *The
Prowler,* Nicholas Ray's *On Dangerous Ground,* Phil Karlson's *99 River Street,
The Phenix City Story,* and *The Brothers Rico,* Joseph H. Lewis's *Gun Crazy* and
The Big Combo, Gerd Oswald's *Crime of Passion,* Edgar G. Ulmer's *Detour* are
only a fraction of the work that has been produced with little means and considerable talent in a style the French have named "le film noir." They conclusively
prove that the quality of a picture can never be measured by its cost—that, in
fact, some of the best work in Hollywood has been done without fanfare, encour-
agement or much hope for reward. The achievements themselves have most often
been their makers' only real satisfaction. Television has a long way to go to
measure up.

The Genre Director: The Films of Donald Siegel

Stuart M. Kaminsky

Every year brings one, sometimes two Hollywood films directed by Donald Siegel. Starting with two Academy Award-winning shorts in 1945 (*Hitler Lives,* a compilation documentary, and *Star in the Night,* a two-reel Christmas story), Siegel's name has appeared on thirty-one films as director. His horror film, *Invasion of the Body Snatchers,* a nightmarish, philosophical feature, is often cited by critics as one of the best and most intelligent films ever made in the horror genre; in addition, it is, according to the film company which owns it, one of the three most requested films on television. *Riot in Cell Block 11* is a powerful, relentless, womanless prison genre picture, against which other prison films are constantly measured. And his *Baby Face Nelson* is a violent gangster film which reminds one of and predates Arthur Penn's *Bonnie and Clyde* by ten years.

With only a few exceptions, Siegel's films are distinct genre works: gangster films, Westerns, war stories, police stories, horror films, melodramas, and comedies. As a genre director, his work received little attention from critics until *Cahiers du Cinéma* singled him out as an auteur in 1964. Retrospective showings of Siegel's films have been held in Paris and London. French director Jean-Luc Godard, a great admirer of the American director, visited him and named a character in one of his films, *Made in U.S.A.,* "Donald Siegel." Godard also drew heavily on *Invasion of the Body Snatchers* in making his film *Alphaville.*

Siegel's popular appeal can be seen in the fact that he is one of the few remaining directors to be under contract to a major studio (Universal), and that his films are consistent money makers. *Dirty Harry,* in fact, is among the top box-office films of the past five years.

Donald Siegel is not an auteur in the accepted sense that, as a film's director, he has had total control over all aspects of each of his films. Until recently. Most often, Siegel has worked with stories he did not select. He was often channeled into film violence by virtue of his second-unit success on many Warner Brothers action films of the 1930s. In addition, studio influence or producer control often have forced him to go in directions, on a particular film, to which he was opposed, and his desire to direct additional films sometimes had led him to compromise where he would have preferred to remain resolute.

Still, the essence of Siegel's creativity can be seen in the extent to which he has been capable of controlling the individual genre films on which he has

From *American Film Genres* (New York: Dell, 1977), pp. 218–226.

worked, often guiding them in directions which allowed him to express himself. Although he might, had he been given the opportunity to do so, well have chosen to work in genres which did not include violence, the fact that he was so channeled does not preclude his self-expression. The manner of expression, and the points of view of such dynamic directors as Howard Hawks or John Ford, frequently have been enhanced by their working in established genres.

The extent to which Siegel is consciously aware of thematic content in his handling of a particular genre is of interest, but not totally relevant to his work. Each film must stand by itself and cannot be judged on the basis of the director's intent. It is not necessary for the genre artist to have a conscious understanding of the underlying themes of his work. Such themes are a part of himself; his culture, existence, and the manner in which he successfully expresses them in his films are a gauge of his artistry. In many of his films, consciously or unconsciously, Siegel has created a generic expression, in popular art, worthy of serious consideration.

Siegel's films show a distinct evolving attitude toward man and his relationship to society, man and his search for meaning, and man and his relationship to women. His treatment of each of these themes shows artistic growth. An understanding of these attitudes and their presentation is essential to an appreciation of Siegel as a serious genre director.

The thematic pattern of Siegel's films, despite occasional variations, involves an initial rash act by the protagonist. This is followed by a sense of guilt and a seeking of justice through personal action. A father-figure is usually present to warn the protagonist by telling him that personal action will not bring justice and peace of mind, even if he comes to understand his impulse; that socially accepted ways of seeking justice are essential; and that if one tries to act like God, he will be defeated. The protagonist does not heed this warning. He plunges ahead in the hope that he can determine his own fate. Usually, the subject of his quest is an antagonist whose character is an extension of his own. The affirmative villain is vibrant—perhaps mad—but his very madness is affirmative, for spontaneous violent madness is pattern-breaking and life-affirming. The hero and villain are both flawed; an act of violence divides the two. The protagonist, to get justice, must destroy the mad villain, the uncontrolled essence of the total personality. The protagonist has little help in his quest for justice, his desire for confrontation with his villainous mirror image. His friends are of value only because of their professional qualities. A Siegel hero makes friends for no reason other than professional competence. Friends also often represent the more conservative aspects of one's personality. Either the villain or the hero can be shown as having friends, who are actually supportive projections of the character's conscience and personality.

Women are of no help at all to either the protagonist or the villain. Siegel's women are tempting, deceitful creatures, forever playing Eve. They can't be denied, but they must never be trusted. Often, in the course of his pursuit of justice and vindication for his mistake, the hero discovers that he can't isolate himself by refusing to feel, or to be affected by others. The hero knows that human existence has no meaning, but he finds that he should not—in fact, that he cannot—insulate himself, protect himself from the pain of life. Violence is not enough. Trust and social affirmation must be tried, even if doomed, for to avoid them is to avoid existence.

Finally, after he attains some kind of justice, the hero finds himself both victorious and defeated at the same time. His wild self is dead; the violent affirmation he once felt has been subdued. The protagonist sinks back into oblivion, lost without his simple course of violent action, his cause of vengeance and feeling of guilt. As the film ends, he is no longer of interest. Siegel is ready to look for another flawed hero, another mad villain to play out another variation of the psychodrama of existence.

Literary analogies to Siegel's films can be found most strikingly in Joseph Conrad, especially in terms of the *Doppelgänger* villain as a psychological mirror image (*The Heart of Darkness*) and of self-vindication for rash action (*Lord Jim*). Strangely, Siegel's concepts of order, society, and the presumptuousness of assuming power are extraordinarily like those of the Swiss writer Friedrich Dürrenmatt (*The Marriage of Mr. Mississippi, An Angel in Babylon, The Pledge,* and *The Quarry*). Cinematically, Siegel's mentors (by his own admission and the evidence of his films) were genre directors Michael Curtiz, from whom he learned much of his cinematic technique, and William Wellman, from whom he learned little technique but whose iconoclastic view of society he admired and accepted.

With this background in mind, one can see that Siegel views man as being torn between two extremes of behavior in his attempt to come to terms with his existence. Although man is drawn toward both extremes, he may be capable of survival—with some semblance of dignity and peace of mind—if he can find a balance between the two extremes. Whether or not this balance is possible is the probing question asked incessantly by Siegel, as he makes use of the icons, themes, and characters of various genres and brings to the foreground those concerns at the core of each genre.

At opposite ends of the spectrum of existence lies madness. On one end is the drive toward conformity, characterized by a protective lack of emotion and involvement, and a seeking of insulation and social acceptance. Those who exist at this end of life's spectrum tend to plunge into hyper-professionalism, have little fear, and display a total disregard for life. In essence, to Siegel, they are pods—a descriptive term for the emotionless, vegetable-humans of *Invasion of the Body Snatchers*. Much of humanity experiences an extreme drive toward this manner of existence, which Siegel despises but toward which he feels drawn. The mad, or extreme, examples of this behavior include all the pods, especially Larry Gates, in *Invasion of the Body Snatchers*, Eli Wallach and Robert Keith in *The Lineup*, and Lee Marvin in *The Killers*. The chief inspector in *No Time for*

Flowers approaches this madness. Contemporary society, in most Siegel films, tends to favor this end of the existence spectrum, as exemplified by the townspeople in *Count the Hours, Flaming Star, Stranger on the Run,* and *No Time for Flowers.*

On the other end of the spectrum is a wild, spontaneous, emotional, life-affirming joyousness which is, nonetheless, mad. The representatives of this end of the spectrum, to which Siegel is also drawn, are spontaneous, violent, free-spirited, without control, vital, filled with exaltation, often humorous, and totally unpredictable. That these unfettered madmen are more psychologically appealing to Siegel than the emotionless pods is clear in their presentation and cinematic interest.

These free spirits are out to destroy whatever stifles society, but they themselves must also be destroyed if any sense of order is to remain within the protagonist and society itself. Such unfettered madmen include Jack Elam in *Count the Hours,* Mark Rydell in *Crime in the Streets,* Mickey Rooney in *Baby Face Nelson,* Mickey Shaughnessy in *Edge of Eternity,* the war lord in *China Venture,* Clu Gulager in *The Killers,* Eddie Albert in *The Gun Runners,* Leo Gordon in *Riot in Cell Block 11,* Steven Ihnat in *Madigan,* and Andy Robinson in *Dirty Harry.*

The human societies which approach this unfettered state without going mad, and which are able to retain their self-affirmation, are the primitive natural societies which have been threatened or subjugated by more dominant and prevalent pod-like societies. Such affirmative primitive societies in Siegel films include the Indians in *Flaming Star,* the mountain people in *Hound Dog Man,* the prisoners in *Riot in Cell Block 11,* and the slum dwellers in *Crime in the Streets.*

The film protagonists, with whom Siegel seeks a sense of balance and a means of accepting and dealing with existence, are pulled in two directions: toward primitivism and unfettered madness on one side, and social order and conformity on the other. Those who choose the primitive extreme—the violent, unfettered course of action—can only meet with defeat in a Siegel film. This is true of Neville Brand in *Riot in Cell Block 11,* John Cassavetes in *Crime in the Streets,* Stuart Whitman in *Hound Dog Man,* and Elvis Presley in *Flaming Star.*

Many of Siegel's protagonists are wild, unpredictable men who make an attempt to accept society and seek the solace of pod existence. Invariably, such protagonists must first overcome their primitive, unfettered urges and then take a step in the direction of emotional involvement—a step which will bring them closer to a balance between the two dominant human drives, but which may not result in personal happiness. Other protagonists begin a Siegel film as pod-like creatures, or as men who seem to seek only the solace of being a pod. By the film's end, they have taken a first tentative step toward emotion and vitality through an act of violence in which they destroy the unfettered madman, the wild side of themselves. This step is a key to possible hope. Such protagonists include Ronald Reagan in *Night Unto Night,* Robert Mitchum in *The Big Steal,*

MacDonald Carey in *Count the Hours,* Richard Kiley in *Spanish Affair,* Henry Fonda in *Stranger on the Run,* and Clint Eastwood in *Coogan's Bluff* and *Dirty Harry.*

At the very center of the spectrum, apparently at peace with existence, are a few Siegel protagonists who appear at the start of some later films. But even in these films, Siegel's conclusion is that if a man is able to come to terms with his own existence, other forces—primarily sexual betrayal—will destroy him. This conclusion is true of the characters portrayed by Clint Eastwood in both *Two Mules for Sister Sara* and *The Beguiled.*

Seen as a whole, Siegel's films do not build toward a thematic solution. Instead, they explore the problem of existence in the terms already discussed. Siegel's films also explore the director's ideas and feelings concerning personality, guilt, madness, and death. His protagonists are plagued by mirror images of themselves: characters who represent a key part of the protagonist's own personality drives, and who force the protagonists to recognize their existence. The villains generally display distorted aspects of the hero's personality, the extremes of pod-like conformity or of unfettered madness. Siegel's skill is such, however, that considerations of psychological structure are not evident on the surface. Even the mad characters are not one-dimensional extensions, psychological equivalents of the generalities encountered by *Everyman* or John Bunyan's Pilgrim. Nor are these characters allegorical creations, like those which appeared in early Ingmar Bergman films. The psychological complexities of character in a Siegel film are totally integrated into the structure of genre entertainment. Siegel's mode of expression lies within the confines of genre and Hollywood, for it is in such contexts that he has learned to express himself. . . .

Invasion of the Body Snatchers

Ernesto G. Laura

One day, in an American small town named Santa Mira, some people suddenly become aware that their fathers or sisters or sons are no longer "themselves." There is no change in their appearance, behavior, or character, but they seem somehow to have been emptied inside, as if they had "no emotion—none—only the pretense of it." Next day, all the people who had this impression about someone in their family are laughing at it, saying they must have suffered from some odd kind of hallucination.

That is the starting point of *Invasion of the Body Snatchers*, a science fiction film that is only now appearing on Italian screens, about a year after its American release. The film is of interest both for the seriousness with which it was made—something unusual in a genre which, while growing in popularity, normally has to be content with second-rate directors and scriptwriters—and for the theme behind its fantastic story. In fact, the allegorical meaning becomes clearer and clearer as the action unfolds. Mysterious pods arrive from some unknown source, and each of them transforms itself into a body identical to that of the nearest human being. It then replaces that person, absorbing his personality without his humanity—since the pods are and remain vegetables. They are also a symbol whose message is easy to read.

Considering the state of public opinion in the United States today, from the recent wave of McCarthyism to the fear of a third World War, it is natural to see the pods as standing for the idea of communism which gradually takes possession of a normal person, leaving him outwardly unchanged but transformed within. This is the kind of simple-minded presentation of the problem that can be found in *Reader's Digest*, but it corresponds to the average American's views as they have been shaped by television and a wide range of periodicals. The memory of Orwell and his *1984* is still very much alive. Anglo-Saxon literature in general shows a predilection for allegory, and so does its more recent popular subdivision, science fiction: H. G. Wells, widely regarded as the founder of modern science fiction, was a typically allegorical writer. The fact that allegory is the key to *Invasion of the Body Snatchers* readily becomes apparent when one looks at the book on which it is based, Jack Finney's *The Body Snatchers*. In this unpretentious popular novel, the arrival of the pods is accounted for as an invasion from outer space, and there are quite detailed pseudoscientific explanations of how the "twinning" is accomplished, how long it takes, and so on.

From *Focus on the Science Fiction Film*, ed. William Johnson (Englewood Cliffs, N.J.: Prentice-Hall, 1972), pp. 71–73. Originally published in *Bianco e Nero* 18, no. 12 (1957):69–71.

Don Siegel has dropped all this, leaving the mystery unexplained. One morning we wake up and find a huge pod in the cellar; it splits open, revealing a blank which develops and takes on the shape of our body; and it waits for the time when our consciousness is at its weakest, when we are asleep at night, to take possession of us. With its atmosphere of unexplained mystery, the action of the film acquires a remarkable power of suggestion which reveals that Siegel, until now a competent craftsman, has a personality of his own. His background, which includes schooling at Cambridge University in England and serious training for the theater, has undoubtedly influenced the careful dramatic structure of the film, full of suspense but at the same time controlled, free of excesses.

In the film as in the novel, Miles, the protagonist, remains the only inhabitant of Santa Mira to hold out, fighting against sleep to preserve his freedom. Then, in the novel, Miles sets fire to the field where the pods are being grown: those that are not destroyed by the flames rise up into the sky, quitting the planet which has shown itself so hostile to them. "We hadn't, and couldn't possibly have been . . . the only souls who had stumbled and blundered onto what had been happening in Santa Mira. There'd been others, of course, individuals, and little groups . . . who had fought, struggled, and simply refused to give up. Some others may have won, many had lost, but all of us who had not been caught and trapped without a chance had fought implacably, and a fragment of a wartime speech moved through my mind: 'We shall fight them in the fields, and in the streets, we shall fight in the hills; we shall never surrender.' " Clearly, having had little success with his allegory, the author of the book falls back on preaching, spelling out the facile McCarthyism of his message.

With better dramatic sense, Siegel ends with Miles running onto a highway. While truck after truck sets out from Santa Mira loaded with pods for the rest of the world, Miles yells the danger to automobile drivers who take no notice as they roar past him. It is a powerful and convincing sequence. While the film is no masterpiece, it is stimulating for its sidelights on the views and attitudes of average Americans, and it is noteworthy for the hallucinatory atmosphere conferred on it by a hitherto minor director.

Watch the Skies

Nora Sayre

The preoccupation with infiltration and mind control was further extended in Don Siegel's *Invasion of the Body Snatchers* (1956). As a result of atomic mutation, plants from another world gain possession of human bodies, which become "hosts to an alien form of life." As our society is converted into a regime of totalitarian vegetables, the survivors exclaim, "They're taking us over, *cell* by *cell*," and "It's a malignant disease spreading through the whole country!" In that era, Communism was often compared to fatal illness: in 1952, Adlai Stevenson said in a campaign speech that Communism was "a disease which may have killed more people in this world than cancer, tuberculosis, and heart disease combined." Stevenson also said that the goal of America's enemies was "total conquest, not merely of the earth, but of the human mind."

In a film like *Invasion of the Body Snatchers,* when a close friend or relative behaves "unlike himself," the image of brainwashing arises—as it did in the consciousness of the Fifties, when many believed that the American prisoners in Korea had been subjected to thought control. (Because none of the seven thousand prisoners had escaped from captivity, and few had attempted to do so, and since subsequent Senate investigations suggested that about 70 percent of them had collaborated with the Koreans to some extent, it was tempting to think that they had been brainwashed.) In the movie, love is abolished, along with all family ties, and the victims are assured that they will be "reborn into an untroubled world"—which has echoes of a baleful utopianism. Humanoids can look just like the rest of us, as Communists do; but they are not in charge of their own souls, and as their numbers multiply, everyone will become alike. (In the Fifties, many believed that Communist governments turned their citizens into robots.) So the political forebodings of the period spilled over into science fiction, where subservience to alien powers and the loss of free will were so often depicted, and the terror of being changed into "something evil" became a ruling passion. The amusing 1978 remake of *Invasion of the Body Snatchers* did not perpetuate the social overtones—instead, it concentrated on conformity and surrendering the capacity to feel, and few of the scenes had the impact of Kevin McCarthy's climax in the original, when he stood on a highway, screaming at passing trucks and cars, "You fools, you're in danger . . . ! They're after us! You're next! You're next!"

From *Running Time* (New York: Dial Press, 1982), pp. 199, 201.

Pods, Blobs, and Ideology in American Films of the Fifties

Peter Biskind

Ever since Georges Méliès sent his rocket to the moon at the turn of the century, science fiction films have been familiar sights on American screens, but it was not until the fifties that they arrived in force. *Destination Moon* and *Rocket Ship X-M,* both released in 1950, inaugurated a flurry of films which, before the decade ended, would produce a veritable invasion of little green men, flying saucers, born-again dinosaurs, predatory plants, diabolical juveniles, and enormous insects.

Ideologically speaking, fifties science fiction films fell into two camps: centrist and radical. Centrist films often presented America in the grip of an emergency, attacked by giant ants in *Them* (1954), or invaded by aliens in *Earth vs. The Flying Saucers* (1956). They did so because they were in the business of dramatizing consensus, the general shared agreement on the basic premises that animated society. Emergencies made it clear that if we wanted to survive to see another day, we had better pull together to overcome our local, petty differences in the common interest.

The ideology of the center was called pluralism, and it held that American society was composed of a variety of interest groups that competed on a more or less equal basis for a piece of the pie. Since this plurality of groups all shared the same assumptions, relations among them were based on compromise, negotiation, and mutual respect. Centrists knew that consensus was more stable if dissenters were inside the magic circle of agreement sharing the pie with Ozzie and Harriet, rather than outside, throwing stones against the picture window. They preferred, if possible, to include their enemies, not cast them into outer darkness. But the scope of the consensus was nothing if not narrow, and centrists did not hesitate to label those who refused to play the game as extremists.

In centrist films extremists were presented as aliens. Who were they? It has long been evident, in fact from the moment the first blob oozed its way across the screen, that the little green men from Mars stood in the popular imagination for the clever red men from Moscow. The media portrayed Russians in such lurid fashion that the connection was inevitable, even if unintended by writers and

From *Shadows of the Magic Lamp,* ed. George E. Slusser and Eric S. Rabkin (Carbondale and Edwardsville: Southern Illinois University Press, 1985), pp. 58–72. A longer version of this essay appeared in *Seeing Is Believing: How Hollywood Taught Us to Stop Worrying and Love the Fifties* (New York: Random House, Pantheon Books, 1983). Copyright © 1983 by Peter Biskind.

directors. But I. F. Stone, among others, pointed out that the Soviet threat was as much a function of the squabbles between Democrats and Republicans as a reality: "The Republicans fight Russians in order to prevent a New Deal, while the Democrats fight Russians as a kind of rearguard action against the Republicans."[1] Indeed, the red nightmare was so handy that had it not existed, American politicians would have had to invent it. Movies did invent it, and it served somewhat the same purpose in Hollywood as it did in Washington. Extremists were not only Russians, but everyone, left and right, who dissented from consensus. More often than not, the communist connection was a red herring, allowing the center to attack the left and right, and the left and right to attack the center, all in the guise of respectable anti-communism, which itself was no more than a smokescreen for a domestic power struggle.

Centrist science fiction adopted an Us/Them framework, whereby that which threatened consensus was simply derogated as "Other." The Other was indeed communism, but it was also everything the center was not, and we can get a good idea of what the center was not by examining the language of pluralism. If the center was modern, the Other was ancient. Sociologist Daniel Bell referred to "archaic Europe" and the "backward colonial system."[2] If the center was civilized, the Other was primitive. Bell criticized the "barbarous" behavior of the radical right[3], and law professor Alan Westin warned against the "spear thrusts of the radicals."[4] If the center was scientific and technological, the Other was magical. Bell accused the right of entertaining the illusion of "the magical rollback of Communism in Europe."[5] Us/Them-ism permeated the whole range of ideas and values. If the center was middle-class, the Other was lower- or occasionally upper-class. If the center was normal, the Other was abnormal. If the center was sane, the Other was insane, and so on.

Pluralists like Bell, Talcott Parsons, Lionel Trilling, David Riesman, and Arthur Schlesinger, Jr., identified the center with no less than civilization itself, with the highest achievements of humanity, with the totality of man-made objects, the aggregate of human production, in short, with culture. Riesman observed that in America, "society is no longer felt as a wilderness or jungle as it often was earlier,"[6] and pluralists invariably imagined it in man-made terms: society was a business, a building, a game, a machine—but rarely nature. Bell spoke of the "fabric of government,"[7] and Parsons of the "institutional machine-

1. I. F. Stone, *The Truman Era,* 2d ed. (New York: Random House, Vintage Books, 1972), p. xxvii.
2. Daniel Bell, "The Dispossessed," in *The Radical Right,* ed. Daniel Bell, 2d ed. (New York: Doubleday Anchor, 1964), p. 19.
3. Ibid., p. 45.
4. Alan Westin, "The John Birch Society" in *The Radical Right,* p. 268.
5. Bell, "The Dispossessed," p. 3.
6. David Riesman, Nathan Glazer, and Reuel Denny, *The Lonely Crowd,* abridged ed. (New York: Doubleday Anchor, 1955), p. 152.
7. Bell, "The Dispossessed," p. 23.

ry" of society.[8] Machines even had God's blessing. "A machine is an assembling of parts according to the law of God. When you love a machine and get to know it, you will be aware that it has a rhythm," wrote Norman Vincent Peale. "It has God's rhythm."[9]

That which is not culture is, more generally, nature, not merely trees, animals, and bugs, but all that is not-human, so that the conflict between centrists and extremists, consensus and the Other, Us and Them, was often presented as a conflict between culture and nature. Since culture was good, nature was generally bad; it was all that threatened to disrupt or destroy culture. Bell, for example, wrote of the "flash-fire spread of McCarthyism,"[10] of the "turbulence" created by the right,[11] and of "a rogue elephant like Huey Long or Joseph McCarthy rampag[ing] against the operations of government."[12] When Billy Graham opened the 1952 session of the United States Senate with a prayer, he warned against the "barbarians beating at our gates from without and the moral termites from within."[13]

In centrist science fiction, the Other is imagined as nature run wild. In *Them* (1954), it is ants. In *The Beginning of the End* (1957), it is grasshoppers, while in *Tarantula* (1955), it is a spider. In the same category are films set in the jungle or remote, wild places, like *The Creature from the Black Lagoon* (1954); *Black Scorpion* (1957); *From Hell It Came* (1957), where the Other is a deranged tree stump; *The Attack of the Crab Monsters* (1957), where the Other is an army of jumbo crabs on a Pacific atoll; or *The Monster That Challenged the World* (1957), where the Other is a school of giant marauding snails.

Since centrist films imagined society as a machine and looked fondly on science and technology, computers and robots—in contrast to nature—were rarely dangerous. In *Forbidden Planet* (1956) and *Tobor the Great* (1954), they are servants or tools, not masters or enemies, while in *Unknown World* (1950), a trip to the center of the earth is facilitated by a giant mechanical mole. When robots appeared to be bad, as in *Earth vs. The Flying Saucers,* they turned out not to be robots at all, but aged humanoids wearing robot-like suits.

Other-izing qualities, ideas, life-styles, or groups that threatened the center was not only a way of discrediting specific alternatives to the status quo, but also a way of discrediting the very idea of alternatives to the orthodox manner of living and being. If alternatives to mainstream institutions were dystopian, there was no place to go but home, that is, back to the center.

The attack on utopias and utopians, dreams and dreamers, was a constant

---

8. Talcott Parsons, "Social Strains in America," in *The Radical Right,* p. 209.
9. Quoted in Douglas T. Miller and Marion Nowak, *The Fifties* (Garden City: Doubleday, 1977), p. 96.
10. Bell, "Interpretations of American Politics," p. 47.
11. Ibid.
12. Bell, "The Dispossessed," p. 43.
13. Quoted in Victor Navasky, *Naming Names* (New York: Viking Press, 1980), p. 24.

refrain in centrist literature. Utopians are our old friends, extremists, and utopianism was worked over so thoroughly that "utopian" and "millenial" became
epithets of abuse, in contrast to adjectives like "realistic," "mature," and "sensible," with which centrists flattered one another. Alan Westin derided "dangerously millenial proposals" of the left and right,[14] while Parsons ridiculed the
"utopianism" of Republican isolationists.

Thus, in centrist science fiction, even if utopias began well, they ended badly,
and were apt to degenerate from the best of all worlds to the worst. Fifties
science fiction was full of futuristic civilizations that had fallen on hard times. In
Forbidden Planet, for example, the Krell were the race that knew too much. In
This Island Earth (1955), the advanced civilization was Metaluna, but its gleam-
ing array of gadgets by no means insured it peace and prosperity; on the contrary,
the Metalunans were locked in a battle to the death with Zahgon, their arch-
enemy, and had to turn to scientists from Earth for help. To judge by these films,
Earth must have been the choicest morsel of real estate in the galaxy, the sweet
center of the Milky Way, because it was repeatedly invaded by advanced civilizations that had fouled up in one way or another—exhausted their resources, over-
populated their cities, nuked one another, and so on. To be an advanced
civilization was to look for trouble; this was not because these films were ambivalent about technology, but because they simply did not like utopias.

If Earth was the place where the hills were always greener, there was good
reason. Centrist science fiction employed a double standard. On one hand, it
attacked utopianism when it cropped up outside the center; on the other, it argued
that Earth, by which it meant the United States, circa 1955, was utopian enough
for anyone. It was there that the contradictions that destroyed advanced civilizations were reconciled. Centrists believed, quite simply, that their country had the
endorsement of the Almighty, the divine seal of approval. A booming consumer
economy offered ample proof that the God who had abandoned twentieth-century
Europe to physical and spiritual destruction was alive and well in America. "God
has set us an awesome mission: nothing less than the leadership of the free
world," said Adlai Stevenson during the 1952 presidential campaign.[15] "Why
should we make a five-year plan," wondered historian Daniel Boorstin in 1952 in
Partisan Review, "when God seems to have had a thousand-year plan ready-made
for us?"[16] It was clear to everyone that God had jumped on the free world
bandwagon.

If America was the City of God on Earth, this meant that God, Christ, and
spiritual values of any kind were immanent, immediate, palpable, familiar, and
accessible in the activities of everyday life, not remote, distant, or unreachable.
Utopia was to be found in our own backyards; salvation lay in humdrum routine.

---

14. Westin, "The John Birch Society," pp. 266–267.
15. Quoted in Miller and Nowak, *The Fifties*, p. 10.
16. Quoted in ibid., p. 222.

Centrist science fiction films were generally more confident and optimistic than radical films of the same genre and often there was no invasion by aliens at all. They were expansion- and exploration-oriented, imperialist rather than paranoid. In *Destination Moon,* the moon is regarded as a potential military base, and "others" must be prevented from exploiting it. The American astronaut takes possession "by the grace of God and in the name of the United States." When trouble came in centrist film, it often came during an expedition, as in *The Thing* (1951), *Forbidden Planet, From Hell It Came,* and *Creature from the Black Lagoon,* another warning not to go poking about for utopian alternatives. Home is safe; danger lurks out there.

Although centrists agreed with one another on the goals of consensus, and presented a common front against extremism, they quarreled among themselves about means, about how best to organize and impose consensus. This disagreement was reflected in centrist science fiction, which can be further divided into corporate liberal and conservative films. Both featured a coalition of scientists and soldiers, but differed on which had the upper hand.

Scientists and soldiers were first thrown together in a big way during the war, in the Manhattan Project, and the romance that blossomed then reached its climax at Hiroshima. In the fifties, when their infant A-bomb grew like a beanstalk into a strong and sturdy H-bomb, scientists became alarmed, and fell to fighting with soldiers (and among themselves) over their child's future. Scientists like Einstein and Oppenheimer began to wish they had strangled him in the cradle, while soldiers (and scientists like Teller) wanted to pack him off to military academy, not reform school. Both scientists and soldiers agreed that only a strong America would deflect the Soviets from their mad path to world conquest, but they disagreed over how much deterrence was enough. Scientists were content to rest on their laurels with the A-bomb, while soldiers wanted a bigger bang for their bucks, and pressed ahead with the H-bomb.

The disagreement over choice of weapons had wider ideological significance. Scientists (and corporate liberals in general) didn't like force, because in their view, society was consensual. Citizens did the right thing because they wanted to, or were persuaded to want to, not because they had to, or were forced to have to. For corporate liberals, moreover, reality was so complex that only scientists or experts were able to decipher it. "The problems of national security," wrote Bell, "like those of the national economy, have become so staggeringly complex that they can no longer be settled by common sense or past experience."[17]

In corporate liberal films, then, brawn deferred to brains, and scientists told soldiers what to do. The prestige of science was so high by the beginning of the fifties that the mad scientists of thirties and forties films, like Doctor Thorkel (Albert Dekker), who had shrunk his colleagues to the size of chickens in *Dr.*

17. Bell, "The Dispossessed," p. 32.

Cyclops (1941), were all working for Bell Labs. They were no longer mad, but on the contrary, rather pleased with the way things had turned out.

When the cops discover patches of sugar strewn all over the desert in *Them*, it "doesn't make sense." Reality is too complex for traditional police procedures to unravel the mystery, and this is clearly a job for "myrmecologist" Doctor Medford (Edmund Gwenn). A far cry from Doctor Thorkel, avuncular Doctor Medford wouldn't hurt a fly, and he has no trouble reading reality. He quickly recognizes that giant ants are the problem, and his expertise puts him at the center of world-shaking events. He meets with the president, lectures top public officials, and is able to command the full resources of the state. An Air Force general is reduced to the role of Medford's chauffeur, and when FBI agent Robert Graham (James Arness) complains that he can't understand Medford's scientific lingo, the film makes us feel that he ought to take a biology course at night school.

Since *Them* is a national emergency film that dramatizes consensus, it valorizes the intervention of the state and favors national over local interests. The alien threat emanates from the heartland and moves against a big city, in this case, Los Angeles. Help, on the other hand, comes from Washington; Gwenn works for the federal Department of Agriculture. Corporate liberals generally favored Big Government, and corporate liberal science fiction expressed the confidence that the government, with its bombs and missiles, was equal to any emergency. In *The Giant Claw* (1957), for example, its federal fighters dispatch "the bird as big as a battleship."

The corollary to the stress on consensus and Big Government was the disciplining of individualism. In these films, individualists—the first one out of an air lock on a strange planet, the first one to investigate a peculiar cavernous pit, like the unhappy scientist in *Invasion of the Crab Monsters*—were rewarded with death.

Similarly, the corollary of favoring experts and scientists was a hierarchical, elitist model of society, where those at the top were better—smarter, more moral, principled, and courageous—than those at the bottom. In *Them*, the average Janes and Joes who are neither scientists nor soldiers are almost as bad as the ants. They spend most of their time, in films like this, fleeing for their lives, obstructing the best efforts of the government to save them from themselves. The war against the ants has to be waged behind closed doors. Reporters, conduits to the people, threaten official secrecy. Like their readers, they have to be kept in the dark. "Do you think all this hush-hush is necessary?" someone asks Doctor Medford. "I certainly do," he replies. "I don't think there's a police force in the world that could handle the panic of the people if they found out what the situation is."

Conservative films, on the other hand, were more inclined to let the soldiers have their way. When Air Force Captain Hendry (Kenneth Tobey) arrives at a remote arctic outpost to investigate odd "disturbances" reported by a team of scientists in *The Thing*, he discovers that he's on alien territory. "Dr. Carrington is in charge here," one of the scientists tells him, referring to the Nobel Prize winner who heads the expedition, and it quickly becomes clear that Hendry's job is to assert the authority of the soldiers over the scientists. *The Thing* is about, among other things, a struggle over turf. It asks the question, which ideology, the conservative ideology of the military, or the corporate liberal ideology of science, is best.

Conservatives were considerably more suspicious of science than were their corporate liberal allies. In 1943, for example, Richard Weaver, author of *The Southern Tradition,* called science a "false messiah."[18] Scientists in conservative films were likely to be brothers beneath the beard of Baron von Frankenstein, which is to say that the mad scientists who had disappeared from the labs of corporate liberal films were alive and well in conservative films. In *It Conquered the World* (1956), for example, the scientist (Lee Van Cleef) helps a group of malicious Venusians do just that. In *The Thing,* the tension between science and the military that was latent in *Them* is not only more pronounced, it is resolved in favor of the military. FBI agent Graham complained in *Them* that he couldn't understand Medford, but he was something of a clod anyway, and it was probably his own fault. But when Captain Hendry asks Carrington (Robert Cornthwaite) a question and gets only mumbo-jumbo in return, it's another matter. "You lost me," he says, and this time it's their fault, a symptom of the arrogance of scientists and intellectuals. In *Them,* Medford's admiration for the "wonderful and intricate engineering" of the ants' nest is reasonable, neither unseemly nor unpatriotic. But in *The Thing,* Doctor Carrington's scientific curiosity is given a sinister twist. He develops an altogether unhealthy interest in the alien. Whereas Medford merely restrains the military because he wants to find out if the queen is dead, Carrington betrays it, defects to the other side. He helps the Thing reproduce itself, finds a warm spot in the greenhouse for it to lay its spores, and sabotages Hendry's efforts to kill it. Carrington is soft on aliens, a Thing-symp, and his behavior justifies the soldiers' mistrust of science, even turns them against the Bomb itself. "Knowledge is more important than life. We split the atom!" Carrington shouts in a transport of enthusiasm. "That sure made everybody happy," comes the sour reply from one of Hendry's men.

Eventually, Carrington is confined to his quarters; when he tells Hendry, "You have no authority here," one of the soldiers pokes a revolver in his face, and he learns that power grows out of the barrel of a gun. Conservative science fiction, in other words, preferred force to persuasion.

But science is by no means rejected wholesale. There are good scientists as well as bad, Tellers as well as Oppenheimers, and the difference between them is that the good scientists side with Hendry, not Carrington. And, at the end of the

18. Quoted in George H. Nash, *The Conservative Intellectual Movement in America* (New York: Basic Books, 1976), p. 39.

film, when the story of the struggle against the Thing is announced to the world, Carrington is singled out for special tribute. Soldiers and scientists, conservatives and corporate liberals may have quarreled among themselves, but it was all in the family, and when the chips were down, they closed ranks in defense of consensus.

Not all conservative films chastised science with the military; in some, religion played the role the military played in *The Thing*. These are the films in which the Faustian mad scientist is warned by a woman or a minister not to tamper with God's work. In Kurt Neumann's *The Fly* (1958), the fifties infatuation with science once again transforms what would earlier have been a mad scientist into a sympathetic victim, but even here, when he exclaims, "I can transport matter!" his wife replies, aghast, "It's like playing God." In these films, the cross is mightier than the test tube.

Fifties conservatives tended to favor local over national interests, the individual over the organization, and displayed considerable skepticism toward large groups of all kinds, including the army, which they regarded as excessively bureaucratic. In *Destination Moon,* for example, the government is a myopic bureaucracy that not only refuses to finance a moon shot, but after a visionary industrialist has seen to it that the rocket is built, tries to abort the launch. In *The Thing,* the conflict between soldiers and scientists is complemented by another, between the individual and the organization, in this case, Captain Hendry and the Air Force. Hendry begins the film as the perfect organization man. He can't blow his nose without clearing it first with headquarters in Alaska, which in turn refers back to Washington. But when Hendry goes by the book, it's a recipe for disaster, and red tape finally immobilizes him altogether. "Until I receive my instructions from my superior officer about what to do," he says, "we'll have to mark time." When his orders finally do come, they are worthless. Although the Thing has been making Bloody Marys out of the boys at the base, Hendry is instructed to "avoid harming the alien at all costs." Eventually, he is forced to disobey orders, take matters into his own hands, and pit his judgment against that of the organization, which is out of touch with reality. Even so he can't go too far; his rebellion is limited, confined to the framework of the organization. He remains a good soldier to the end.

Because *The Thing* is critical of bureaucracy and sympathetic toward individualism and initiative, it is more populist and less elitist than *Them*. While people in *Them* obstruct authority, authority in *The Thing* frustrates people. Within the community of soldiers and scientists at the base, relationships are more egalitarian than they are in *Them*. Decisions are not made behind closed doors, and the Thing is not destroyed by the power of the federal government, nor incinerated by soldiers wielding flamethrowers, as are the ants in *Them*, but rather by means of a do-it-yourself electric chair improvised on the spot out of spit and chewing gum.

In the fifties film, radical science fiction upended the conventions of centrist science fiction, turned them inside out, held them up to a mirror. If centrist films dramatized consensus, radical films dramatized conflict, polarization, and the antagonism between the self and society. If centrist films dramatized the views of insiders, radical films dramatized the views of outsiders. It was, of course, possible to attack the center from the right or left, so that radical science fiction in the fifties broke down into right-wing films and left-wing films.

Right-wing films were considerably more paranoid than centrist films. Their heroes did not have to go looking for trouble in strange and exotic places; trouble came to them, right here at home. These films resolved the ambivalence that afflicted conservative films, took the attitudes they displayed and pushed them to extremes. If conservative films were more sympathetic to individualism than corporate liberal films, right-wing films went further. They endorsed vigilantism and do-it-yourself justice, because society was not only corrupt, but anathema to the individual. They focused on the struggles of the self beseiged.

There was no question that giant ants were crawling all over Los Angeles in *Them,* or that a homicidal carrot was stalking the arctic base in *The Thing.* Everyone could see it. The focus of these films was not the strenuous efforts of those who knew to alert those who didn't to the fact that there was trouble afoot, a blob in the basement or green slime in the attic. Right-wing science fiction, on the contrary, dramatized the struggle of the outsider, the kook, the end-of-the-worlder to force the community to acknowledge the validity of the self's private vision, even if it violated the norms of credibility that governed the expectations of experts and professionals. When average Joe saw a flying saucer land in his bean field, nobody believed him. An abyss opened up between him and society. Far worse than invasion, these films anxiously imagined the loss of community, the estrangement of the one-who-knows from those that didn't, Us from Them, but this time Us were the so-called "extremists," and Them was the center.

In *Invasion of the Body Snatchers* (1956) Kevin McCarthy, as small town doctor Miles Bennell, is beseiged by patients telling him that their friends and neighbors are not what they seem to be; they are imposters. At first, Bennell advises them to see a psychiatrist. "The trouble's inside you," he tells one patient. But gradually, as the whole town, including the psychiatrist and police are taken over by pods, Bennell begins to change his mind. In one scene, he and a pal argue with the psychiatrist about whether or not the pods exist. Suddenly, the cops burst in. "I have a good mind to throw you both in jail," says the first cop, pointing to Bennell and pal. But the psychiatrist intervenes: "These people are patients, badly in need of psychiatric help." The cops and docs (in this film analogous to the soldiers and scientists of *Them* and *The Thing*) argue about whether Bennell and his pal are felons or patients, but we know they are both wrong. In *Invasion,* the doctors are sick and the cops are criminals. (Bennell is a doctor too, of course, but he's only a general practitioner, and he is not operating in the capacity of a doctor. His pal asks him, "Would you be able to forget you're a doctor for awhile?" Bennell: "Yes.")

In right-wing films, both cops and doctors, the twin pillars of the centrist authority, are vilified. The center itself is the enemy; taken over by aliens, it becomes alien. When Bennell finds an oversized pod in the greenhouse, he finally realizes that his patients have been right all along, that he must have faith in his own perceptions of the world, and not let experts mediate between himself and reality, convince him that he's wrong, crazy, or criminal.

Since the enemy in right-wing science fiction was the center, it was not too surprising that the form in which this enemy was imagined was not nature but culture, and specifically technology. If people betrayed technology in centrist films like *Forbidden Planet,* where disaster was caused by "human error," in right-wing films (and some conservative films), technology betrayed people; disaster was caused by "mechanical error." The editors of *The National Review,* for example, writing in the late sixties about John Glenn's space flight, preferred men to machines. "This and that went wrong with the mechanism, and man took over and brought Friendship 7 to its strange harbor," they wrote. "No machine, on land, in sea, air or space, can do man's job for him."[19] For the right, "robot" and "mechanical" were epithets of scorn, and the center, perceived from the right as dehumanized and technocratic, was represented in science fiction by a whole army of robots, androids, and mechanical pod people that trudged across the screens of the fifties with their characteristic jerky motions. Whereas in centrist films robots like Robby were friendly, they were dangerous in right-wing (and some left-wing) films like *The Twonky* (1953), *Target Earth* (1954), *Gog* (1954), and *Kronos* (1957).

Susan Sontag first called attention to this fear of robots, which she contrasted to the older fear of the animal. "The dark secret behind human nature used to be the upsurge of the animal—as in King Kong. The threat to man, his availability to dehumanization, lay in his own animality," she wrote. "Now the danger is understood as residing in man's ability to be turned into a machine."[20] But Sontag was only partly right. While it is true that in the fifties the imagination of disaster took a mechanical turn, this new metaphor for dehumanization did not supersede the older one of animality. Rather, they coexisted. There were a number of films, such as *Forbidden Planet,* in which dehumanization was imagined either as the eruption of the primitive, the return of the repressed unconscious—the monster from the *id*—or an attack by the natural world deranged by radiation. The alien as primitive, animal, and natural was a centrist fantasy, while the alien as mechanical and technological was a right-wing fantasy. In fact, since right-wing films used the past to flog the present, the primitive was often sentimentalized in the retrospective glow of nostalgia. The past was not barbarous, as it was to the center, but rather, a simpler, purer time. *Invasion of the*

19. Bell, "The Dispossessed," p. 9.
20. Susan Sontag, "The Imagination of Disaster," in *Against Interpretation* (New York: Dell, 1966), p. 222.

Body Snatchers is suffused with nostalgia for the past, for the old-fashioned, pretechnological family doctor, rather than the newfangled psychiatrist with his glib theories. The family is no longer what it seemed; traditional bonds have eroded. "He was always like a father to me," complains one woman about her spaced-out uncle. "Now there's no emotion." Science has upset the natural order of things. Wondering about the peculiar behavior of the townies, Bennell says, "So many things have been discovered in the last few years, it could be anything."

Invasion presents us with a vision of the perversion of small-town life without the saving cross-cutting to Washington that characterized *Them.* In fact, Washington presents no help at all. Bennell calls the FBI, but the operator tells him that there is no answer. In right-wing films, the federal government, the state, either cannot be reached or is ineffectual. When the government tries to destroy the aliens, it fails. Its weapons are useless against their superior powers.

It is because the government (the center) is either useless or itself evil in these films, that individuals have to take the law into their own hands. After Bennell finally realizes that the pods pose a threat, he spends the rest of the film trying to convince others that he is telling the truth, but they do not believe him. At the end of much right-wing science fiction, average Joe, once regarded by everyone as a loony, finally convinces his friends and neighbors that he has been correct all the time. Community is restored, but on his terms, not theirs. They have been converted to his paranoid vision, and what is more, they have been mobilized for action. These films push the populist sentiments evident in conservative films like *The Thing* to extremes. The alien is destroyed by the resourceful citizens of Smallville without the benefit of federal aid.

In *Them* and *The Thing,* no one expressed a yen for utopias, except perhaps for Carrington, and he was a villain. Alternative forms of life were simply monsters, while alternative societies like the matriarchy of ants were dystopias. But this did not matter, since utopian aspirations were realizable within the institutions of the center. In *Them,* the FBI agent will marry Medford's daughter, just as in *The Thing,* Hendry will marry his girlfriend. But in right-wing films like *Invasion,* Bennell and the heroine have been married and divorced, which is to say, both have discovered that their aspirations cannot be realized within society. For the right, utopian aspirations did not inhere in everyday life; they were transcendent, not immanent. Eric Voegelin, in a book called *The New Science of Politics* (1952), decried the liberal tendency to "immanentize" Christianity, to reduce its otherworldly perspective to an "intramundane range of action," while at the same time striving for the "redivinization of society."[21] These films found their utopia in the new community, the transformed society based on their own principles. This utopia favored the heart over the head. Nature-within is not a monster

21. Quoted in Nash, *The Conservative Intellectual Movement in America,* p. 49.

from the *id,* as it is in a centrist film like *Forbidden Planet,* but "natural" human warmth, normal emotion. "I don't want a world without love or faith or beauty," wails Bennell's sweetheart, and later when she tries to pass for a pod-person and attempts to merge with the crowd, she gives herself away by expressing her feelings, screaming when a dog is run over.

Left-wing films shared the outsider perspective of right-wing films, but they differed from them (and from centrist films as well), in one significant respect. They did not fear aliens. In these films, the alien was neutral, benevolent, superior, or victimized.

It Came from Outer Space (1953) begins like a right-wing film. As in *Invasion of the Body Snatchers,* aliens take over earthlings, and the center—the scientists and police, the guardians of the public weal—are incompetents with their heads in the sand. We are firmly behind John Putnam (Richard Carlson) in his attempts to convince the authorities that a spaceship has indeed landed. But in this film, unlike *Invasion,* the aliens do not mean humans any harm. They have "borrowed" their bodies, not "taken" them. These visitors from outer space have merely had a flat tire and landed on Earth to repair their ship. Nobody yells, "If you don't like it here, go back to outer space," and at the end, when they do, we feel sad. We have learned a lesson in peaceful co-existence.

In *The Day the Earth Stood Still* (1951), the aliens are alternately victimized by, and superior to, humans. Space emissary Klaatu (Michael Rennie) is shot dead, but miraculously resurrects himself in time to warn us to shape up, or our planet will be burnt to a cinder. And in *The Space Children* (1960), the alien is a disembodied brain that floats to earth on the end of a rainbow to frustrate America's launch of a "doomsday missile."

Then there is the poor Creature, hero of *The Creature Walks among Us* (1956), the concluding film of the Creature trilogy. In the first installment, made in 1954, the Creature was mildly sympathetic, more sinned against than sinning, almost a noble savage tormented beyond endurance by the arrogant scientists who mucked about in his lagoon, driven into a frenzy by the spectacle of Kay Lawrence (Julia Adams) swimming above him in a one-piece bathing suit. In *The Creature Walks among Us,* "he" has been removed from his natural habitat entirely, taken in chains to a cage on land where mad scientists perform all sorts of grim experiments on his body. They transplant this, amputate that, move a fin here, a gill there, until his own mother would not recognize him. One of the scientists even tries to frame him for murder, and in the end, he is killed.

Whereas the heroes of right-wing films were Paul Reveres who tried to stir people up to take things into their own hands, these same figures in left-wing films were villains—hysterical vigilantes, dangerous paranoids, and the "people" (as in corporate liberal films) were no better than a mob. Instead of mobilizing people against the alien threat, these films pacified them, protected the aliens from the people. Justifiable alarm to the right was hysteria to the left. In the context of the Red Scare, these were anti–witch-hunt films.

In *It Came from Outer Space,* the fire-eater is a deputy sheriff. "I'd get some rifles into the hands of some men and clean it up, whatever it is," he says fiercely, but he is just a fool. The right-wing whistle-blower in *The Day the Earth Stood Still* is an insurance salesman (Hugh Marlowe) who turns Klaatu over to the authorities. But in this film, he is not treated like a hero; rather, he is a petty, jealous man, and the proper behavior is displayed by Helen Benson (Patricia Neal), who in effect defects to the other side.

Like the right-wing variety, left-wing science fiction polarized the center into a conflict between the individual and the community. The heroes of these films, who saw the spaceship land or shook hands with little green men, were also estranged from society, but whereas right-wing heroes were just average Joes, the left-wing heroes were more likely to have been estranged in the first place. They were Einsteins and Oppenheimers, the eggheads who thought for themselves. The special knowledge of the alien they came to possess merely ratified their pre-existing alienation. Therefore, they were not interested in recasting the community in their own image, as were their right-wing counterparts. Left-wing heroes just wanted to get out.

To the left, like the right, Christianity and utopian aspirations were transcendent, not immanent. They did not inhabit the center, but on the contrary, existed without, in future worlds, or within, beating in the breasts of the disaffected heroes. At the end of *The Day the Earth Stood Still,* Klaatu simply up and left, went back to the galaxy from whence he came. He did not marry Helen Benson, get a job at Brookings, and settle down in Chevy Chase. But unlike the right, the left was pessimistic about the possibility of transforming the community into a utopia—a reflection of its bitter, disillusioned anti-populism.

While the ideological configuration of center, right, and left held throughout the fifties, in the sixties, under the pressure of Vietnam, the center gave way, and films were increasingly polarized between right and left. At the same time, science fiction in film went into a precipitous decline, and it was not until the mid-seventies that *Star Wars,* in the cinematic vanguard of the Carter Restoration, picked up the pieces, reconstructed the center, and initiated a vigorous revival of the genre.

Danse Macabre

Stephen King

If horror movies have redeeming social merit, it is because of that ability to form liaisons between the real and unreal—to provide subtexts. And because of their mass appeal, these subtexts are often culture-wide.

In many cases—particularly in the fifties and then again in the early seventies—the fears expressed are sociopolitical in nature, a fact that gives such disparate pictures as Don Siegel's *Invasion of the Body Snatchers* and William Friedkin's *The Exorcist* a crazily convincing documentary feel. When the horror movies wear their various sociopolitical hats—the B-picture as tabloid editorial—they often serve as an extraordinarily accurate barometer of those things which trouble the night-thoughts of a whole society.

But horror movies don't always wear a hat which identifies them as disguised comments on the social or political scene (as Cronenberg's *The Brood* comments on the disintegration of the generational family or as his *They Came from Within* treats of the more cannibalistic side-effects of Erica Jong's "zipless fuck"). More often the horror movie points even further inward, looking for those deep-seated personal fears—those pressure points—we all must cope with. This adds an element of universality to the proceedings, and may produce an even truer sort of art. It also explains, I think, why *The Exorcist* (a social horror film if there ever was one) did only so-so business when it was released in West Germany, a country which had an entirely different set of social fears at the time (they were a lot more worried about bomb-throwing radicals than about foul-talking young people), and why *Dawn of the Dead* went through the roof there.

This second sort of horror film has more in common with the Brothers Grimm than with the op-ed page in a tabloid paper. It is the B-picture as fairy tale. This sort of picture doesn't want to score political points but to scare the hell out of us by crossing certain taboo lines. So if my idea about art is correct (it giveth more than it receiveth), this sort of film is of value to the audience by helping it to better understand what those taboos and fears are, and why it feels so uneasy about them.

A good example of this second type of horror picture is RKO's *The Body Snatcher* (1945), liberally adapted—and that's putting it kindly—from a Robert Louis Stevenson story and starring Karloff and Lugosi. And by the way, the picture was produced by our friend Val Lewton.

As an example of the art, *The Body Snatcher* is one of the forties' best. And as an example of this second artistic "purpose"—that of breaking taboos—it positively shines.

From *Stephen King's Danse Macabre* (New York: Berkley Books, 1983), pp. 130–132, 5–7.

I think we'd all agree that one of the great fears which all of us must deal with on a purely personal level is the fear of dying; without good old death to fall back on, the horror movies would be in bad shape. A corollary to this is that there are "good" deaths and "bad" deaths; most of us would like to die peacefully in our beds at age eighty (preferably after a good meal, a bottle of really fine *vino,* and a really super lay), but very few of us are interested in finding out how it might feel to get slowly crushed under an automobile lift while crankcase oil drips slowly onto our foreheads.

Lots of horror films derive their best effects from this fear of the bad death (as in *The Abominable Dr. Phibes,* where Phibes dispatches his victims one at a time using the Twelve Plagues of Egypt, slightly updated, a gimmick worthy of the Batman comics during their palmiest days). Who can forget the lethal binoculars in *Horrors of the Black Museum,* for instance? They came equipped with spring-loaded six-inch prongs, so that when the victim put them to her eyes and then attempted to adjust the field of focus . . .

Others derive their horror simply from the fact of death itself, and the decay which follows death. In a society where such a great store is placed in the fragile commodities of youth, health, and beauty (and the latter, it seems to me, is very often defined in terms of the former two), death and decay become inevitably horrible, and inevitably taboo. If you don't think so, ask yourself why the second grade doesn't get to tour the local mortuary along with the police department, the fire department, and the nearest McDonalds—one can imagine, or I can in my more morbid moments, the mortuary and McDonalds combined; the highlights of the tour, of course, would be a viewing of the McCorpse. . . .

There is nothing really physically horrible in the Siegel version of *Invasion of the Body Snatchers;* no gnarled and evil star travelers here, no twisted, mutated shape under the façade of normality. The pod people are just a little different, that's all. A little vague. A little messy. Although Finney never puts this fine a point on it in his book, he certainly suggests that the most horrible thing about "them" is that they lack even the most common and easily attainable sense of aesthetics. Never mind, Finney suggests, that these usurping aliens from outer space can't appreciate *La Traviata* or *Moby Dick* or even a good Norman Rockwell cover on the *Saturday Evening Post.* That's bad enough, but—my God—they don't mow their lawns or replace the pane of garage glass that got broken when the kid down the street batted a baseball through it. They don't repaint their houses when they get flaky. The roads leading into Santa Mira, we're told, are so full of potholes and washouts that pretty soon the salesmen who service the town—who aerate its municipal lungs with the life-giving atmosphere of capitalism, you might say—will no longer bother to come.

The gross-out level is one thing, but it is on that second level of horror that we often experience that low sense of anxiety which we call "the creeps." Over the years, *Invasion of the Body Snatchers* has given a lot of people the creeps, and all sorts of high-flown ideas have been imputed to Siegel's film version. It was seen as an anti-McCarthy film until someone pointed out the fact that Don Siegel's political views could hardly be called leftish. Then people began seeing it as a "better dead than Red" picture. Of the two ideas, I think that second one better fits the film that Siegel made, the picture that ends with Kevin McCarthy in the middle of a freeway, screaming "They're here already! You're next!" to cars which rush heedlessly by him. But in my heart, I don't really believe that Siegel was wearing a political hat at all when he made the movie (and you will see later that Jack Finney has never believed it, either); I believe he was simply having fun and that the undertones . . . just happened.

This doesn't invalidate the idea that there is an allegorical element in *Invasion of the Body Snatchers;* it is simply to suggest that sometimes these pressure points, these terminals of fear, are so deeply buried and yet so vital that we may tap them like artesian wells—saying one thing out loud while we express something else in a whisper. The Philip Kaufman version of Finney's novel is fun (although, to be fair, not quite as much fun as Siegel's), but that whisper has changed into something entirely different: the subtext of Kaufman's picture seems to satirize the whole I'm-okay-you're-okay-so-let's-get-in-the-hot-tub-and-massage-our-precious-consciousness movement of the egocentric seventies. Which is to suggest that, although the uneasy dreams of the mass subconscious may change from decade to decade, the pipeline into that well of dreams remains constant and vital.

This is the real danse macabre, I suspect: those remarkable moments when the creator of a horror story is able to unite the conscious and subconscious mind with one potent idea. I believe it happened to a greater degree with the Siegel version of *Invasion of the Body Snatchers,* but of course both Siegel and Kaufman were able to proceed courtesy of Jack Finney, who sank the original well.

Kiss Me Deadly:
Communism, Motherhood,
and Cold War Movies

Michael Paul Rogin

When President Reagan insisted that movies show us how we feel, he collapsed the distinction between the producers and consumers of movies. That collapse had a social and psychological intention as well as a political one; it absorbed the world outside movies into film. We were to learn how we already felt by seeing our (ideal) selves reflected on the screen. If successful, that process would obliterate our subversive, hidden interiors and render the need for political surveillance obsolete. (Should movies fail in showing us how we felt, an emissary from Hollywood not altogether successful in them would have to enter politics and go to Washington.) But that very process, the loss of the self to its manufactured and controlled double, recurred as nightmare within one movie genre of the 1950s. Cold war science fiction generalized film as secret influence from the restricted homologies of family and state and depicted the spread of that secret influence throughout society.

If we use movie attendance figures to chart the intersection of popular feelings and Hollywood anxiety, then we must turn from explicitly anti-Communist films to science fiction. The American masses went to movies that raised anxieties not about politics but about mass society. Science fiction films presented an undifferentiated, homogeneous social world in which reality offered little resistance to the takeover by dream. Having examined the first two layers of American domestic anxiety—mom's identification with Communism and her replacement by the state—we look finally at the return of the repressed. Just as cold war movies made mom a condensation symbol and scapegoat for political and familial worries, science fiction films generated mass society not from movie but from female influence.

Aside from its anti-Communist films, Hollywood avoided political themes in the 1950s. Monogram Studios dropped plans for a movie on Hiawatha; it feared that his efforts for peace among the Iroquois nations would be seen as aiding Communist peace propaganda. Judy Holliday, called before HUAC for supporting Henry Wallace, insisted, "I don't say 'yes' to anything now except cancer, polio, and cerebral palsy, things like that." By listing diseases as the only safe evils to oppose, Holliday unwittingly suggested the logic of countersubversion that equated Communism with disease. She also inadvertently explained the popularity of those films whose alien invaders came not from political conspiracies

From *Ronald Reagan, the Movie and Other Episodes in Political Demonology* (Berkeley and Los Angeles: University of California Press, 1987), pp. 262–267.

but from outer space. Jack Warner attacked "ideological termites" before HUAC, "subversive germs hiding in dark corners." Gordon Douglas, who directed *I Was a Communist* in 1951, made the giant-ant movie *Them!* three years later. It was one of Warner Brothers' highest grossing movies of 1954. The "germs of death for society" that Truman's attorney general said were carried by Communists spread from Hollywood through science fiction.[1]

Biology is out of control in such movies as *Them!*, *The Thing,* and *Invasion of the Body Snatchers.* Promiscuous, undifferentiated, vegetable reproduction threatens family bonds. Reproduction dispenses with the father in *Body Snatchers* and *The Thing.* The aliens multiply promiscuously, through detachable body parts in *The Thing* (1951) and through generative pods in *Body Snatchers* (1956). Like the opened box in *Kiss Me Deadly* [1955], the ovarian pods spread destruction.

The monster was a sympathetic character in the classic monster movie. Embodying savage or aristocratic masculine desire, he stood against genteel, feminine culture. *The Thing* seems at first to carry on that tradition. Its monster, a lone, male descendant of King Kong, is menaced by the forces of civilization. But earlier monsters like Dracula and the werewolf were hungry males who fed off female bodies. The Thing reproduces himself; severed parts of his own body grow into new monsters. When we are shown the planter boxes in which these Things are multiplying, we lose all sympathy for the monster. We do not see simulacra of the male Thing, moreover, but plants with ovarian pods. The movie has transformed a single male monster into multiple, reproductive vegetables.[2]

The Thing is transitional between the classic movie monster and his 1950s female descendants. Male insects are present in *Them!* (1954); they fertilize the queen ants and die. A mutation from atomic testing has produced the giant ants, and a scientist working with the police destroys most of them. But a single queen, fertilized by the male members of her court, can give birth to enough ants

1. Robert Justin Goldstein, *Political Repression in Modern America* (Cambridge, Mass.: Schenkman, 1978), pp. 362, 377; University Art Museum, *Calendar* (October 1982), 9.
2. On the contrast between the classic monster movie and the 1950s creature feature, see Andrew Griffin, "Sympathy for the Werewolf," in *The Borzoi College Reader,* ed. Charles Muscatine and Marlene Griffith, 4th ed. (New York: Alfred A. Knopf, 1980), pp. 508–512.

A complementary transition is visible in the contrast between the two 3-D monster movies of the 1950s, *Creature from the Black Lagoon* (1954) and *It Came from Outer Space* (1953). *Creature* is in the classic tradition; the monster is supposed to be threatening; like the bad explorer who tracks him, he attacks the female lead. Until he is provoked by the explorer, however, the monster wants only to be left alone, and he is finally allowed by the good explorer to return to the sea to die. *It Came from Outer Space,* by contrast, intends to create sympathy for the aliens; they only need time to repair their spaceship and leave an earth that is not yet ready for them. But since the aliens take over human bodies (foreshadowing *Body Snatchers*) and since their symbol is an enormous (surveilling) eye, the audience rightly shares the townspeople's terror. The creature from the lagoon emerges from primitive and fecund nature; that presocial past is more sympathetic in American 1950s iconography, whatever the filmmakers thought they were doing, than the blankness of the desert in the other film and the outer space future to which it points. On the films' intentions, see Peter Biskind, *Seeing Is Believing: How Hollywood Taught Us to Stop Worrying and Love the Fifties* (New York: Random House, Pantheon Books, 1983), pp. 107–108, 147–151.

to destroy all humanity. The danger of reproductive world destruction hangs over the movie.

Female ants undergo the transformation from "Cinderella" to mom that Philip Wylie depicted for women. Each female, a "princess" until she mates, then lays eggs for fifteen years. Never leaving her nest, she presides over an aggressive collectivist society. Ants are "chronic aggressors, [who] make slave laborers out of their captives," and a scientist shows movies to emphasize the "industry, social organization, and savagery" of the ants. "Unless the queens are destroyed," he warns, "man as the dominant species on this planet will probably be destroyed." The scientist is warning the audience within the film about ants; he is warning the audience outside the film about Communism. As in *My Son John* [1952] and *The Manchurian Candidate* [1962], however, the sexual threat absorbs the political one.

Two surviving queen ants fly off with their "consorts" after the first giant-ant colony is destroyed. "They are gone on their wedding flight," explains the scientist. These ants are enacting the dark side of the John Wayne–Janet Leigh romance in *Jet Pilot* [1957]. The flying planes engaged in sexual foreplay, which first threatened the man but finally domesticated the woman. The male ants will die in the service of the mother. An observer who sees one of the airborne wedding parties describes "one big one [the queen] and two little ones [her consorts]." He is hospitalized for hallucinating, and his belt is removed so he cannot escape. The man who saw the queen ant clutches at his pants as he tells his story; he has become, like the male ants, her victim. We are shown the ants' world, which lies deep within the bowels of the earth early in the movie, deep within the Los Angeles storm drain system at its climax. That world is a matriarchy.

Traced to their cloacal sanctuary, the giant ants are finally destroyed. "Has the cold war gotten hot?" a reporter wants to know when the army is sent to Los Angeles. His words name the political allegory, anty-communism, but the action supplants it with the sexual allegory. Modern fire power is mobilized against the reproducing monsters as flame-throwing bazookas and other long guns invade the ants' inner space. The army penetrates to the "egg chamber," with its strong "brood odor," and destroys it in a holocaust of fire. Soldiers rescue two boys whom the ants have kidnapped and brought to the queen's chamber. The ants have killed the boys' father; they also kill the policeman (James Whitmore), the protagonist of the movie. But by restoring the boys to their mother, the army saves the (truncated) American family.

The ants are bad mothers who breed in storm drains instead of the home. But breeding itself is the problem in these films. The ants, the pods, and the Thing proliferate identities. The creatures they create are interchangeable parts, members of a mass society. Freed of the name of the father and of the mother's singular love, these creatures lack the stamp of individuality. They replace individual identities (identity as difference) with identities identical and out of control.

The mother in domestic ideology made her son feel loved by sacrificing her identity to his. *My Son John* exposed that special bond as the source of Communist influence. But if unique individual identity is suspect, its obverse is just as bad. Mothers in *Them!* claim direct power. The consequence (seen also in *Body Snatchers*) is the multiplication of identical selves. Deprived of maternal love, one identity is not different from another. The division of the products of labor has entered the reproductive labor process, mobilizing fears of procreation without love. The body snatchers replicate townspeople, who now function efficiently and interchangeably. Both *Them!* and *Body Snatchers* evoke the nightmare of uncontrolled female generativity. The two films join nature's revenge against man to the triumph of mass society.

Body Snatchers, unlike *Them!*, is a self-aware film; Don Siegel made it in protest against pressures for political and social conformity. Since socialization is triumphant both in McCarthyism and Communism (in the 1950s liberal view), "the malignant disease spreading through the country, cell for cell, atom for atom" can represent either danger. *Body Snatchers* could be a McCarthyite warning against Communism, like *Them!*; it could be a protest against what one writer has called the "unnatural, menacing, even alien . . . bloblike growth of the postwar," self-replicating suburbs. "I wanted to end the picture at the point where McCarthy is standing in the highway," Siegel has said. "He turns, points his finger at the audience and yells, 'You're next.' " Siegel was referring to Kevin McCarthy, who starred in the movie; but the actor has the politician's name, as if to raise doubts about whether Joe McCarthy is the movie's hidden hero or villain. *Body Snatchers* may reflect awareness (unlike *Them!*) that fears of foreign, Communist influence displaced fears of mass domestic conformity. Nonetheless, its political consciousness, like that in cold war cinema generally, is subordinate to its sexual unconsciousness.[3]

Anti-Communist films demand eternal vigilance to protect self and country from invasion. Self-surveillance in *Body Snatchers* makes sleep itself impossible. Humans must stay awake forever, for they are replaced by pods when they sleep. The film deprives sleep of its function as social escape, for sleep makes the relaxed self vulnerable. Danger may come from without in *Body Snatchers,* but what needs to be defended against is the wish from within. The unconscious takes over from self-vigilance in sleep. And the dream wish of the 1950s was to escape from the anxiety of separate identity and to merge with society.

As if in support of Emile Durkheim's identification—"Society is the . . . nourishing mother"[4]—a woman is the unconscious's source of temptation in

---

3. University Art Museum, *Calendar* (November 1982), 9; Ron Rosen, "The House That Levitt Built," *Esquire* (December 1983), 380. For interpretation of *Body Snatchers* as a right-wing film, see Biskind, *Seeing Is Believing,* pp. 137–144.
4. Quoted in Christopher Lasch, *Haven in a Heartless World: The Family Besieged* (New York: Basic Books, 1977), p. 13.

Body Snatchers. The film's heroine succumbs to sleep. Now a pod, she tries with a kiss to draw the hero into sleeping with her. Her kiss is deadly, however, as he can tell from the dead feel of her lips. Totally alone, McCarthy must flee the sleep that would cost him his identity. Advertisements for *Body Snatchers* depicted the kiss as if it united the lovers. But alongside the copy, which presented them alone against the world, a menacing female reaches out to envelop her man. *Body Snatchers*, like *Manchurian Candidate*, united deceit with bodily invasion and located both in female influence.

Human beings are "hosts to an alien form of life" in *Body Snatchers*. Just as the Communists in *I Was a Communist* want "not just our bodies but our minds," so the body snatchers are "taking us over, cell by cell."[5] Matt Cvetic, pretending to be taken over by a Communist cell, represents Communism's threat to personal identity. That threat is deepened in *Body Snatchers* and *Invaders from Mars* (1953). Cvetic alienated his family by masquerading as a Communist. The pods in *Body Snatchers* and the people implanted with electronic control devices in *Invaders from Mars* alienate their families by pretending still to be themselves. Reds were visibly alien in earlier Red Scares; they were the others. They moved inside our minds and bodies in the 1950s, and one could not tell them from anyone else. The vulnerability of the self to influence, upon which domestic ideology had hoped to capitalize, resulted in Communist influence instead. Surveillance and inquisition exposed domestic forces that had taken possession of the nation and the self. No longer part of a conflict between contrasting classes, 1950s Communists were the invisible members of (and thereby exposed anxieties about) American mass society.

Hollywood both responded to and encouraged the retreat to private life, the depoliticization of America encouraged by the Red Scare. But in the Hollywood films of private life, the promised family sanctuary is problematic; it is threatened by invasion from without and seduction from within. Families under siege generated anxieties about who was to blame, anxieties that could take the form of anti-Communism. But anti-Communist films, in spite of their conscious intentions, exposed the connections between an endangered private life and a fear of political subversion.

5. Nora Sayre, *Running Time* (New York: Dial Press, 1982), p. 201.

Women and the Inner Game of Don Siegel's *Invasion of the Body Snatchers*

Nancy Steffen-Fluhr

> To strive, to seek, to find, and not to yield.
>
> Tennyson, "Ulysses"

> There is no joy but calm.
>
> Tennyson, "The Lotus Eaters"

Sometimes I teach my students; sometimes they teach me. Consider the case of *Invasion of the Body Snatchers* (1956; dir. Don Siegel). I was screening it for my SF class one crisp autumn afternoon not long ago; I was going to tell them what it was all about. They were reacting pretty much the way I wanted them to—snickering at first at the baggy suits, the big cars, the grainy film stock. (The '50s were as strange as Mars to them.) But then the sheer pace and energy of the film caught and held them rapt. The chase was on . . .

Once again Kevin McCarthy and Dana Wynter ("Miles" and "Becky") are scrambling up the foothills outside mythical Santa Mira, pursued by the pod people. She, the weaker vessel, is faint from lack of sleep. (Mustn't sleep or the pods will steal your mind.) He carries her in his arms like a child. They reach an abandoned mine tunnel high up the hill. The camera freezes them for a second in a low angle silhouette, framed by the key hole of the shaft entrance.[1] They enter the dark tunnel and bury themselves under the floor boards. When the danger passes, they emerge and splash their faces with water. (Mustn't sleep.) Suddenly they are mesmerized by a sound they have not heard for a long time: human music, a wordless lullaby in a high maternal croon. Miles is drawn irresistibly toward that sound, and, for the first time since the crisis began, he separates from Becky, leaving her in the cave while he follows the music to its source: alas, a radio in a pod truck. When he returns to the cave, he finds her asleep. (Mustn't sleep.) He shakes her awake and drags her down the tunnel. Spent, they fall together in the muddy water. He embraces her with desperate passion. Hovering above, we see her white arm coil about his neck. Then Siegel, who has saved his quota of close-ups for just this moment, suddenly gives us two very tight shock

From *Science-Fiction Studies* 11 (July 1984): 139–151.
1. A popular shot that year: cf. John Ford's *The Searchers* (Warner Brothers, 1956), especially the climactic sequence in which John Wayne lifts Natalie Wood in his arms.

shots in rapid succession: her face, empty Gorgon's eyes staring quietly; his face, recoiling, eyes saucered open in terror. He has just kissed a pod! She—his partner, his soul-mate, his other half—is one of Them now. "Stop acting like a fool, Miles, and accept us," she snaps. "No." His eyes are shut tight; his lips, a thin hard line. "Never." She turns on him, denouncing, screaming out to the other pods. He bolts and runs from her. We see his back in long shot as he flees the tunnel and scuttles down the hill, growing smaller and smaller. Voice-over: "I'd been afraid a lot of times in my life, but I didn't know the real meaning of fear until I kissed Becky."

Here, quite unaccountably, my students laughed again—not a titter but a big explosive boff that shook the classroom. I was taken aback; then I was taken over. For in that laughter, implicit and complete, was a critique all the more perceptive for its innocence. They had seen the film more honestly than I had. What, their laughter asked, what *is* so scary about Becky? What *is* so scary about a kiss?

Let us rewind the film's metaphors and ask those questions again in proper context. *Invasion of the Body Snatchers* is a *film noir,* a male nightmare in black and grey; but it begins in broad daylight on Main Street, Santa Mira, California. The occasion is a homecoming of sorts. Dr. Miles Bennell, returning after a trip to the big city, discovers that the old town isn't what it used to be. A sort of decay has set in: shops closed, businesses gone to seed. Moreover, an increasing number of otherwise solid citizens seem to be going crazy, convinced that their friends and relatives are false faces, impostors. Little Jimmy Grimaldi runs from his home screaming, "She's not my mother! She's not!" Sensible Wilma Lenz accuses her Uncle Ira:

> Miles, he looks, sounds, acts, and remembers like Uncle Ira. . . . But
> there's something missing. He was like a father to me since I was a baby,
> and always when he talked to me there was a special look in his
> eyes. . . . That look's gone. . . . There's no emotion—none—only the pre-
> tense of it. The words, the gestures, the tone of voice, everything else is the
> same—but not the *feeling*.

Dan Kaufman, the town psychiatrist, is reassuring, philosophic. It's just a little touch of mass hysteria, he says—"worry about what's going on in the world, probably." He'll take Wilma into therapy and persuade her that her feelings are silly. He advises Miles to drop the matter, but Miles has a hunch that there's more to it; and he follows his hunch . . . into a suburban heart of darkness.

Something else is new in Santa Mira; or rather, something old is new again. Becky Driscoll, Miles's college sweetheart, has returned home from a sojourn in England, like Miles freshly divorced. She turns up unexpectedly in his life—at precisely the same time that the impostor trouble does—and they are immediately drawn to each other. As the crisis grows, so does their passion. Like the impostors, their intimacy is at once familiar and yet infinitely strange—a fine madness which parallels and comments upon the general madness sweeping Santa Mira.

Still tender from the pain of their recent divorces, neither Miles nor Becky especially wants to fall in love; love simply happens to them, as the alien invasion simply happens, unanticipated, unprovoked, a force beyond their control. Their inability to control their feelings troubles them both; they dig their heels in against it, especially Miles, who spends almost as much time exhorting Becky "not to get involved with a doctor" as he does ogling her cleavage.[2]

At first sight, Miles's coyness—indeed, the whole Miles-Becky relationship— seems to be an afterthought, a conventional love-interest grafted onto the main plot stem. In fact, it is Siegel's essential text. The come-close/go-away pulse of Miles's emotions is the heartbeat of the film.[3] It is his burgeoning intimacy with Becky, not the burgeoning pods, which is the hidden source of his fear. She is the familiar stranger, alien flesh to which he is about to bond himself, and he is worried that this merger may entail some loss of freedom and identity. The pod plot is, at least in part, simply a surrealistic projection of these unacknowledged anxieties, of a man's terror of falling helplessly in love.

Criticism of the film has tended to ignore its *liebestod* motif, concentrating instead on the political implications of the prologue and epilogue.[4] However,

2. Wynter's first-reel costume is a reflection of 1950s' sexism: it is a strapless sun-dress in demure gingham except for the bra-style white bodice. This bodice seems to expose her breasts to our gaze, even as it rigidly restrains them from any natural movement.
3. Heterosexual tension is a much more obvious theme in Philip Kaufman's 1978 remake. Kaufman's blatant sexual imagery has been analyzed perceptively by a number of critics, including Sumiko Higashi (*"Invasion of the Body Snatchers*: Pods Then and Now," *Jump Cut* 24/25 [1981]:3–4). Higashi, however, takes a traditional view towards Siegel's film, regarding it primarily as a '50s mood piece whose "basic network . . . is the family and apprehension about threats to its survival" (p. 3).
4. As Siegel originally shot it, the film begins when Miles returns to Santa Mira and ends with him on a highway bridge screaming out his warnings to the passing cars. However, after previewing the film, Allied Artists executives insisted on adding a prologue and epilogue. Ostensibly, they were afraid that audiences wouldn't understand the plot, although their motivation is often seen as political. Producer Walter Wanger, supported by Daniel Mainwaring, apparently persuaded Siegel to shoot the additional footage himself, in order to enhance his control over the final product. (See Guy Braucourt, "Interview with Don Siegel" [1970], reprinted in *Focus on the Science Fiction Film*, ed. William Johnson [Englewood Cliffs, N.J., 1972], pp. 74–75; and also Stuart Kaminsky, "Don Siegel on *Invasion of the Body Snatchers*," *Cinéfantastique* 2 (1972/73):17.
This new narrative frame (in which the entire plot is a story told by an ostensibly crazy Miles to his doctors) has tempted some allegorical-minded interpreters to decode the film as a right-wing validation of Joe McCarthy's accusations: the pods are real! For instance, Rob Baker, reviewing the film during a retrospective showing, called it "Invasion of the Pinkos" and derided it as "one of the most mind-boggling right-wing diatribes against the Red-Menace" (*Soho Weekly News*, Aug. 18, 1977, p. 48). Others have concluded that *Invasion* is a surreptitious *left-wing* satire of anti-Communist paranoia: they note that Kevin McCarthy and Joe McCarthy share a common surname and that even with the epilogue in place, Miles can be regarded as an unreliable narrator, in the mode of Dowell in Ford

Siegel's own statements make it clear that love, not Cold War, was his primary subject in *Invasion*. Although he tried to capture the mood of the '50s, its nervousness and buttoned-down repressions, he was not making a political allegory but, rather, a defense of passion, risk-taking, and active engagement. "All of us who worked on the film believed in what it said—that the majority of people in the world are pods, existing without any intellectual aspirations and incapable of love."[5]

Insofar as Siegel is asserting the primacy of emotion against the false lure of security and conformity, his stance is admirable. Yet there is a sour, judgmental undertone in his statement, a disturbingly elitist conception of human life. Strident, devoid of humor and humility, intolerant of ordinary fears and everyday helplessness, it suggests a mind not quite at ease with itself.

That fundamental uneasiness, masked as bravado, is the inner voice of *Invasion,* a male voice crying out in a world grown weary and womanish. This is not a John Sayles film in which She and He are part of a lively, humane dialectic of the self. In *Invasion* the relationship is between Them and Us, and I and Thou. Thus, although Becky is one of the most important characters in the film, she is a mute object rather than a controlling consciousness. "She" has no voice in this male chorus. From the very first, not merely at the climax, She is the Other, an alien.

In short, the inner game of *Invasion* is a very traditional version of the War Between the Sexes in which overt antagonism has been suppressed and reprojected as a War of the Worlds.[6] As in the narratives of Mickey Spillane, which serve Siegel as a tacit paradigm, gender conflicts begin as a Cold War which gradually heats up as the romance between Miles and Becky catches fire. At first there is merely vague anxiety, a sense of change and strangeness. Then there is a palpable problem, a mystery to be solved: a body.

Incongruously, this particular body problem inverts the usual rules in mysteries. It is not a living being which has become an inert object but an inert object on the verge of becoming a living being. Something strange and new is growing, coming to life in Santa Mira, just as Miles and Becky are growing together, coming to life emotionally.

Maddox Ford's *The Good Soldier.* More usually, however, *Invasion* is treated, not as a strict allegory, but as a kind of fractured mirror of the 1950s. (See Ernesto G. Laura, "Invasion of the Body Snatchers" [1957], reprinted in *Focus in the Science Film, ed. cit.,* pp. 71–73; Stuart Samuels, "Invasion of the Body Snatchers" [1956], in *American History/American Film,* ed. John E. O'Connor & Martin A. Jackson (New York: 1979), pp. 204–217; and Arthur Le Gacy, "*Invasion of the Body Snatchers*: A Metaphor for the Fifties," *Literature/Film Quarterly* 1 [1978]:285–292.) For a view of *Invasion* somewhat closer to my own, see J. P. Telotte, "The Doubles of Fantasy and the Space of Desire," *Film Criticism* 7 (1982):61–63.
5. Guy Braucourt, "Interview with Don Siegel," p. 75.
6. Cf. Joanna Russ, "*Amor Vincit Foeminam*: The Battle of the Sexes in Science Fiction," *SFS* 7 (1980):2–15.

Miles's best friend, the mystery writer, Jack Belicec, and Jack's wife, "Teddy," discover this strange body neatly laid out on their basement pool table, as if it had dropped in for a nap. Perhaps because his profession has inured him to corpses, Belicec is more curious than disconcerted. He examines the body, finds it uninjured yet inert, perfect in every part yet oddly lacking something; he cannot say quite what. All of which moves him quietly to call for help—not to the authorities but to Miles.

The timing of Belicec's call is as important as its content. It interrupts an intimate dinner which Miles had arranged as part of his plan for seducing Becky, the focus of his teenage lusts. It is the first of many such interruptions which will prevent Miles and Becky both from sleeping and from sleeping with each other.

On the one hand, the pod crisis stimulates the passion between them. It accelerates the pace of life, reminding both that time is precious, cautioning them against coyness. In effect, this is a war-time romance, undercranked, almost desperate in its urgency. On the other hand, the pod crisis offers a convenient rationale for postponing sexual intimacy. In other words, the pods are associated simultaneously with both a sudden heightening of sexual desire and also with a heightened fear of the consequences of that desire, that sleep: loss of self, loss of individuality, surrender. In the second half of the film, Miles's fear of surrendering to the aliens—and all they represent—is precisely parallel to his unarticulated fear of other surrenders: to Becky and all that she represents; to his own passion; and, most importantly, to his own desire for surcease.

Belicec's call also serves to emphasize Miles's essential puritanism. He immediately stops the music, snuffs out the candles, and prepares to leave. Work before pleasure. ("Never get involved with a doctor, Becky.") The intellectual lure of this new "body problem" readily supersedes (even as it subtly parallels) the lure of Becky's body. When duty calls, emotions will have to get out of the way.

The scene in the Belicecs' basement is one of the oddest in this rather odd and fascinating film, charged with unarticulated anxieties. Miles, ever the calm professional, strips back the tarp and cooly examines the body on the pool table. It is a little unusual: perfect yet somehow incomplete; its facial features indistinct, like a blank coin waiting to be stamped; it has no fingerprints: lacking in identity. Curiouser and curiouser.

Like over-aged Alices in a rec-room underground, both couples agree to let things lie, as it were, to see if anything develops. Incredibly, they cover up the body and go off to the bar in the opposite corner for drinks and chitchat. Something does develop almost immediately, although its significance won't be clear until much later. Teddy casually observes that the "blank" body looks a lot like Jack. In sudden shock, he reacts, cutting himself with a glass, producing a bloody longitudinal gash along the palm of his left hand.

The bloody gash is one of several disturbing visual synecdoches for "woman" with which this film is littered—graffiti-like cartoons which represent in the abstract what men regard as the salient features of the female genitals. For instance, as Miles will shortly discover, the inert male body on the pool table and thousands of others like it initially grow in large seed pods. When they are actively reproducing, these pods strongly resemble ovaries in both form and function. When they are not active, when they are closed, awaiting the touch of mind necessary to fertilize them, they resemble closed female pudenda—oval shapes bisected by a longitudinal seam.

Throughout the second half of the film, these pods, especially in their closed, passive state, are objects of such horror that Miles's eyes dilate in terror every time he sees them. In terms of the film's overt plot, of course, this terror is perfectly rational. These pods are aliens come to conquer Earth and make it their own. They are the progeny of beings from another part of the universe who have been forced to abandon their dying world and to seek a new home. Like Wells's Martians in *The War of the Worlds,* they are all brain, no heart, hyper-Victorians, a *reductio ad absurdum* of the Protestant Work Ethic. Emotionless, conformist, they obey orders from totalitarian leaders. In a desperate bid for survival, they have shot their seed into space. After eons of aimless drifting, it has fallen to Earth like warm rain and taken root in the soil of Santa Mira. The pods themselves are merely a transitional and transitory life-form, designed solely for reproduction.

The story of the alien pods is an artfully disguised version of certain ancient patriarchic myths about reproduction. In these myths, it is asserted that the fetus is a *homunculus,* complete at conception, and the pregnant woman merely a pod. Human life, the immortal spirit which animates mere matter and makes it grow, is deemed to come from the male sperm alone. The female body is mere mortal clay, the loamy substratum upon which the male soul does its work. From this theory logically flows a misogynistic caricature of Woman-as-Body and therefore Woman-as-Death. The She, synecdochized as a vagina, is the Yeatsian "dying-beast" to which the male soul is chained. In short, this patriarchic myth of conception begins as a pathological denial of women's central role in reproduction. This denial serves to cover up terrible doubt about the male role in procreation, the fear that women might be able to do the whole thing by themselves, might not need men at all. But fears as powerful as these don't stay covered up; and thus the initial, suppressed vision of women as all-powerful creatures resurfaces in extreme ascetic versions of this myth, in which Woman's body is deemed to be the locus of death.[7]

The role of the pods in *Invasion* is precisely parallel to the role of women in these patriarchic myths. Paradoxically, they are both sources of new life and sources of death. Indeed, it is their very fecundity which makes them so

---

7. Similar analyses appear in many histories of misogyny, including: Katherine M. Rogers, *The Troublesome Helpmate* (Seattle, 1966), pp. 36–37; and Wolfgang Lederer, *The Fear of Women* (New York, 1968), pp. 154–158.

dangerous. They want to take over, to make everybody like them, to make everyone the same.

The fear of sameness which pervades *Invasion* ("alike as two peas in a pod") is a direct expression of Siegel's vaunted disdain for conformity. Less obviously, perhaps, this fear also reflects the impact of socio-economic changes on traditional gender roles. To repeat a now-familiar story: during the Second World War, faced with an acute shortage of civilian male labor, the government implemented a propaganda campaign to persuade women to leave their normal role as homemakers and to take up occupations previously reserved for men—e.g., as welders and riveters, to cite a clichéd but important example. For the first time in their lives, many women became breadwinners, doing socially important work for adequate pay. However, after V-J Day, when the men came home and the need for a female labor force had ceased, most of these women were summarily fired. The government initiated a new propaganda campaign designed to coerce women back into the home. They went, by and large, but their experience engendered considerable bitterness.[8] Propaganda tracts notwithstanding, family life never returned to pre-war norms. Faced with major demographic shifts and prolonged periods of recession, many men, too, found it difficult to take up their old lives, to find work. These economic changes, complicated by the existential fears generated by the Cold War, served to make the 1950s an exceptionally anxious time for most Americans, despite a great deal of cheery whistling in the dark.

Inevitably, much of this anxiety focused on gender roles. Confronted with a vaguely articulated but nonetheless palpable threat to their traditional dominant status, many men returned with renewed vigor to old patriarchal verities, the first and foremost of which is a belief in the intrinsic inferiority of women. Yet, paradoxically, this ancient dictum tended to exacerbate rather than to allay male anxiety. For once the specter of gender role reversal has been raised, however tacitly and quietly, the definition of women as persons who "lack" something becomes a terrible void into which men themselves may fall, or be pushed.

To reverse Professor Higgin's famous sexist lament: Why can't a man be more like a *woman*? Why? Because, according to the patriarchy, a woman isn't much of anything at all—at best, she is a sort of man manqué. Sigmund Freud was quite correct when he argued that the female genital is perceived by men not as an organ in its own right, complex and complete, but as a mutilated male crotch. A *vagina* is what a man would have if he didn't have his penis and testicles. However, the equation of *Woman* with *lack* is more extensive than Freud, ever the literal-minded materialist, detected.

If the vulva is perceived as an absence rather than a presence, so, too, are a whole set of human characteristics and capabilities with which woman is traditionally associated and often thought to personify. Thus, intuitive, holistic thinking is perceived as an absence of analytical logic; emotional motility is perceived

8. See Connie Field's telling documentary film, *The Life and Times of Rosie the Riveter* (1980).

as an absence of self-control; openness and receptivity as an absence of strength; passivity as an absence of self-assertion.

I take it for granted that little girls intrinsically are no more intuitive, emotional, open, or passive than are little boys. But the belief that they are has had the force of a self-fulfilling prophecy—i.e., little girls have been routinely trained to accept passivity in themselves, just as little boys have been trained to abhor it in themselves. The result of this training is that the traditional, Ideal Woman is only half a person, just as the Ideal Man is only half a person—both genders estranged from many of their most important desires. In fictions, as in dreams, these estranged desires reassert themselves in powerful and distorted form as the Alien, the Monster, the Other, the fatal *Doppelgänger*.[9]

The body on the Belicecs' pool table is just such a *Doppelgänger*. Its principal characteristics are lack and passivity, and it is precisely these characteristics which so unhinge Jack when his wife suggests that "it" resembles him—or worse, that he resembles "it." Teddy (an onomastic androgyne) has thought the unthinkable: why *can't* a man be more like a woman? Her husband responds with a phatic gesture (the cut on the palm) which expresses both the dimensions of his terror and its content. He is not merely "acting out" a castration fear, as Freud would have it. (After all, Jack is a fictional construct, not a person, and therefore not subject to psychoanalysis.) He is the vehicle through which Siegel and his scriptwriter, the late Daniel Mainwaring, first begin to assert their resolute rejection of womanish passivity.

Remember that, thus far, Jack knows nothing at all about the alien invasion. He has no rational reason to feel so threatened. His terror, therefore, is a direct measure of his (and Siegel's) horror of the body *qua* body, vulnerable, quiet, active-less, perhaps even penis-less. (What, exactly, does Miles see, or not see, when he lifts the tarp and peers at the body? Siegel conceals the precise topography of the pod's body from us.)

Odder still is the nature of the gesture in which Jack's fear is conveyed—the cut. Like the visual paradoxes of dream structures, it confirms precisely what he seeks to deny: the identity between him and it. Significantly, it is Teddy who is the lone witness to this confirmation. Later that night, while Jack sleeps, she sees the stigmata appear on the pod-body's left palm.

At this point in the film, it is Jack and Teddy, the vehicles of the ostensible subplot, who carry Siegel's main theme. But their interaction is adumbrated by a night-world drama between Miles and Becky. She has gone back to her father's house to sleep. Miles, disturbed by what he has seen, resists sleep. A sudden intuition strikes him: perhaps Becky's father, like Wilma's Uncle Ira, is an impostor of some sort. He rushes to the Driscoll house and, while she dreams in her bedroom above, he prowls through her basement. He discovers a coal bin,

---

9. For a Marxist view of the Alien as "the return of the repressed," see John Rieder, "Embracing the Alien: Science Fiction in Mass Culture," *SFS* 9 (1982):26–37.

coffinlike, amid the garden tools. When he lifts the lid, he sees Becky inside—or, rather, sees Becky's body, inert, with eyes closed, a nimbus of foam framing her head. Siegel gives us only the briefest glimpse of this inert form; he holds instead on a close shot of Miles's reacting face. Miles had been calm and reassuring earlier when Jack had his moment of terror; now it is his turn to be afraid. The sight of that female body, waiting, overwhelms even his formidable defenses. He slams down the lid and flees from "it" to "her"—the upstairs, spiritual her, asleep in her childhood bed. Roughly, he shakes her awake, forces her out of her night-time passivity.

This is the first instance of what soon becomes the major theme of *Invasion*: a dialectic between sleep and wakefulness, between deadly "alien" passivity and passionate human activity (i.e., between stereotypical female and male modes.) This dialectic is further complicated because, in *Invasion*, "to sleep" is linked to the euphemism for sexual intercourse, "to sleep with." Like Metaphysical poets, Siegel and Mainwaring thus yoke together two antithetical human experiences: the "little death" of orgasm and the Big Death we share with everything that breathes and has being, including plants.[10]

Becky's wakening brings on the dawn, and, with it, the threatening androgynous *noir* world is washed out by a steadier consciousness. This consciousness is personified by none other than Doc Kaufman, the psychiatrist, to whom Miles and Jack have turned for help. At the tail end of the night, the three men gather in the Belicecs' basement to examine the body again. But it has vanished! There is nothing but a tarp and a pool table. Kaufman reassures Jack and Miles the way he had earlier reassured Wilma. Their fears are silly. Yes, there was a body on the pool table, but there was nothing mysterious or extrater-

---

10. Siegel has always hated the title the studio gave to the film and would have much preferred Kevin McCarthy's suggestion that it be called "Sleep No More." (See Shakespeare's *Hamlet*, III.i.60–70 and also *Macbeth*, II.ii.56.) And a wry suggestion on McCarthy's part it was, for he probably knew that Siegel, a chronic insomniac, equated sleep and death. Interestingly enough, I was not at all aware that Siegel was an insomniac when I wrote the first draft of this essay. I was simply reacting to the emotional patterns which I had intuited in the film itself. Thus it was with a peculiar *frisson* of pleasure, and confirmation, that I subsequently happened upon this quotation from Siegel: "One of the reasons insomniacs are afraid to sleep is that they fear they won't wake up. The parallel is there. Ironically, at times I have suffered so much from chronic insomnia that I would have liked to turn into a pod" (cited by Le Gacy, "Invasion of the Body Snatchers," p. 287). In other words, Siegel is someone who has a rather strong need for conscious control and therefore is also someone who is driven in equal measure by an estranged desire to let go. No wonder Finney's novel, with its sleep-is-death motif, appealed to him so immediately. And no wonder that the structure of his film adaptation is so replete with powerful, projective images of forbidden surrender.

These days it is rather fashionable to argue that not only Andrew Sarris-inspired Auteurism, but all author-expressive approaches to criticism are logically flawed, indeed, profoundly naïve. (See Stephen Crofts, "Authorship and Hollywood," *Wide Angle* 5 [1983]:16–22.) As a member of the passionate opposition to such critical trends, I offer this citation in particular and my essay in general as a way of raising the flag for a kind of textual analysis which is at once rigorous, humanistic, intuitive, and idiomatic. By their works, ye shall know them.

restrial about it. It was just an average corpse, the product of an average small-town murder. Nothing to get excited about. It will turn up eventually along with a rational explanation for what they have seen. Miles protests: what about the body in Becky's basement? An hallucination, Kaufman explains, and offers to prove his assertion. He leads the men back to the Driscoll basement and artfully stages a discovery scene. While Jack and Miles stand behind him, he dramatically raises the "coffin" lid: "There's a body here all right," he says. "It's Becky's double!," Miles shouts. "It sure is!" Belicec echoes. Kaufman smiles and steps back, letting them come closer. "Take another look." The box is empty. "Now you see it; now you don't." "I saw it here! It was real!" Miles insists. "You saw her all right . . . but only in your mind." The local police chief appears suddenly, as if on cue, to back Kaufman with apparently irrefutable evidence: the missing body has been found on a farmer's haystack, a routine murder victim, just as Kaufman had predicted. This is a matter for the authorities, not for over-imaginative sleuths. Go home and get some sleep!

In the morning, the terror is gone and order restored. The two couples have breakfast together in the Belicecs' cozy kitchen. Both genders relax back into their traditional roles. A good *balabusta,* Becky busies herself at the stove while Miles waits happily to be served. She is in charge of the eggs, but she boils them to his specifications. The night-fear he felt when he saw her body in the cellar is forgotten, and Miles is his old seductive self again. She responds, coyly wrapping her arms around his neck.

Yet frankly, where seduction is concerned, Miles talks a better game than he plays. This becomes clear when night falls again. Miles and Becky join the Belicecs for a traditional suburban barbeque, full of booze and reassuring forgetfulness. Then suddenly, 'twixt the hors d'oeuvres and the steak, comes a terrible revelation, palpable confirmation of their worst fears. In the Belicecs' greenhouse there are giant seed pods, great ovaries popping with latent energy, inside of which, growing, are humanoid bodies! Pop, pop, the blank bodies become more recognizable by the second—another Becky body, a Teddy body, and clones of Miles and Jack, too. Looking at the blank, passive form, Teddy screams, "Is that me? Is that *me*?"

The men arm themselves for action with phallic props: pitchforks. And yet a curious hesitancy intervenes between intent and action. Looking down at Becky's inert pod-body, tendrils coiling from its scalp, Miles is unable to plunge his weapon into her flesh, though moments later, he stabs his own duplicate body—by all calculations the more psychologically difficult of the two acts. In this, Miles is both a quintessential Victorian and a more modern androgyne-manqué, too fearful to embrace his other half, yet unwilling to kill it off even though it threatens his conception of himself.

Frightened now, his calm bedside manner wavering, Miles tries to call for help. Alas, the pods control the means of communication. In desperation, he sends the Belicecs out of town for assistance while he and Becky retreat to the safety of his office. But there is no escape even there. Hearing Jack's voice, expecting rescue, Miles opens the door, only to discover that Jack is one of Them now, as are all of his neighbors, including Doc Kaufman, who, as it turns out, was one of the very first pod converts. What has seemed to be Doc's common sense is really the blank serenity of a lobotomy victim, a zombie. In counseling Miles and Becky to cease their resistance, to join the majority, Kaufman clearly defines the pods as pro-security and anti-passion: "There's no need for love . . . You've been in love before; it didn't last."

Here Kaufman is articulating Siegel's stated theme, that "the majority of people in the world are pods . . . incapable of love." And yet, as I have already suggested, Siegel's text and his subtext don't necessarily support each other. As in most *noir* films which have a male voice-over narration, the words in *Invasion* profoundly conflict with the images.

The infinitive "to sleep" is the seam along which the two schizoid halves of *Invasion* have been stitched together. Sleeping and waking, passivity and activity, are dichotomies and yet also part of a larger whole. Each mode is fully human, essential to an intra-psychic balance of forces.[11] The quirk which makes *Invasion* so odd and so difficult to talk about is that its male authors (Finney, Mainwaring, and Siegel) are so skewed towards fight-or-flight thinking that they are unable to make any conscious connection at all between human passion and human passivity. Their collective desire for surcease, which is powerfully represented by the fertile pods, is incompatible with the thrusting macho definition of manhood which structures their vision of the intensely-lived life. To take is to thrive; to be taken is to die.

The ambivalent meaning of the pods in *Invasion* follows the general rule for SF plots: that "anything alien is inhuman to me." Aliens in SF invariably represent some internal human capability which the author or *auteur* is trying to reject. Moreover, since until recently the vast majority of SF authors/*auteurs* were male, aliens tend to be distorted projections of *anima*—not women-as-women but women-as-symbols of the "fem" components of the male psyche.[12]

---

11. This vision of psychic wholeness, of the fruitful compenetration of opposites, is powerfully represented in the fiction of Ursula Le Guin, among others. (See Robert Galbreath, "Holism, Openness, and the Other: Le Guin's Use of the Occult," *SFS* 7 [1980]:36–48; Douglas Barbour, "Wholeness and Balance in the Hainish Novels of Ursula K. Le Guin," *SFS* 1 [1974]:64–73; Darko Suvin, "Parables of De-Alienation: Le Guin's Widdershins Dance," *SFS* 2 [1975]:265–274; and George Sluser, *The Farthest Shores of Ursula K. Le Guin* (San Bernardino, Calif., 1976). And, of course, see Le Guin's novels themselves, especially the "On the Ice" chapter of *The Left Hand of Darkness* [1969].)

12. There has been much skillful commentary on the androgynous vision in the work of women SF writers, especially Ursula Le Guin. (See Pamela J. Annas, "New Words: Androgyny in Feminist Science Fiction," *SFS* 5 [1978]:143–156; and Susan Gubar, "C. L. Moore and the Conventions of Women's Science Fiction," *SFS* 7 [1980]:16–27.) Somewhat less attention has been paid to the importance of covert androgynous yearnings in the work of male SF writers. *Snatchers,* which its

The pods are difficult to decode as symbols because they are a condensed dialectic, a thesis and an antithesis rolled into one. They are like one of those gestalt pictures in which one sees either a pretty young woman or an old crone depending on whether one perceives the dark area as figure or as ground. On the one hand, the pods represent depression. They are caricatures of people who deny their passionate feelings in a vain search for perfect security. This is most clear when the pods speak and explain the appeal of their way of life. On the other hand, the pods also represent all those passionate feelings which have been repressed and which, therefore, are reasserting themselves in powerful estranged form, trying to take over. (Feelings are not a matter of will; they simply exist, whether we like them or not. The less we accept and embrace a feeling, the more strenuously it drives us, owns us.) All this is most clear when we ignore the pods' words and look at their form, their fecundity, and their ultimate connection with the beloved "Becky."

This dialectic between feelings and denial of feelings—between anxiety and anxiety-avoidance—determines the peculiar surrealistic plot structure of *Invasion,* especially its later reels. That is, this is a film which substitutes a physical *invasion* for an intra-psychic *evasion.* It is a *psychomachia* designed by and for beleaguered males of the mid-1950s.

The principal evader is Miles, or, more precisely, the macho authorial consciousness for which he is the voice. His alliance with Becky, his "other half," is a powerful, life-enhancing configuration. So long as it lasts, it protects him against the forces of depression—against Doc Kaufman and his cohorts. But this androgynous configuration, without adequate precedent in '50s' culture, is too unstable to endure. Thus, in the end, Miles (and the film for which he speaks) turns against intimacy and androgyny and reasserts the simpler, though more sterile values of the American patriarchy. Back to the raft again, Huck honey.

All of which brings us back to where we began: the muddy water in the tunnel. In entering the tunnel with Becky, Miles metaphorically enters into sexual intercourse with her. (His breathless ascent up the hill is his erection.) But there is no relief in this painfully-postponed consummation, no "Ode to Joy," but rather, a dreary *liebedstod* in which passionate intimacy is equated with being buried alive. Miles and Becky hide from the pods on the floor, pulling a layer of planks over them as if sealing the lid of a coffin-built-for-two. Gone is Miles's confident repartée and Becky's coy ripostes. There is little dialogue now at all, merely the tinny echo of their breathing. Claustrophobia, vulnerability, paranoia, terror, a desire to flee: this is such stuff as love is made of in *Invasion.* Siegel is not being

ambivalent presentation of the estranged, alien "Other half"—its hidden desire for surcease—offers a characteristic paradigm of SF as a genre, from H. G. Wells through the "Golden Age" of the 1950s at least. This becomes even clearer when one compares "classical" SF plot structures to the programmatically subversive work of J. G. Ballard, a writer for whom the Lotus Eaters, not Ulysses, are the bearers of ultimate wisdom.

especially misogynic here (that will come in a minute); he is merely trying to find honest visual correlatives for the great anxiety that invariably accompanies a surrender to great passion. In this sense, Doc Kaufman is perfectly correct when he warns Miles that love is painful and insecure.

On the other hand, orgasm isn't really death (it just feels like it a little); and so, the danger past, Miles and Becky emerge intact from their coffin-built-for-two. They are still themselves. Indeed, they're twice themselves: as they wash their faces, we see both them and their twinned faces reflected in the water. One is now two; two are four. In the darkness, they have grown. And this doubling, in turn, suggests another contradiction at the heart of the film. Though deemed alien and inimical, the pods are advocates of growth. Moreover, the growth process which the pods purvey is very much like a mating, a marriage—a union of strangers (or, perhaps, a union of estranged halves of the psyche). In the 1978 remake of *Invasion* (dir. Philip Kaufman), the withering and destruction of the old human body, as the pod absorbs the brain, is rendered in horrific detail. But in Siegel's film, significantly, there is nothing left over—no detritus, no husk, no visible evidence at all that any real destruction has taken place. The alien and the human simply, seamlessly merge into a new unitary identity. One plus one equals one.

If the pods are associated with growth and union, Miles is associated with stasis and the past, the old town, the old values. In Jack Finney's novel, on which the film was based, the Oedipal nature of Miles's allegiance to the past is made much more specific than it is in Siegel's film. He has never really grown up, it seems. At twenty-eight, he is still his daddy's little boy. He lives alone in his dead parents' house, amid his parents' things. He repeatedly summons up nostalgic memories of his boyhood, especially of his doctor father, whose place he has taken but whose power remains undimmed. A central prop in Miles and Becky's escape from the pods is a pair of skeletons, male and female, which once belonged to his father. Miles substitutes those skeletons for his and Becky's bodies and sprinkles them with their hair and blood. While the pods are busy cloning the skeletons, he and Becky are able to anesthetize their pod guards with syringes of morphine (Becky's idea) and to flee to freedom.[13]

This business with the skeletons, hair, and blood is a primitive but effective ritual which allows Miles to exorcise the ghost of his father (whose puritanical force is embodied in Kaufman) and to achieve his manhood. Until Becky comes along, Miles has been a suburban Oedipus of sorts, frozen in time-space. His frequently stated reluctance to "get serious" with her is not only the natural hesitation of a recent divorcé but also the psychological foot-dragging of an emotional virgin.

Daniel Mainwaring's screenplay omits the skeleton sequence and Miles's ref-

13. Jack Finney, *Invasion of the Body Snatchers* (London: Sphere Books, 1978), 1:9 and 18:151–155.

erences to his parents but makes him, if anything, more reluctant to "get serious" with Becky. Seduction, yes; commitment, no. Over and over, he warns her not to get involved with a doctor. She doesn't listen, of course, but in the end it is his horror of intimate entanglement which the plot validates.

Here the film differs from the novel. Throughout most of his screenplay, Mainwaring has followed Finney very closely, often lifting dialogue word for word. But at the climax, the screenplay and the novel suddenly and significantly diverge. At the juncture of this divergence stands the figure of Becky. In the novel, Becky is a full-fledged heroine. She not only saves Miles's life, literally and emotionally; she saves the whole of mankind. In her will to prevail and in her ingenuity, she is every bit Miles's equal, and then some. Partners, working as a team, she and he offer such fierce and clever resistance that the aliens are at last persuaded to leave Earth altogether and to seek a planet with more tractable hosts.

> Quite simply, the great pods were leaving a fierce and inhospitable planet. I knew it utterly and a wave of exultation so violent it left me trembling swept through my body; because I knew Becky and I had played our part in what was now happening. . . . [A] fragment of a wartime speech moved through my mind: *We shall fight them in the fields, and in the streets, we shall fight in the hills; we shall never surrender.* . . . Now I felt that nothing in the whole vast universe could ever defeat us.
>
> Did this incredible alien life form "think" this, too, or "know" it? Probably not, I thought, or anything our minds could conceive. But it had sensed it. . . . And Becky and I, in refusing to surrender, but instead fighting their invasion to the end, had provided the final conclusive demonstration of that truth.[14]

In short, Becky and Miles conquer the aliens, and love conquers all. We leave them happily settling into married life. The pod duplicates still exist, but they are a dying breed; and slowly the old town is resurging. The hearty Bennell-Driscoll genes, not the green genes, will inherit the Earth.

Against these rosy new-dawn colors, the black misogyny of Siegel's ending emerges all the more clearly.[15] In Mainwaring's screenplay, Becky becomes, not a savior, but a Judas who betrays her lord with a kiss. "I never really knew what

---

14. *Ibid.*, 21:168.

15. It is often stated that Sam Peckinpah, who played the pod meter-reader in *Invasion*, made uncredited contributions to the filmscript. (See Walt Lee, *Reference Guide to Fantastic Films: Science Fiction, Fantasy, and Horror* [Los Angeles, 1972], II:220.) This would be interesting, were it true, because Peckinpah's subsequent work as a director is exceptional, even in macho-Hollywood, for the intensity of its misogyny (e.g., in *Straw Dogs*). However, Siegel says that Peckinpah merely "made suggestions" to Mainwaring: Kaminsky, "Don Siegel on *Invasion*" p. 21.

fear was until I kissed Becky." And yet, although Becky gets the blame, it is Miles's fearful faithlessness which sets up her fall.

Until the climax in the tunnel, Miles's and Becky's capacity to survive has been enhanced by their being together, by their working as a team, by their mutual passion. But Miles is so seduced by the far-off music he hears outside the tunnel—a maternal lullaby—that he leaves Becky alone just when she needs him most (and just when he needs her most). As it turns out, the lullaby is an illusion. There is no warm human voice behind it, no rescuing mama, merely more machinery and pods. But if he can't go home again, he can't go forward again either. When he returns to the cave, "Becky" is no longer really there. In her place is a mere thing, a pod. The feelings which have given him the will to live have disappeared. This is all Becky's fault, of course; she is a weak woman, unable to stand alone. But in a deeper sense, it is Miles's failure of nerve which has occasioned this irreparable loss: his inability to bear the anxiety contingent upon great sexual passion; his yearning for maternal security (the pod come-on); his reluctance to embrace the estranged feminine components of his personality; his horror of the "little death" that is orgasm. Although the plot asserts otherwise, when he leaves Becky (and thus leaves a precious part of his own identity), it is *he* not she, who has chosen to become an alien, a depressive, passionless drone.

The epilogue confirms this conclusion. In trying to beat Them, Miles has unwittingly joined Them. He began the film as a leader of men and a potent seducer of women, confident, knowing, in control of his emotions and, for that matter, in control of other people's emotions as well. (He prescribes a tranquilizer for little Jimmy Grimaldi and masterfully talks Wilma Lenz out of her fears about Uncle Ira.) But when he meets Becky he begins to trust his intuition and to release his control. In effect, he joins forces with the women and the children against his own kind. He is a traitor to his sex. In the end, however, he suffers for his treason. Helpless, in a puddle of tears, out of control, vulnerable, he is utterly dependent for his salvation upon the male Authorities, personified by J. Edgar Hoover and his F.B.I. The psychiatrists who attend him are indistinguishable from Doc Kaufman. Both are committed to a disbelief in the reliability of hunches, of feelings. They will accept only palpable, logical proof.

Proof comes. There is a highway accident. A truck from Santa Mira spills weird pods on the roadway. The aliens are real! But simultaneously, the emotional realities which the pods have represented disappear from the film. A wonderfully complex, androgynous configuration has ceased to be. The familiar polarities reassert themselves, and all is well. Yet somehow life is diminished thereby.

Thus the ostensibly up-beat note on which *Invasion of the Body Snatchers* ends—a call to action, to busy-ness, and to conquest—is really a vision of a future bleak and blank and not at all the paean to passion that Siegel has said he intended. For what is a world without pods but a world committed resolutely to macho principles—dangerously narrow, only half-human, a world devoid of rest, receptivity, growth, and an empathetic acceptance of otherness?[16]

We know what that world is like. Alas, we live in it.

16. Cf. Scott Sanders, "Women as Nature in Science Fiction," in *Future Females: A Critical Anthology,* ed. Marlene Barr (Bowling Green, Ohio, 1981), p. 58.

Filmography and Bibliography

Siegel Filmography, 1945–1982

The following credits are based on those in Stuart M. Kaminsky's *Don Siegel, Director* (New York: Curtis Books, 1974) and Alan Lovell's *Don Siegel, American Cinema* (London: British Film Institute, 1975) and updated through a variety of other sources.

1945   *Star in the Night* (dramatic short)
Screenplay by Saul Elkins.

1945   *Hitler Lives* (documentary short)
Screenplay by Saul Elkins.

1946   *The Verdict*
Screenplay by Peter Milne.

1949   *Night Unto Night*
Screenplay by Kathryn Scola.

The Big Steal
Screenplay by Daniel Mainwaring (as Geoffrey Homes) and Gerald Drayson Adams.

1952   *No Time for Flowers*
Screenplay by Laszlo Vadnay and Hans Wilhelm.

Duel at Silver Creek
Screenplay by Gerald Drayson Adams and Joseph Hoffman.

1953   *Count the Hours*
Screenplay by Doane R. Hoag and Karen de Wolf.

China Venture
Screenplay by George Worthington Yates and Richard Collins.

1954   *Riot in Cell Block 11*
Screenplay by Richard Collins.

Private Hell 36
Screenplay by Collier Young and Ida Lupino.

1955   *An Annapolis Story*
Screenplay by Dan Ulman and Daniel Mainwaring (as Geoffrey Homes).

1956   *Invasion of the Body Snatchers*
Screenplay by Daniel Mainwaring.

Crime in the Streets
Screenplay by Reginald Rose.

1957   *A Spanish Affair*
Screenplay by Richard Collins.

Baby Face Nelson
Screenplay by Daniel Mainwaring.

1958   *The Gun Runners*
Screenplay by Daniel Mainwaring and Paul Monash, based on Ernest Hemingway's *To Have and Have Not.*

The Lineup
Screenplay by Sterling Silliphant.

1959   *Edge of Eternity*
Screenplay by Kurt Swenson and Richard Collins.

Hound Dog Man
Screenplay by Fred Gipson and Winston Miller.

1960   *Flaming Star*
Screenplay by Clair Huffaker and Nunnally Johnson.

1962   *Hell Is for Heroes*
Screenplay by Robert Pirosh and Richard Carr.

1964   *The Killers*
Screenplay by Gene L. Coon from Hemingway's story.

The Hanged Man
(*Ride the Pink Horse*)
Screenplay by Jack Laird and Stanford Whitmore.

1967   *Stranger on the Run*
Screenplay by Dean Riesner.

1968   *Madigan*
Screenplay by Henri Simoun (Howard Rodman) and Abraham Polonsky.

1969   *Coogan's Bluff*
Screenplay by Herman Miller, Dean Riesner, and Howard Rodman.

Death of a Gunfighter
Screenplay by Joseph Calvelli. After twenty-five days of shooting by

Robert Totten, Siegel assumed the directorship.

1970   *Two Mules for Sister Sara*
Screenplay by Albert Maltz.

1971   *The Beguiled*
Screenplay by John B. Sherry and Grimes Grice (Albert Maltz).

Dirty Harry
Screenplay by Harry Julian Fink, R. M. Fink, and Dean Riesner.

1973   *Charley Varrick*
Screenplay by Howard Rodman and Dean Riesner.

1974   *The Black Windmill*
Screenplay by Leigh Vance.

1976   *The Shootist*
Screenplay by Miles Hood Swarthout and Scott Hall.

1977   *Telefon*
Screenplay by Sterling Silliphant and Peter Hyams.

1979   *Escape from Alcatraz*
Screenplay by Richard Tuggle.

1982   *Jinxed*
Screenplay by Brian Blessed (Frank D. Gilroy).

Television Credits

1954   "The Doctors." Three half-hour episodes.
"The Lineup." Half-hour pilot.

1955   "The Bogeyman." Episode of the United States Steel Hour. Teleplay by Don Siegel and Francis Rosenwald.

1961   "Frontier." First episode.
"Code Three." Pilot.
"The Man from Blackhawk."

Pilot episode teleplay by Don Siegel and Herb Meadows.

1963 "Bus Stop." Fifty-minute pilot.
"Breaking Point." First episode.

1964 "Twilight Zone." Two episodes, "Uncle Simon" and "Self-Improvement of Salvadore Ross."

"The Lloyd Bridges Show." One episode.

1965 "Destry." One-hour pilot, "Johnny I Hardly Knew You."
"Convoy." Fifty-minute pilot.

1966 "The Legend of Jesse James." Produced and directed the half-hour pilot.

Selected Bibliography

Biskind, Peter. "Pods, Blobs, and Ideology in American Films of the Fifties." In *Shadows of the Magic Lamp*, ed. George E. Slusser and Eric S. Rabkin, pp. 58–72. Carbondale and Edwardsville: Southern Illinois University Press, 1985.

———. *Seeing Is Believing*. New York: Pantheon, 1983.

Boddy, William. "Daniel Mainwaring." In *Dictionary of Literary Biography*, vol. 44, *American Screenwriters*, 2nd ser., pp. 207–215. Detroit: Gail Research Co., 1986.

Ceplair, Larry and Steven Englund. *The Inquisition in Hollywood*. Berkeley and Los Angeles: University of California Press, 1983.

Grant, Barry Keith, ed. *Planks of Reason: Essays on the Horror Film*. Metuchen, N.J. and London: The Scarecrow Press, 1984.

Higashi, Sumiko. "*Invasion of the Body Snatchers:* Pods Then and Now." *Jump Cut* 24/25 (1981): 3–4.

Johnson, Glen M. "'We'd Fight . . . We Had To': *The Body Snatchers* as Novel and Film." *Journal of Popular Culture* 13 (Summer 1979): 5–16.

Johnson, William, ed. *Focus on the Science Fiction Film*. Englewood Cliffs, N.J.: Prentice-Hall, 1972.

Kaminsky, Stuart M. *American Film Genres*. New York: Dell, 1977.

———. *Don Siegel, Director*. New York: Curtis Books, 1974.

———. "Don Siegel on the Pod Society." In *Science Fiction Films*, ed. Thomas R. Atkins, pp. 73–82. New York: Monarch Press, 1976.

———. "*Invasion of the Body Snatchers*: A Classic of Subtle Horror." In *Science Fiction Films*, ed. Atkins, pp. 63–72.

Kass, Judith M. "Don Siegel." In *The Hollywood Professionals*, vol. 4. London and New York: A. S. Barnes, 1975.

King, Stephen. *Stephen King's Danse Macabre*. New York: Everett House, 1981.

Laura, Ernesto G. "Invasion of the

Body Snatchers." In *Focus on the Science Fiction Film,* ed. W. Johnson, pp. 71–73. Originally published in *Bianco e Nero* 18, no. 12 (1957): 69–71.

Le Gacy, Arthur. *"Invasion of the Body Snatchers:* A Metaphor for the Fifties." *Literature/Film Quarterly* 1 (1978): 285–292.

Lovell, Alan. *Don Siegel, American Cinema.* London: British Film Institute, 1975.

Polan, Dana B. "Eros and Syphilization: The Contemporary Horror Film." In *Planks of Reason,* ed. Barry Keith Grant, pp. 201–211. Metuchen, N.J. and London: The Scarecrow Press, 1984.

Rogin, Michael Paul. "Kiss Me Deadly: Communism, Motherhood, and Cold War Movies." In *Ronald Reagan, The Movie and Other Episodes in Political Demonology,* pp. 236–271. Berkeley and Los Angeles: University of California Press, 1987.

Samuels, Stuart. "The Age of Conspiracy and Conformity: *Invasion of the Body Snatchers.*" In *American History/American Film: Interpreting the American Image,* ed. John O'Connor and Martin A. Jackson, pp. 203–217. New York: Frederick Ungar Publishing Co., 1979.

Sayre, Nora. *Running Time.* New York: Dial Press, 1982.

Steffen-Fluhr, Nancy. "Women and the Inner Game of Don Siegel's *Invasion of the Body Snatchers.*" *Science Fiction Studies* 11 (July 1984): 139–151.

Sobchack, Vivian. *The Limits of Infinity.* South Brunswick, N.J., and London: A. S. Barnes, 1980.

———. *Screening Space: The American Science Fiction Film.* New York: Unger, 1986.

Telotte, J. P. "The Doubles of Fantasy and the Space of Desire." *Film Criticism* 7 (1982): 61–63.

Whyte, William H., Jr. *The Organization Man.* New York: Simon and Schuster, 1956.

Wood, Robin. "Don Siegel." In *Cinema: A Critical Dictionary,* vol. 2, *The Major Filmmakers,* ed. Richard Roud, pp. 921–924. New York: Viking, 1980.

Yacowar, Maurice. Audio essay on the film on laserdisk. Los Angeles: The Criterion Collection, 1986.